THE BEST OF NEWSPAPER DESIGN

Thirteenth Edition

Contents

Introduction 2
Best of Show 4
Judges 8
Overall Design 11
News 21
The Persian Gulf War 49
Features 79
Magazines 115
Special Sections 129
Design Portfolios 145
Photojournalism 167
Illustration 187
Informational Graphics 209
Miscellaneous 241
Index of Winners 253

© 1992 THE SOCIETY OF NEWSPAPER DESIGN

ROCKPORT PUBLISHERS

FIRST PUBLISHED IN THE U. S. A. BY ROCKPORT PUBLISHERS, INC. • PRINTED IN SINGAPORE
HARDCOVER: ISBN: 1-56496-027-7 • SOFTCOVER: ISBN: 1-878107-02-X

Introduction

For the first time since the Ninth Edition, judges in this year's annual Society of Newspaper Design competition awarded Best of Show recognition.

Best of Show is, of course, the highest possible award and is awarded entirely at the discretion of the judges. The 18 judges from the United States and Spain awarded Best of Show to:
- The New York Times Magazine for photojournalism.
- The Washington Times for its Arts sections.

(SND contest watchers will remember the last Best of Show also went to The Washington Times, for John Kascht's design and illustration.)

And this year's competition restored a an award of merit. All of which presented a challenge to the judges who spent three days evaluating of more than 7,500 entries from four continents.

Judging included scrutiny from folio line to jump line. Six entries were awarded Judges' Special Recognition, along with six Gold Awards, 56 Silver Awards, 126 Bronze Awards and 610 Awards of Excellence.

The Bronze award, last presented in the Second Edition, was resurrected by the SND Competition Committee to recognize entries that merited judges' discussion for possible Gold or Silver award consideration.

In addition to the Bronze awards and separate Best of Show awards in this book, which is the annual publication based on contest winners, a 30-page section of Persian Gulf War pages is included beginning on page 49.

Judging, as usual, took place at the S. I. Newhouse School of Public Communication in Syracuse, N. Y. For their help, I want to thank:

C. Marshall Matlock and the students of the Newhouse School who worked long hours – not only during the actual judging, but in the weeks prior – preparing the site so everything operated with precision; G.W. Babb, David Gray and Alan Jacobson, who helped coordinate the judging teams; Randy Stano of The Miami Herald, president of SND; Ray Chattman, executive director of the Society; the photographic and art departments of the Lexington Herald-Leader, which helped respond to the hundreds of telephone calls concerning this contest; and the art department of the Detroit Free Press, which gave time and talent to produce this contest's entry materials.

– *Jim Jennings, Thirteenth Edition Chair*

Por primera vez desde la Novena Edición, los jueces de este concurso anual de la Sociedad de Diseño de Periódicos entregaron el premio Best of the Show.

Este premio, naturalmente, es el más prestigioso y se entrega a completa discreción de los jueces. Los 18 jueces de Estados Unidos y España otorgaron el premio a:
- The New York Times Magazine por fotoperiodismo.
- The Washington Times por su sección de Arte.

(Los observadores del concurso de la Sociedad recordarán que el premio Best of the Show del año pasado también fue otorgado a The Washington Times, por el diseño e ilustración de John Kascht.)

Y el concurso de este año reinstauró un premio al mérito.

Todo esto constituyó un reto para los jueces, que dedicaron tres días a la evaluación de más de 7,500 inscripciones de cuatro continentes en el concurso de este año.

La tarea de los jueces incluyó evaluar todo, desde el folio hasta las líneas de pase. Se otorgaron seis premios en la categoría de Reconocimiento Especial de los Jueces, conjuntamente con seis Premios de Oro, 56 Premios de Plata, 126 Premios de Bronce y 610 Premios de Excelencia.

El Premio de Bronce, otorgado por última vez en la Segunda Edición, fue resucitado por el Comité de Competencia de la Sociedad de Diseño de Periódicos para premiar presentaciones que merecieron la discusión de los jueves para el posible otorgamiento de premios de Oro y Plata.

Además de los premios de Bronce y los galardones Best of the Show separados incluidos en este libro, que es la publicación anual que incluye a los ganadores, se incluyó una sección de 30 páginas sobre la guerra del Golfo Pérsico a partir de la página 49.

La labor de los jueces, como es costumbre, se realizó en la Escuela de Comunicaciones Públicas S.I. Newhouse, en Syracuse, Nueva York. Por su ayuda, quisiera agradecer a las siguientes personas:

C. Marshall Matlock y los estudiantes de la Escuela Newhouse que trabajaron tantas horas – no sólo durante la labor del jurado sino también durante las semanas anteriores – preparando el lugar para que todo funcionara debidamente; G.W. Babb, David Gray y Alan Jacobson, quienes ayudaron a coordinar los equipos de jurados; Randy Stano, de The Miami Herald, presidente de la Sociedad de Diseño de Periódicos; Ray Chattman, director ejecutivo de la Sociedad; los departamentos de arte y fotografía del Lexington Herald-Leader, que ayudó a responder los cientos de llamadas telefónicas sobre este concurso; y al departamento de arte del Detroit Free Press, que ofreció tiempo y experiencia para producir los materiales de inscripción de este concurso.

– *Jim Jennings, presidente de la Decimotercera Edición.*

Best of Show

The Washington Times
John Kascht, Art Director, Designer & Illustrator

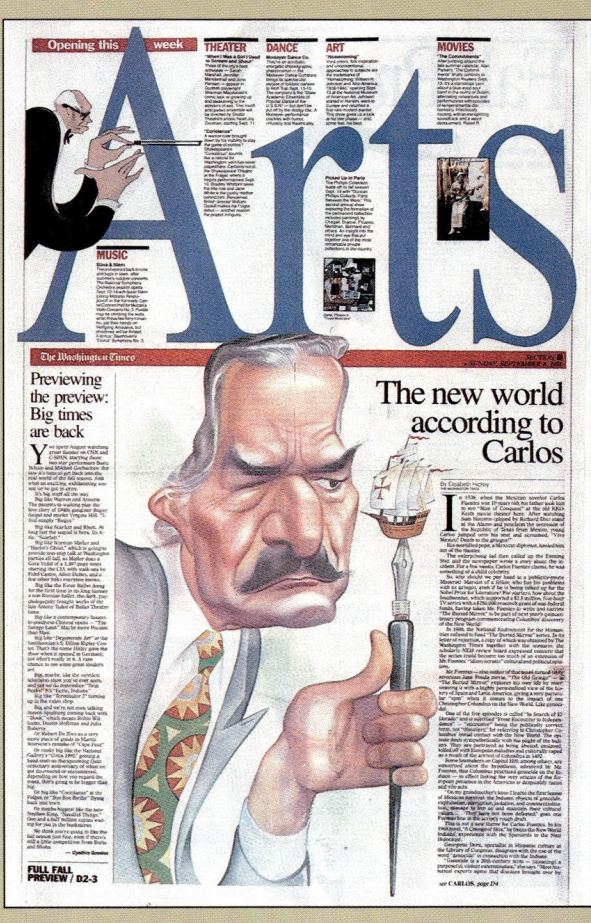

THIRTEENTH EDITION 5

Best of Show

The New York Times Magazine
Janet Froelich, Art Director & Designer; Sebastiao Salgado, Photographer; Kathy Ryan, Photo Editor; Tom Bodkin, Design Director

The work is exhausting. It all must be done by hand because a stray spark from power equipment could re-ignite the well. For two days, these men have been trying to remove a well head that was blown up by Iraqi explosives.

THE NEW YORK TIMES MAGAZINE / JUNE 9, 1991   25

Like ants moving a mountain, the oil workers struggle from well to well. When they arrived, it was estimated that the unchecked flow of Kuwaiti oil equaled a tenth of the world's total production.

THIRTEENTH EDITION   7

Core Judges

Tim Atseff
is managing editor of the Syracuse Herald-Journal and Syracuse Herald American. Previously, he worked as deputy managing editor, director of graphics and design, editorial cartoonist and illustrator.

Tim Atseff
es director gerente del Syracuse Herald-Journal y del Syracuse Herald American. Anteriormente, fue subdirector gerente, director de gráficas y diseño, caricaturista político e ilustrador.

Carmelo Caderot
is design director of El Mundo, in Madrid, Spain.

Carmelo Caderot
es director de diseño de El Mundo, de Madrid, España.

Susan Casey
is deputy art director of Esprit de Corp. in San Francisco, responsible for the creation and development of print-media images. Before joining Esprit she was creative director at the Globe and Mail.

Susan Casey
es subdirectora artística de Esprit de Corp. en San Francisco, responsable de la creación y desarrollo de imágenes para medios impresos. Antes de comenzar en Sprit, fue directora creativa de The Globe and Mail.

Stephen Cvengros
is illustrations editor for the Chicago Tribune, responsible for news graphics and photos. He was graphics editor of The Detroit News, an artist and designer at Newsday and special sections editor and reporter for Sliger-Livingston Publications in Michigan.

Steven Cvengros
es director de ilustraciones del Chicago Tribune, responsable de las gráficas y fotografías noticiosas. Fue director de gráficas de The Detroit News, artista y diseñador en Newsday y director de secciones especiales y reportero de Sliger-Livingston Publications en

Greg Leeds
is design director of special projects for The Wall Street Journal. Formerly he was design director of the Journal, art director at The New York Times, GEO magazine, People magazine and The Real Paper.

Greg Leeds
es director de diseño de proyectos especiales de The Wall Street Journal. Anteriormente fue director de diseño del Journa l, director artístico de The New York Times, la revista GEO y The Real Paper.

Galie Jean-Louis
is the art director and designer of the Impulse section of the Anchorage Daily News. Prior to joining the Daily News she was an advertising art director and editorial freelancer.

Galie Jean-Louis
es directora artística y diseñadora de la sección Impulse del Anchorage Daily News. Antes de comenzar a trabajar en el Daily News, fue directora artística de publicidad y colaboradora

8 THE BEST OF NEWSPAPER DESIGN

J. Keith Moyer
is editor at the Democrat and Chronicle and the Times-Union in Rochester, N. Y. He was editor at the Fort Myers News-Press, managing editor of Gannett's Westchester, N.Y. newspapers, features editor at the Times-Union, features and special projects editor at the News-Press and assistant city editor and reporter at the Lakeland (Fla.) Ledger.

J. Keith Moyer
es director del Democrat and Chronicle y del Times-Union en Rochester, Nueva York. Fue director del Fort Myers News-Pres, director gerente de los periódicos Westchester de Gannett, director de reportajes especiales del Times-Union, director de reportajes y proyectos especiales en el News-Press y subdirector y reportero de noticias locales del Lakeland Ledger, en la Florida.

J. F. Paschal
is an associate professor at the H. H. Herbert School of Journalism and Mass Communication, at the University of Oklahoma in Norman. He also is a freelance photographer and design consultant.

J. F. Paschal
es profesor auxiliar en la Escuela de Periodismo y Comunicaciones Masivas H. H. Herbert, en la Universidad de Oklahoma, en Norman. También es fotógrafo y consultor de diseño independiente.

Trish Redman
is art director of the St. Petersburg Times. She has worked as art director of the Jackson Hole News and as a staff artist at The Orange County Register.

Trish Redman
es directora artística del St. Petersburg Times. Ha sido directora artística del Jackson Hole News y artista de The Orange County Register.

Joseph W. Scopin
is assistant managing editor for photography / graphics at The Washington Times. He has been graphics editor at UPI, art director at The Washington Times, art director of The Washington Post Style section and art director of The Washington Star's Life and Calendar sections.

Joseph W. Scopin
es director gerente a cargo de fotografía y gráficas en The Washington Times. Ha sido director de gráficas en la UPI, director artístico en The Washington Times, director artístico de la sección Style de The Washington Post y director artístico de las secciones Life y Calendar de The Washington Star.

Janet Shaughnessy
is a staff artist at The Virginian-Pilot and The Ledger-Star in Norfolk and art director for the Sunday magazine, Hampton Roads Woman. Prior to Norfolk she worked at The San Diego Union and the Democrat and Chronicle in Rochester, N. Y.

Janet Shaughnessy
es artista gráfico de The Virginian-Pilot y de The Ledger-Star en Norfolk y directora artística de la revista dominical, Hampton Roads Woman. Antes de empezar en Norfolk trabajó en The San Diego Union y el Democrat and Chronicle en Rochester, Nueva York.

Randy Stano
is president of the Society of Newspaper Design and director of editorial art and design at The Miami Herald. He was graphics editor for the Democrat and Chronicle in Rochester, N. Y., and assistant editorial art director for The Kansas City Times. He also taught journalism and directed student publications in Austin, Texas.

Randy Stano
es presidente de la Sociedad de Diseño de Periódicos y director de arte y caricaturas políticas en The Miami Herald. Fue director de gráficas del Democrat and Chronicle en Rochester, Nueva York, y director adjunto de caricatura política de The Kansas City Times. También fue profesor de periodismo y dirigió publicaciones estudiantiles en Austis, Texas.

Specialty Judges

Alan Berner is a staff photographer at The Seattle Times. He has worked as a photographer, picture editor and graphics editor for five other papers.

J. Bruce Baumann is the assistant managing editor / graphics at The Pittsburgh Press, responsible for overall design. He has worked as a photographer, reporter, designer, picture editor, lifestyle editor, and director of photography in California, Indiana, Iowa, Michigan and Pennsylvania and at National Geographic.

J. Bruce Baumann es director gerente encargado de gráficas en The Pittsburgh Press, responsable del diseño general. Ha trabajado de fotógrafo, reportero, diseñador, director de gráficas y fotografía, director de secciones de entretenimiento y director de fotografía en California, Indiana, Iowa, Michigan y Pennsylvania, además de en National Geographic.

Alan Berner es fotógrafo de The Seattle Times. Ha trabajado de fotógrafo, director de fotografía y director de gráficas en otros cinco periódicos.

Thea Breite is the chief picture editor for the Providence Journal. She is responsible for designing page one and news and sports photo editing. She was a picture editor at the Boston Globe, The Orange County Register and a picture editor / photographer at the Journal Tribune in Biddeford, Maine.

Thea Breite es la directora principal de gráficas y fotografía del Providence Journal. Es responsable del diseño de la primera plana y de la edición de fotografías de deportes. Fue directora de fotografía en el Boston Globe, The Orange County Register y director de fotografía y fotógrafa del Journal Tribune en Biddeford, Maine.

Tony O. Champagne is a staff artist at The Times-Picayune in New Orleans. His work has also appeared in The Los Angeles Times, The Quill and in campaigns for McDonald's and the National Football League.

Tony O. Champagne es artista gráfico de The Times Picayune en Nueva Orleans. Sus trabajos también han sido publicados en The Los Angeles Times, The Quill y en campañas publicitarias de McDonald's y la National Football League.

Bert Fox is the art director of The Philadelphia Inquirer's Sunday magazine. He was photo editor and chief photographer of the Mail Tribune in Medford, Ore., the World Newspapers in Coos Bay, Ore., and a reporter and photographer at the Standard-Examiner in Ogden, Utah.

Bert Fox es director artístico de la revista dominical de The Philadelphia Inquirer. Fue director de fotografía y fotógrafo principal del Mail Tribune en Medford, Oregon, World Newspapers en Coos, Oregon y reportero y fotógrafo del Standard-Examiner, en Ogden, Utah.

David Pierce is assistant graphics editor of The Detroit News. He has worked on the art staff at The Rocky Mountain News, The Philadelphia Inquirer and The Fort Lauderdale News and Sun-Sentinal.

David Pierce es director asistente de gráficas de The Detroit News. Ha trabajado en el departamento artístico de The Rocky Mountain News, The Philadelphia Inquirer y The Fort

CHAPTER ONE

Overall Design

OVERALL DESIGN 250,000 Plus

BRONZE

The New York Times

Staff

Detroit Free Press
Staff

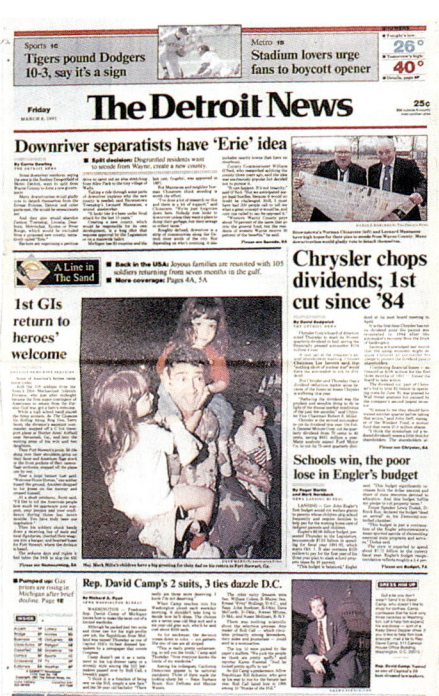

The Detroit News
Staff

THIRTEENTH EDITION 13

OVERALL DESIGN 100,000 – 249,000

BRONZE

The Christian Science Monitor
Boston, MA

John Van Pelt, Design Director; Robert Harbison,
Photo Editor; Staff

14 THE BEST OF NEWSPAPER DESIGN

BRONZE

El Sol
Madrid, Spain

Staff

OVERALL DESIGN 100,000 – 249,999

BRONZE

The Washington Times

Joseph Scopin, AME Design; Michael Keating, AME/News; James Fiedler, Director of Photography; Gil Roschuni, Art Director

16 THE BEST OF NEWSPAPER DESIGN

Gazette Telegraph
Colorado Springs, CO
Staff

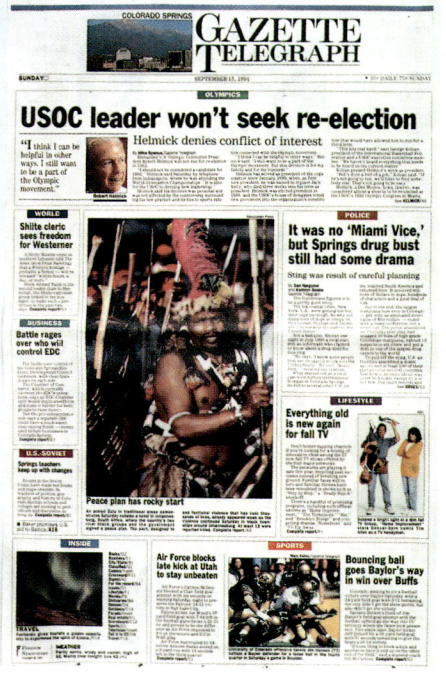

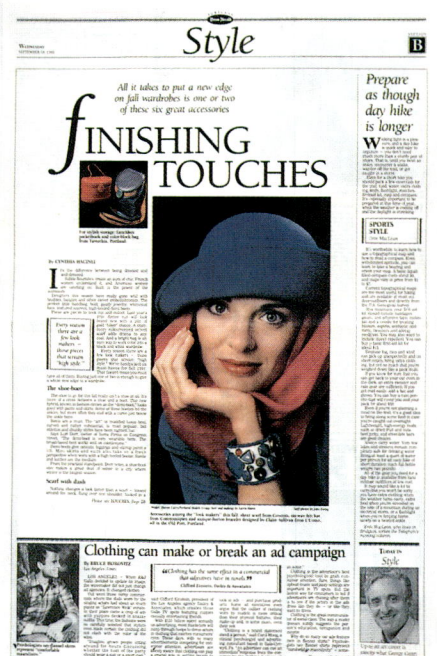

Maine Sunday Telegram &
Press Herald
Portland, ME

Warren Watson, Art Director; Andrea Philbrick, Designer; Rick Wakely, Designer; Steve Dandy, Designer; Bob Dixon, Designer; Sandy Shriver, Photo Editor

THIRTEENTH EDITION 17

OVERALL DESIGN 100,000 – 249,999

The Virginian-Pilot / Ledger Star
Norfolk, VA

Alan Jacobson, Design Director; Staff

BRONZE

Eastsideweek
Kirkland, WA

Sandra Schneider, Art Director; Mark Widmer, Illustrator; Jerry Gay, Photographer; Sandra Hoover, Photographer

OVERALL DESIGN | Non-daily

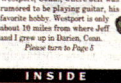

The Wall Street Journal Classroom Edition

Karl Hartig, Design Director; Orlie Kraus, Art Director; Karin Siciliano, Art Director

20 THE BEST OF NEWSPAPER DESIGN

CHAPTER TWO

IN THIS CHAPTER:

**Judges'
Special
Recognition**

The Detroit News,
for breaking news
presentation.

News

NEWS Front Section

BRONZE

The Orange County Register
Santa Ana, CA

Kevin Byrne, News Editor/Design; John Fabris, Assistant News Editor/Design; Mark Yemma, Assistant News Editor/Design; Staff

Berlingske Tidende
Copenhagen, Denmark

Staff

Detroit Free Press

Randy Miller, Deputy Managing Editor; John Goecke, Design Director; Wayne Kamidoi, Designer; Ken McDonald, Designer; Sue Parker, Designer; Lee Yarosh, Designer

The Detroit News

Dale Peskin, AME; Sue Burzynski, AME News; Dierck Casselman, AME Graphics/Design; Nancy Hanus, Assistant News Editor; Beth Valone, Assistant News Editor; Joe Gray, Assistant News Editor; Cathy Anderson, Assistant News Editor

The Washington Times

Michael Keating, AME/News; Joseph Scopin, AME Design; James Fiedler, Director of Photography; Greg Groesch, Art Director; Paul Woodward, Artist; Henry Christopher, Artist

Local News • Sports • Business • Other Sections

(LOCAL NEWS SECTION)
The Washington Times
Don Renfroe, Deputy News Editor

(SPORTS SECTION)
Gazette Telegraph
Colorado Springs, CO
Dan Cotter, Designer

(BUSINESS SECTION)
Dayton Daily News
John Thomson, AME Graphics; Kristin Herzog, Art Director & Designer; June Herold, Coordinator; Laura Dempsey, Copy Editor; Tim Borgert, Illustrator; Randy Palmer, Illustrator

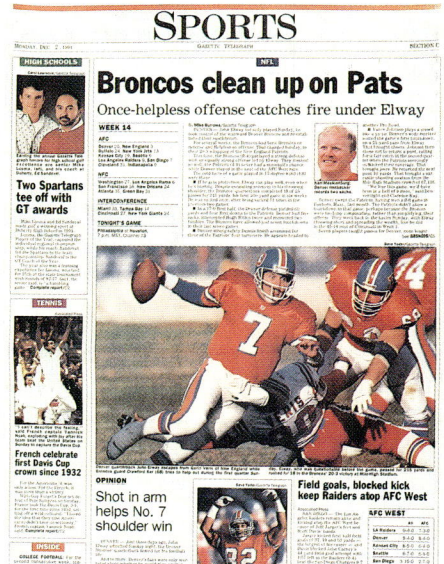

The Detroit News
Felix Grabowski, Graphics Director; Mark Lett, AME/National and Business; Steve Kaskovich, Asst. Business Editor; Patrick Sedlar, Artist; Glynnis Sweeny, Artist; Mary Harris, Copy Editor; Aaron Hightower, Artist

(OTHER SECTION)
The Orange County Register
Brenda Shoun, Designer; Staff

BRONZE
The Orange County Register
John Fabris, Assistant News Editor/Design; Brenda Shoun, Designer; Nanette Bisher, Art Director; Staff

THIRTEENTH EDITION 23

NEWS Front Page

BRONZE
Aftenposten
Oslo, Norway
Layout Staff

BRONZE
Newsday
Jeff Massaro, Art Director & Designer; Bob Brandt, Managing Editor; Ken Irby, Photo Editor

BRONZE
The Times-Picayune
George Berke, Design Director; Tom Gregory, Associate News Editor; Kurt Mutchler, Graphics Editor

BRONZE

The Washington Times

Michael Keating, AME/News

BRONZE

The Wichita Eagle

Alice Sky, Design Director; Jeff Tuttle, Photographer; Randy Tobias, Photographer

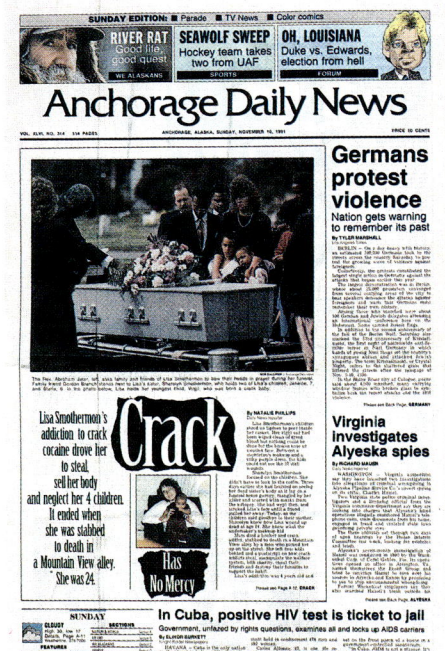

Anchorage Daily News

Mike Campbell, Designer; Bob Hallinen, Photographer; Richard J. Murphy, Photo Editor; Frank Gerjevic, Designer

NEWS Front Page

Detroit Free Press
Sue Parker, Designer; John Goecke, Design Director

The Providence Journal
Thea Breite, Designer & Picture Editor; William K. Daby, Photographer

The Virginian-Pilot
Norfolk, VA

Alan Jacobson, Design Director; Nelson Brown, AME/News; Pam Smith-Rodden, News Editor; Pat Thomas, Designer; Alex Burrows, Photo Editor

San Francisco Examiner
Staff

San Jose Mercury News
Staff

The Spokesman-Review & Spokane Chronicle

Scott Sines, Photo Editor; Neal Pattison, AME; John Kafentzis, News Editor; Kit King, Chief Photographer; Kevin Graham, Copy Desk Chief; Vince Grippi, Graphics Editor; Molly Quinn, Graphics Artist

Syracuse Herald-Journal
Tim Atseff, Managing Editor

El Sol
Madrid, Spain
Juan Varela, Chief Editor

The Washington Times
Michael Keating, AME/News

THIRTEENTH EDITION 27

26 EL SOL Domingo, 8 de diciembre de 1991   MADRID

PAISAJES URBANOS

GIMNASIO MARAVILLAS

■ Construido en 1961 ■ Solar con un desnivel de 12 metros ■ Dificultad: hacer tres espacios distintos ■ Coste: ocho millones de pesetas ■ Elemento principal: las cerchas invertidas

▶ EL SOL/EQUIPO DE ANALISIS DE LA ESCUELA DE ARQUITECTURA

Cuando Alejandro de la Sota fue a visitar el solar donde le habían encargado levantar un gimnasio, lo primero que tuvo que levantar fue la vista: doce metros de desnivel separaban las calles que limitaban el espacio disponible.

Corría el año 1961 y el proyecto se lo habían encargado los propietarios del colegio Maravillas, situado entre las calles de Joaquín Costa y Guadalquivir, que necesitaban ampliar sus instalaciones con un gimnasio, un patio de recreo, nuevas aulas, una pista de hockey, vestuarios y laboratorio.

Se trataba de un edificio encajonado. La única pared que da a la calle debía actuar como una membrana, es decir, tenía que dejar pasar la luz y el aire pero impedir la invasión del ruido del tráfico de la transitada vía de Joaquín Costa.

Otra condición impuesta a De la Sota era que el patio del colegio debía estar al mismo nivel que la calle más elevada, por lo que el techo del gimnasio debía ser a la vez el suelo de ese patio. La altura del edificio era, por tanto, limitada.

¿Dónde colocar entonces las aulas?

Lo original en la resolución que aplica De la Sota es *abombar* el techo del gimnasio para ubicar las aulas en ese espacio. De paso consiguió dar a esas clases una estructura de auditorio aprovechando la inclinación del suelo, lo que favorece la visibilidad.

Consigue dos espacios distintos donde en teoría sólo cabía uno, gracias a la utilización de *cerchas* –vigas gigantes con forma curvada que permiten soportar el peso de las aulas sobre el gimnasio– que coloca en sentido contrario a lo habitual.

Abajo, en el sótano, queda la piscina, que aprovecha la pendiente que va de derecha a izquierda del terreno.

Luz selectiva

Los espectadores que se sientan en las gradas, que permanecen en penumbra, pueden seguir los movimientos en la cancha sin que la luz les deslumbre.

Aulas y cancha rivalizan para atrapar la luz, que sólo se filtra en el interior por ventanales superiores de la única fachada que da a la calle. Al contrario, la inclinación de la bóveda invertida dirige la atención del público hacia abajo, donde se desarrollan los acontecimientos deportivos.

Enormes vigas actúan a la vez de paredes para las clases y de aislantes del ruido exterior. La frialdad de estos materiales –hierro y hormigón– se contrapone a los materiales utilizados para el gimnasio: la madera contribuye a dotar de calor y color a

1 Sótano (piscina)
2 Planta baja (polideportivo-gimnasio)
3 1ª planta (Aulas)
4 Nivel superior (Patio-canchas de juego)
5 Entradas de luz natural (Al gimnasio y a las aulas)
6 Colegio
7 Reja protectora (Calle Joaquín Costa)

Una lección de lógica arquitectónica

Como una fachada de ladrillo más en la ciudad, el gimnasio Maravillas ha pasado desapercibido a los madrileños durante 30 años. Sin embargo, aún hoy es visitado por arquitectos de todo el mundo, que lo consideran genial.

un ámbito aparentemente frío.

En cuanto a la fachada, no deja traslucir el contenido del interior. El ladrillo se ve intercalado por bandas horizontales acristaladas y balcones de forma rectangular que sobresalen hacia fuera.

Arriba, ya en el patio, la fachada se remata con una tela metálica sostenida por puntales inclinados. Esta es la estructura que se divisa desde la calle de Joaquín Costa y que apenas apunta el complejo y estudiadísimo interior.

La estructura del Colegio Maravillas se asemeja a un aparato de gimnasia de proporciones gigantescas tensado al igual que los músculos de los deportistas que lo utilizan.

El espíritu

Dicen que cuando se entra en el gimnasio del Maravillas lo primero que se dice es: "Bueno, no se podría haber hecho de otra forma, ésta es la única solución posible".

En esta apreciación parece estar la clave del gallego Alejandro de la Sota, un arquitecto que recurre a las soluciones más ingeniosas pero, en apariencia, más sencillas.

De hecho, una de sus máximas es que no se debe trazar una sola línea hasta que el proyecto no esté totalmente ideado en la cabeza.

Alejandro de la Sota no se distingue por la monumentalidad de sus obras.

Al igual que su carácter, sus edificios se definen por la aparente sencillez: cómo coger una serie de elementos, jugar con ellos y conseguir lo que al final parece la única solución posible. Como él mismo dice, la arquitectura es emoción, y esta emoción hace sonreír.

Entre las calles de Joaquín Costa y Guadalquivir, De la Sota exhibe desde hace 30 años un leve y magnífico apunte de su emocionante obra.

▶ *Esta serie de artículos ha sido coordinada por las redactoras Carlota Lafuente y Cristina Díaz. Los estudiantes de arquitectura que han colaborado en el primer artículo son: José Vela, Pedro Rodríguez Miranda, Felipe Lozano, Marta Mediavilla, José de Coca, Fernando Fernández, Pablo Berzal, María Linares, Alberto Morell, Carmen Moreno Balboa y Susana García.*

ARQUITECTO

ALEJANDRO DE LA SOTA
■ Nació en Pontevedra en 1913
■ Premio Nacional de Arquitectura
■ Titulado por la ESA de Madrid
■ Otra obra: pueblo de Esquivel (Sevilla)
■ Filosofía: la arquitectura lógica

BRONZE

The New York Times

Tom Bodkin, Art Director & Design Director;
Margaret O'Connor, Designer; Sam Reep, Designer;
Anne Cronin, Graphics Editor; Nancy Weinstock,
Photo Editor

The New York Times

Tom Bodkin, Art Director & Design Director;
Margaret O'Connor, Designer

The New York Times

Tom Bodkin, Art Director & Design Director;
Margaret O'Connor, Designer

THIRTEENTH EDITION 29

NEWS Local News Page

Aftenposten
Oslo, Norway

Rolf Chr. Ulrichsen, Photographer; Layout Staff

Newsday

Don Forst, New York Editor; Jeff Massaro, Designer; John Mancini, News Editor

Times Advocate
Escondido, CA

Michael Quinn, Designer

The Washington Times

Don Renfroe, Deputy News Editor

The Washington Times

Don Renfroe, Deputy News Editor

30 THE BEST OF NEWSPAPER DESIGN

Sports Page

THURSDAY, MAY 2, 1991 — San Francisco Chronicle — D1

CITYLINE: 24-Hour Sports (415) 512-5000
- Pro Sports, enter 6200
- College Sports, enter 6300

SPORTING GREEN

LOWELL COHN — PAGE D3
C.W. NEVIUS — PAGE D7
SPORTS DIGEST — PAGE D8

939

Henderson Gets His Record-Setting Steal

By David Bush
Chronicle Staff Writer

As Rickey Henderson wrapped his arms around third base in the fourth inning at the Coliseum yesterday, he knew that he had run perhaps the longest 90 feet of his life. He was now baseball's career leader in stolen bases.

Henderson has 939 steals, Lou Brock has 938, and nobody else matters.

"I said to myself, 'It's all over,'" Hender-

FOR THE RECORD
SPECIAL SOUVENIR PAGE / See Page D2

son said later. "I'm No. 1 now. A lot of the pressure had left. I had become lighter. I think I was carrying so much weight and so much pressure by trying to get it over

See Page D6 Col. 5

With a trademark headfirst lunge, Rickey Henderson kicked up some dirt in the fourth inning yesterday at the Coliseum and slid toward the 939th stolen base of his career, one more than Lou Brock had

BY DEANNE FITZMAURICE/THE CHRONICLE

7 Ryan Does It Again, No-Hits Blue Jays

Associated Press

Arlington, Texas

Nolan Ryan pitched his seventh major-league no-hitter last night in one of the most dominating performances of his amazing quarter-century career.

Ryan struck out 16 in shutting down the best-hitting team in the major leagues, and the Texas Rangers beat the Toronto Blue Jays, 3-0.

"I had the best command of all three pitches. This is the best," Ryan, 44, said of his no-hit collection. "This is my most overpowering night."

Ryan, who became the oldest player to pitch a no-hitter last season with his record sixth, against the A's at the Coliseum, had only two runners reach base against him last night, and neither made it past first base. He walked Kelly Gruber on a 3-2 pitch in the first inning and walked Joe Carter on a full-count pitch in the seventh.

That was all as Ryan pitched the first no-hitter of the season. After taking part in a record nine no-hitters last year,

INSIDE
- Brewers take 19 to win. PAGE D4
- Giants lose again, 4-1. PAGE D6
- Celtics take 2-1 series lead. PAGE D7

Earlier in the day, Ryan didn't expect to last more than a few innings, let alone make more history. Before the game, he told Rangers pitching coach Tom House: "I feel old today. My back hurts, my heel hurts, I don't feel good.

"I didn't think I would be out there very long," Ryan said after the game. "I'm going home straight to bed. I've got a busy day tomorrow."

"That's Nolan Ryan," Texas catcher Mike Stanley said. "He complains all day and then goes out and throws a no-hitter."

The Blue Jays, leading the majors with a .276 average, did not hit a single ball hard and flailed helplessly at Ryan's assortment of 96-miles-per-hour fastballs, sharp curves and change-ups.

Ryan threw 122 pitches, 83 for strikes. He tied his own team record for strikeouts, set April 26, 1990, against Chicago.

The closest Toronto came to a hit

See Page D3 Col. 1

Nolan Ryan was all smiles last night after he got the final out of his seventh no-hitter

BY UNITED PRESS INTERNATIONAL

Warriors Go 1 Up On Spurs

By George Shirk
Chronicle Staff Writer

The Warriors last night seized control of their best-of-five, first-round playoff series against favored San Antonio, but to do it, they had to make an emergency rescue.

Twice they took 14-point leads in the first half, and they had a pair of 11-point leads in the fourth quarter. But all that melted away, and with 57 seconds left in the game, they led by only two. The Warriors hung in, though, and finally won it, 106-106.

"It almost looked like it was slipping away," said guard Tim Hardaway, "but we had enough poise from all those other leads we blew in the regular season. Tonight, nobody panicked, nobody took bad shots. We did what we had to do."

With the victory, the Warriors took a two-games-to-one lead in the

See Page D7 Col. 5

SILVER

San Francisco Chronicle

John Curley, Sports Editor/Designer; Hulda Nelson, Art Director

NEWS Sports Page

BRONZE

Asbury Park Press

James Denk, Illustrator & Designer

BRONZE

The San Diego Union

Stan McNeal, Designer

Asbury Park Press

Tim Oliver, Designer; Sean McNaughton, Artist; Greg Henderson, Editor; Joe Sullivan, Editor; Mike Rafferty, Photo Editor; Noah K. Murray, Photographer; Bill King, Illustrator

32 THE BEST OF NEWSPAPER DESIGN

The Detroit News

Michael Green, Photographer; Jim Russ, Asst. Sports Editor

The Detroit News

Patrick Sedlar, Illustrator; Jim Russ, Asst. Sports Editor

Gazette Telegraph
Colorado Springs, CO

Dan Cotter, Designer

Los Angeles Times /
Orange County Edition

Chuck Nigash, Art Director & Designer

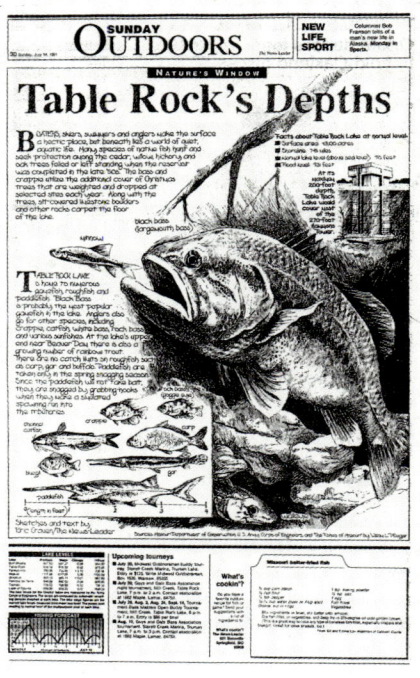

The News-Leader
Springfield, MO

Eric Craven, Graphics Artist & Reporter; John L. Dengler, Graphics Editor; Mary Ulmer, Sports Editor; George Benge, Managing Editor

THIRTEENTH EDITION 33

NEWS Sports Page

The New York Times

Fred Norgaard, Art Director & Designer; Tom Bodkin, Design Director

The New York Times

Staff

The New York Times

Margaret O'Connor, Designer; Tom Bodkin, Art Director & Designer

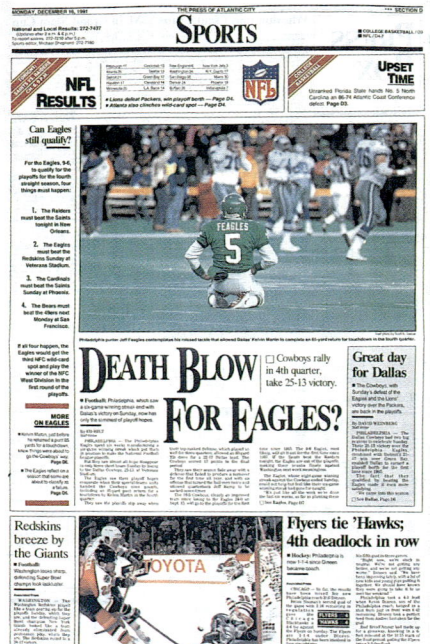

The Atlantic City Press

Peter M. Brophy, Assistant Sports Editor

The Providence Journal

Stephanie Gay, Picture Editor & Designer; Mary Murphy, Photographer

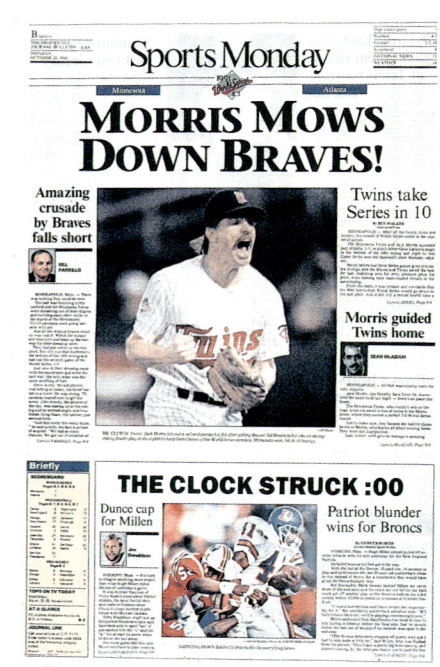

The Providence Journal

Susie Stevens, Picture Editor & Designer; Bill Ostendorf, Art Director; Glenn Osmundson, Photographer

34 THE BEST OF NEWSPAPER DESIGN

Business Page

Akron Beacon Journal
Dennis Gordon, Page Designer

Asbury Park Press
James Denk, Illustrator & Designer

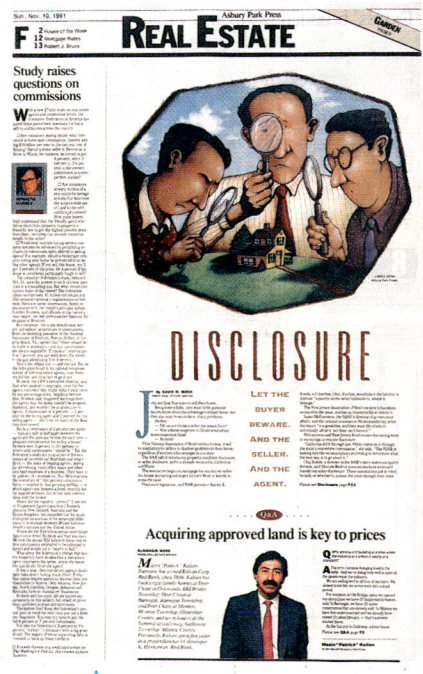

Asbury Park Press
James Denk, Illustrator & Designer

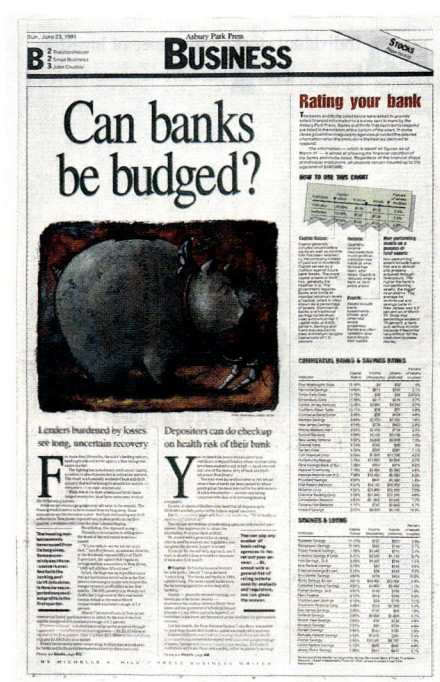

Dayton Daily News
John Thomson, AME Graphics; Kristin Herzog, Art Director; Randy Palmer, Illustrator and Designer

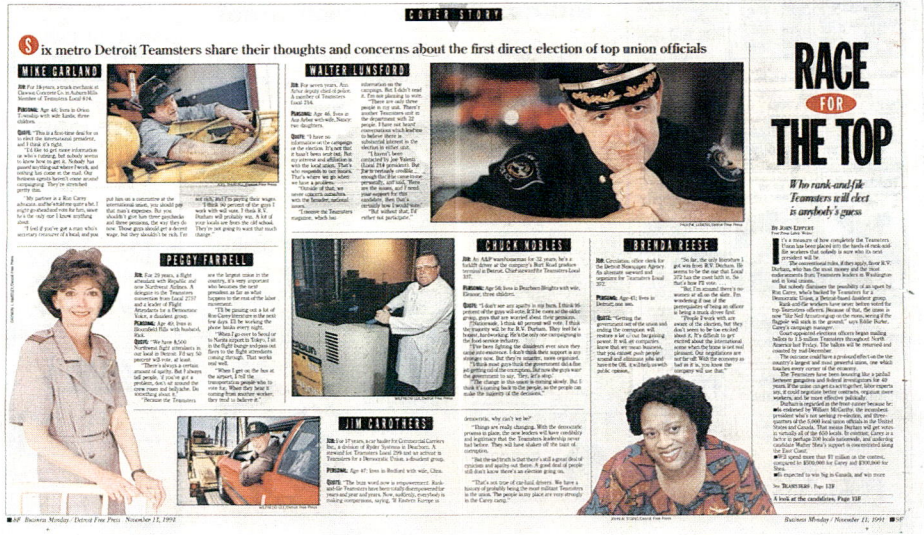

Detroit Free Press
Steve Anderson, Designer; Deborah Withey, Design Director

THIRTEENTH EDITION 35

NEWS Business Page

The Detroit News
Patrick Sedlar, Illustrator & Designer; Felix Grabowski, Graphics Director

The Detroit News
Felix Grabowski, Graphics Director; Steve Kaskovich, Asst. Business Editor

The Miami Herald
Ana Lense Larrauri, Editorial Artist; Jim Watters, Business Monday News Editor; Randy Stano, Director of Editorial Art & Design

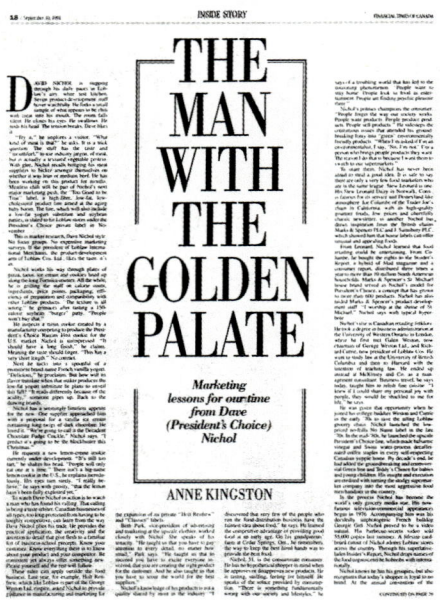

Financial Times of Canada
Toronto, ON, Canada

Barbara Hyland, Publisher; Steve Lawrence, Editor; Gary Hall, Art Director; Anne Kingston, Writer; Edward Gajdel, Photographer

The Miami Herald
Woody Vondracek, Editorial Artist; Jim Watters, Business Monday News Editor; Randy Stano, Director of Editorial Art & Design

The New York Times

Anne Leigh, Art Director & Designer; Tom Bodkin, Design Director

The New York Times

Greg Ryan, Art Director & Designer; Tom Bodkin, Design Director; Culver Pictures, Photographer

Newsday

Bozena Syska, Designer; Don Bruce, Editor

Newsday

Bozena Syska, Designer; Ned Levine, Illustrator; Rick Green, Editor

Saint Paul Pioneer Press

Lauri Hopple Treston, Designer; Stacy Sweat, Art Director; Scott Takushi, Photographer

The Times-Picayune

Tony O. Champagne, Illustrator & Designer; Jean McIntosh, Art Director

NEWS Other Page

Akron Beacon Journal
Dennis Gordon, Page Designer

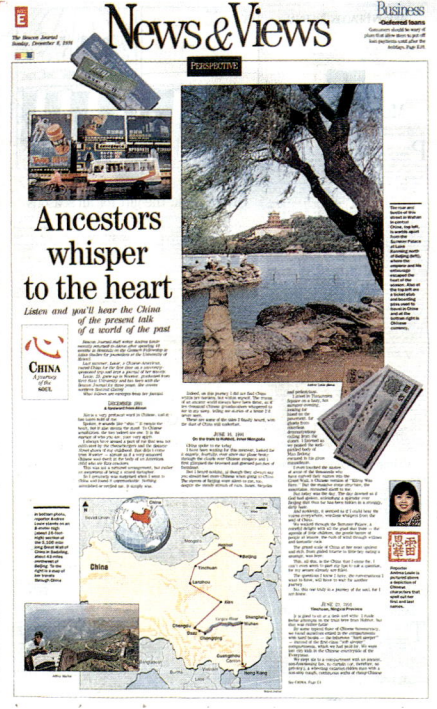

The Columbus Dispatch
Julia Barry Bell, Designer & Infographics Artist; Tom Mattix, Infographics Artist; Doug Miller, Infographics Artist; Nancy McCloud, Infographics Coordinator; Scott Minister, Art Director

The Orange County Register
Santa Ana, CA

John Fabris, Assistant News Editor/Design; Nanette Bisher, Art Director

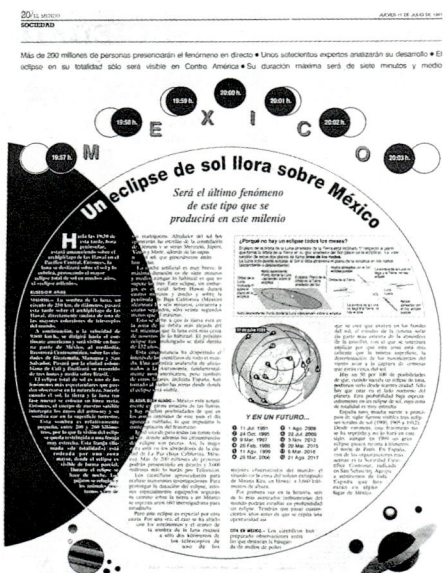

El Mundo
Madrid, Spain

Carmelo Caderot, Art Director & Designer; Manuel de Miguel, Assistant Art Director

Diario 16
Madrid, Spain

Carlos Perez, Art Director & Designer; Roberto Hernandez, Illustrator

38 THE BEST OF NEWSPAPER DESIGN

Other • Inside Pages

The Orange County Register

Don Wyatt, Designer; Staff

BRONZE

The Orange County Register

John Fabris, Assistant News Editor/Design; Nanette Bisher, Art Director

The Orange County Register

Brenda Shoun, Designer; Staff

(INSIDE PAGE)

The Orange County Register

Paul Carbo, Designer

The Orange County Register

Nanette Bisher, Art Director; Staff

Chicago Tribune

Stephen Ravenscraft, Illustrator & Researcher; Julie Sheer, Researcher; Dennis Odom, Art Director; Stephen Cvengros, Illustration Editor

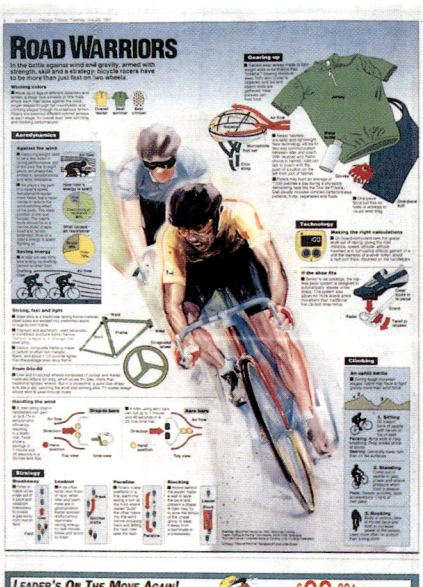

THIRTEENTH EDITION 39

NEWS Inside Page

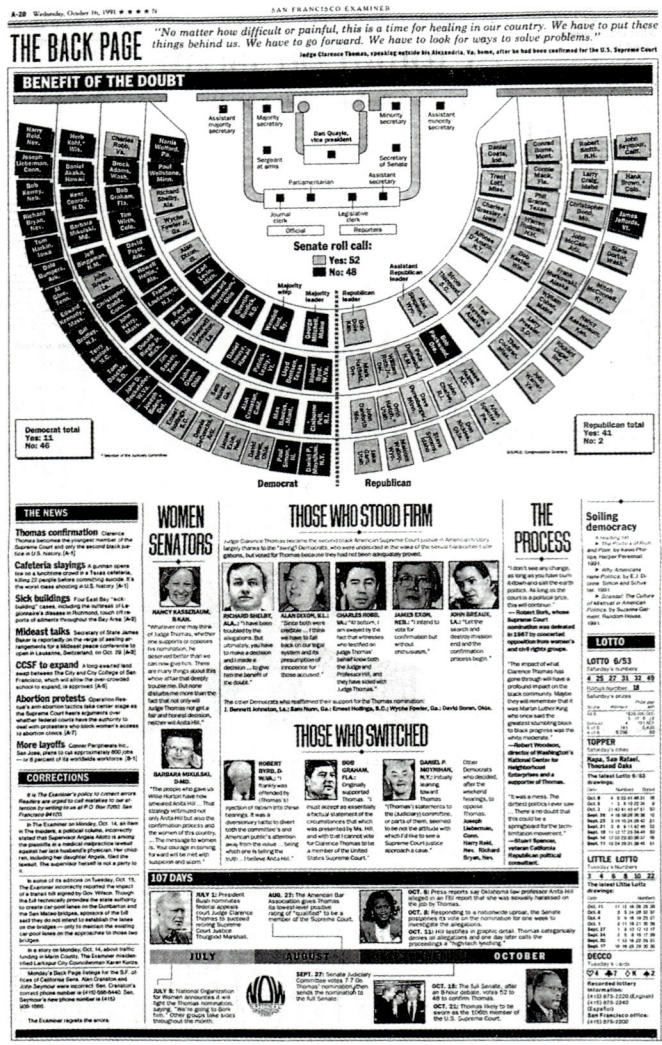

SILVER
San Francisco Examiner

Kelly Frankeny, Graphics Editor; Andrew Ross, Back Page Editor; Joe Shoulak, Artist

San Jose Mercury News

Albert Poon, Designer; Sam Hundley, Features Design Director; Edmundo Macedo, Asst. Sports Editor

BRONZE
The San Diego Union

Ken Marshall, Designer & Writer; Hank Wesch, Writer; Sean M. Haffey, Photographer

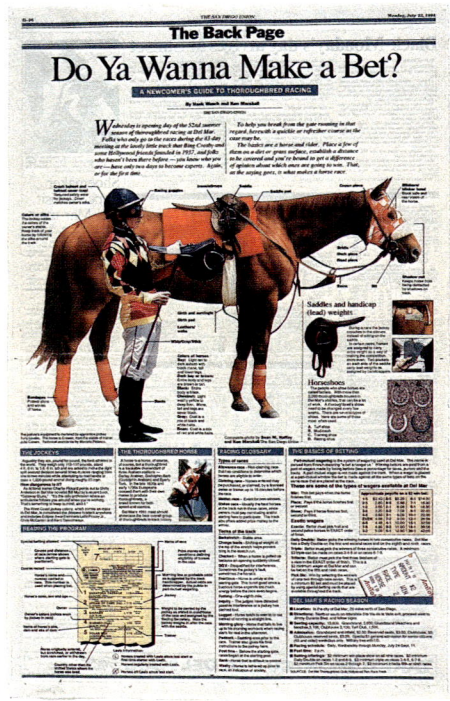

San Jose Mercury News

Albert Poon, Designer; Sam Hundley, Features Design Director; Edmundo Macedo, Assistant Sports Editor

Inside Page • Breaking News: Soviet Coup

BRONZE
Syracuse Herald-Journal

Tim Atseff, Managing Editor

The Sacramento Bee

Merrill Oliver, Asst. Director of Photography

(SOVIET COUP)
BRONZE
The Orange County Register

Kevin Byrne, News Editor/Design; John Fabris, Assistant News Editor/Design; Mark Yemma, Assistant News Editor/Design; Bernadette Finley, Assistant News Editor/Design; Tia Lai, Graphics Editor; Staff

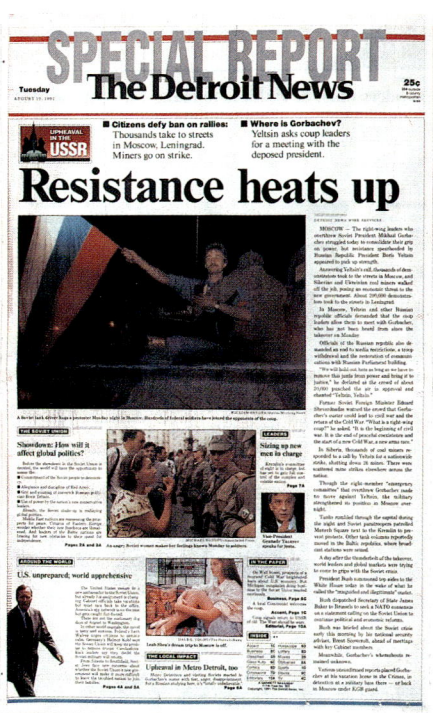

The Detroit News

Dale Peskin, AME; Dierck Casselman, AME Graphics/Design; Nancy Hanus, Asst. News Editor; Beth Valone, Asst. News Editor; Robert Graham, Graphics Art Director

Los Angeles Times

Ligaya Gritz, Art Director; Jon Thurber, News Editor; Dan Fisher, Section Editor

THIRTEENTH EDITION 41

NEWS   Breaking News: Soviet Coup • Solar Eclipse

The Seattle Times
Greg Rasa, News Page Designer; David Miller, Art Director

Syracuse Herald-Journal
Tim Atseff, Managing Editor

The Washington Times
Michael Keating, AME News; Joseph Scopin, AME Design; James Fiedler, Director of Photography; Greg Groesch, Art Director; Paul Woodward, Artist; Henry Christopher, Artist

El Sol
Madrid, Spain

Juan Varela, Chief Editor; Staff

The Times-Picayune
George Berke, Design Director; Tom Gregory, Associate Editor/News; Kurt Mutchler, Graphics Editor; Michael Jantze, Staff Artist; Mike S. Henry, Staff Artist

(SOLAR ECLIPSE)

Filha de São Paulo
São Paulo, Brazil

Luiz Gustavo Pauli, Graphics Designer; Teresa Nunes, Assistant for Graphics; Eliane Stephan, Art Director

Breaking News: Editor's Choice

The Atlanta Journal & Constitution
Mike Gordon, Design Director; Tony De Feria, Art Director; Ron Feinberg, 1A Editor

El Mundo
Madrid, Spain

Carmelo Caderot, Art Director & Designer; Manuel de Miguel, Assistant Art Director

Gazette Telegraph
Colorado Springs, CO

Scott Hiestand, Art Director; Staff

Austin American-Statesman
Mike Sutter, Designer; Ralph Barrera, Photographer; Karen Warren, Photographer; Zach Ryall, Photography Director; Cliff Vancura, Graphics Artist; Linda Swanson-Scott, Graphics Researcher; Mark Freistedt, Graphics Editor; G.W. Babb, Design Director

The Dallas Morning News
News Art Staff

The Detroit News
Dale Peskin, AME; Joe Gray, Asst. News Editor; Felecia Henderson, Copy Editor; Kenneth Knight, Artist; David Pierce, Artist; Robert Richards, Artist; Patrick Sedlar, Artist

NEWS   Breaking News: Editor's Choice

(TOP ROW)

SILVER & JSR

The Detroit News

Dale Peskin, AME; Dierck Casselman, AME Graphics/Design; Phil Laciura, Sports Editor; Rob Alstetter, Asst. Sports Editor; Brian Hanley, Asst. Sports Editor; Joe Gray, Asst. News Editor; Cathy Anderson, Asst. News Editor

(BOTTOM ROW)

El Mundo
Madrid, Spain

Carmelo Caderot, Art Director & Designer; Manuel de Miguel, Assistant Art Director; Pedro J. Ramirez, Editor in Chief; Gorka Sampedro, Infographics Artist; Mario Tascon, Infographics Director; Jeff Goertzen, Art Consultant; Ulises Culebro, Illustrator; Samuel Velasco, Illustrator; Modesto Carrasco, Infographics Artist

44 THE BEST OF NEWSPAPER DESIGN

NEWS Breaking News: Editor's Choice • Topic: Editor's Choice

Saint Paul Pioneer Press

Richard Marshall, Photographer; Stacy Sweat, Art Director; Joe Sevick, Designer; Peter Weinberger, Photo Director

San Francisco Examiner

Kelly Frankeny, Graphics Editor; Bill Prochnow, Design Director; Stewart Huntington, Graphics Coordinator; Staff

BRONZE

The Wichita Eagle

Alice Sky, Design Director; Brian Corn, Director of Photography; Dave Williams, Photographer; Kim Johnson, Photographer; Randy Tobias, Photographer; Fernando Salazar, Photographer; Laura Rauch, Photographer; Jeff Tuttle, Photographer; Paul Soutar, Graphics Director

(TOPIC: EDITOR'S CHOICE)

Detroit Free Press

Ted Williamson, Assistant Graphics Editor; Laura Varon Brown, Graphics Director; John Goecke, Design Director; Moses Harris, Chief Artist; Martha Thierry, Artist; Hank Szerlag, Artist; Peter Gavrilovich, Reporter; Chip Visci, AME/Local News

El Sol
Madrid, Spain

Juan Valera, Chief Editor; Staff

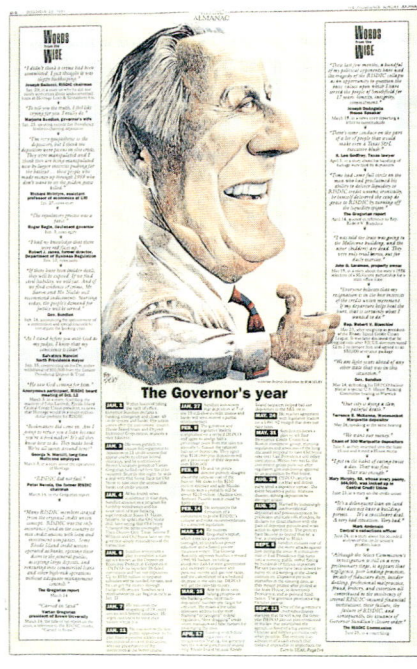

The Providence Journal

Mick Cochran, Art Director & Designer; Bob Shelby, Illustrator

46 THE BEST OF NEWSPAPER DESIGN

Topic: Editor's Choice

San Francisco Examiner

Kelly Frankeny, Graphics Editor; Bill Prochnow, Design Director; Stewart Huntington, Graphics Coordinator; Staff

San Jose Mercury News
Staff

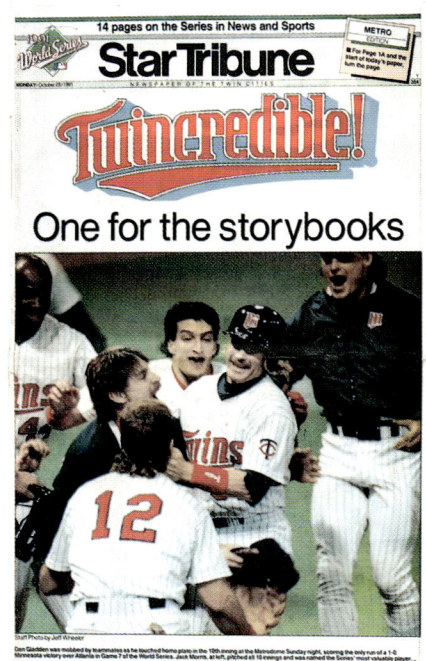

Star Tribune
Minneapolis, MN
Staff

The Tribune
Fort Pierce, FL

Wade E. Wilson, News Editor/Designer; Diane Wilson, Photographer

The Christian Science Monitor
Boston, MA
Staff

THIRTEENTH EDITION 47

NEWS   Topic: Soviet Unrest • Abortion

SILVER
The Dallas Morning News
Kathleen Vincent, Art Director; Ben McConnell, Graphics Editor; Betsy Bock, Graphics; Don Huff, Graphics; Linda Hawks Oistad, Graphics; Carol Zuber Mallison, Graphics; Charles Ealy, Layout Editor; John Davidson, Photo Editor; William Snyder, Photographer; Jim Landers, International Editor

The Orange County Register
Santa Ana, CA

Kevin Byrne, News Editor/Design; John Fabris, Assistant News Editor/Design; Mark Yemma, Assistant News Editor/Design; Don Wyatt, Assistant News Editor/Design; Tom Porter, AME; Staff

(TOPIC: ABORTION)
The Wichita Eagle
Sara Quinn, Staff Artist; Dan Holder, Layout Editor; Alice Sky, Design Director; Paul Soutar, Graphics Director; Photo Staff

The New York Times
Jim Quinlan, Art Director; Tom Bodkin, Design Director; Carol Bakinowski, Makeup Editor; John Hyland, Makeup Editor; Jim Mones, Makeup Editor; Dave Pitt, Makeup Editor; Peter Putrimas, Makeup Editor

CHAPTER THREE

IN THIS CHAPTER:

Judges' Special Recognition

The Detroit News, for breaking news presentation.

Los Angeles Times, for its informational graphics.

The Persian Gulf War

THE PERSIAN GULF WAR

SPECIAL NEWS TOPIC: THE GULF WAR
GOLD & JSR
The Detroit News

Dale Peskin, AME; Nancy Hanus, Assistant News Editor; Cathy Anderson, Assistant News Editor; Beth Valone, Assistant News Editor; Joe Gray, Assistant News Editor; Dierck Casselman, AME Graphics/Design; Felix Grabowski, Graphics Director; Mike Brown, Director of Photography; Graphics Staff

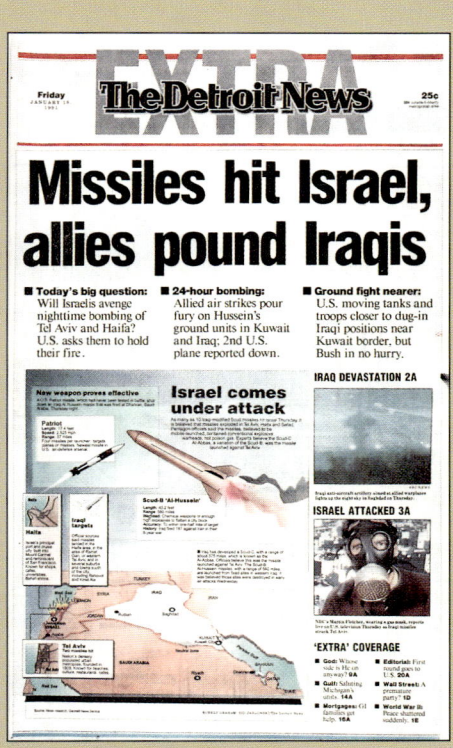

THIRTEENTH EDITION 51

THE PERSIAN GULF WAR

SPECIAL NEWS TOPIC: THE GULF WAR
GOLD & JSR
The Detroit News
(CONTINUED)

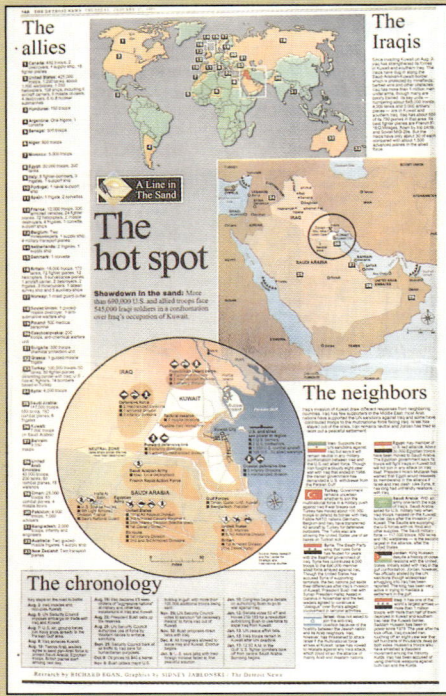

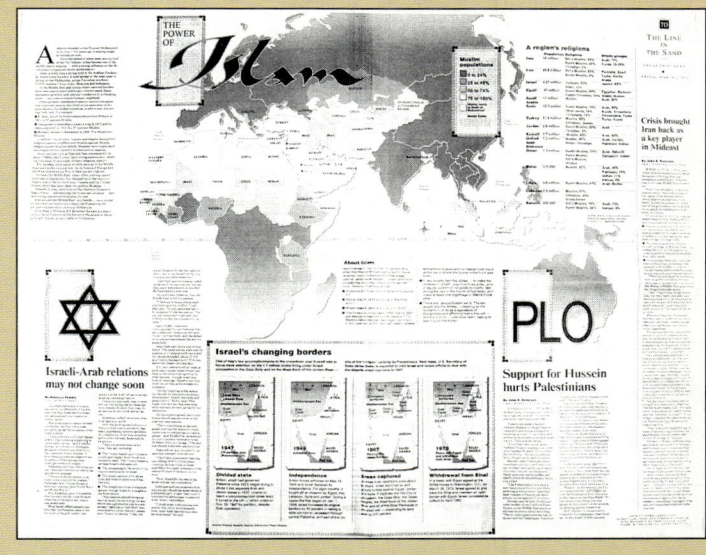

THE PERSIAN GULF WAR

BREAKING NEWS: U.S. BOMBING OF IRAQ
The Detroit News
Dale Peskin, AME; Dierck Casselman, AME Graphics/Design; Nancy Hanus, Assistant News Editor; Beth Valone, Assistant News Editor; Joe Gray, Assistant News Editor; Felix Grabowski, Graphics Director; Robert Graham, Graphics Art Director; Sidney Jablonski, Graphics Artist; Mike

BREAKING NEWS: ALLIES GROUND WAR ATTACK
The Detroit News
Christy Bradford, Managing Editor; Dierck Casselman, AME Graphics/Design; Nancy Hanus, Asst. News Editor; Joe Gray, Asst. News Editor; David Pierce, Graphic Artist; Sidney Jablonski, Graphic Artist; Robert Richards, Graphic Artist; Aaron Hightower, Graphic Artist

BREAKING NEWS: EDITOR'S CHOICE
The Detroit News
Dale Peskin, AME; Dierck Casselman, AME Graphics/Design; Felix Grabowski, Graphics Director; Nancy Hanus, Asst. News Editor; Beth Valone, Asst. News Editor; David Pierce, Graphic Artist; Mike Brown, Director of Photography

BREAKING NEWS: EDITOR'S CHOICE
The Detroit News
Dale Peskin, AME; Nancy Hanus, Asst. News Editor; Beth Valone, Asst. News Editor; Mike Brown, Director of Photography

BREAKING NEWS: EDITOR'S CHOICE
BRONZE
The Detroit News
Dale Peskin, Assistant Managing Editor; Joe Gray, Assistant News Editor; Dierck Casselman, AME Graphics/Design; Mike Brown, Photo Editor; Joan Rosen, Assistant Photo Editor; Sidney Jablonski, Graphics Artist; Felix Grabowski, Graphics Editor; Robert Graham, Graphics Artist

BREAKING NEWS: END OF GULF WAR
The Detroit News
Dale Peskin, Assistant Managing Editor; Dierck Casselman, AME Graphics/Design; Nancy Hanus, Assistant News Editor; Beth Valone, Assistant News Editor; Joe Gray, Assistant News Editor; Felix Grabowski, Graphics Director; Robert Graham, Graphics Art Director; Sidney Jablonski, Graphic Artist; David Pierce, Graphic Artist; Mike Brown, Director of Photography

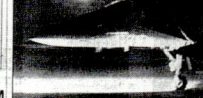

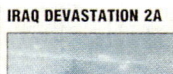

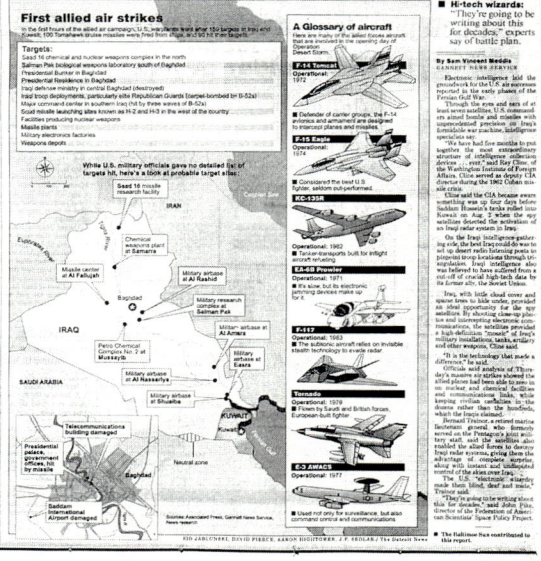

BREAKING NEWS: IRAQ BOMBING OF ISRAEL

SILVER

The Detroit News

Dale Peskin, AME; Dierck Casselman, AME Graphics/Design; Nancy Hanus, Asst. News Editor; Beth Valone, Asst. News Editor; Joe Gray, Asst. News Editor; Felix Grabowski, Graphics Director; Robert Graham, Graphics Art Director; Sidney Jablonski, Graphics Artist; Mike Brown, Director of Photography

THIRTEENTH EDITION 55

THE PERSIAN GULF WAR

BREAKING NEWS GRAPHIC: COLOR

The Detroit News

Robert Graham, Artist; David Pierce, Artist; Dierck Casselman, AME Graphics/Design; Felix Grabowski, Graphics Director; Patricia Vegella, Researcher; Michele Fecht, Asst. Graphics Editor

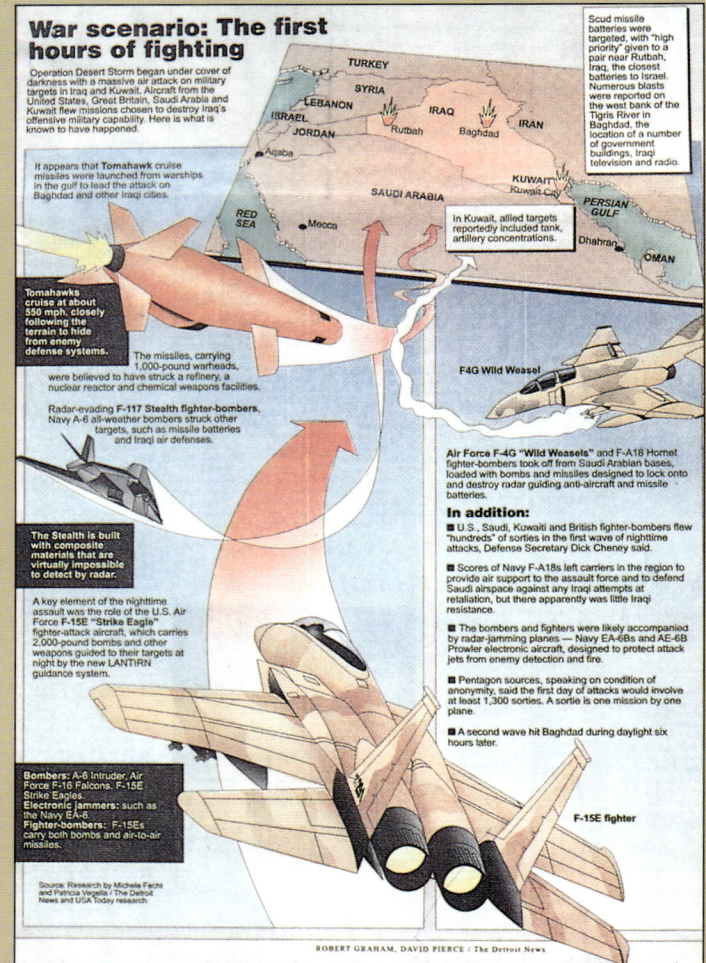

INFORMATIONAL GRAPHIC: BLACK & WHITE

The Detroit News

Kenneth Knight, Artist; Aaron Hightower, Artist; Robert J. Richards, Artist; Robert Graham, Graphics Art Director; Patricia Vegella, Researcher; Michele Fecht, Asst. Graphics Editor; Scott Faust, Asst. City Editor

INFORMATIONAL GRAPHIC: COLOR

BRONZE

The Detroit News

David Pierce, Artist; Marla Camp, Graphics Editor

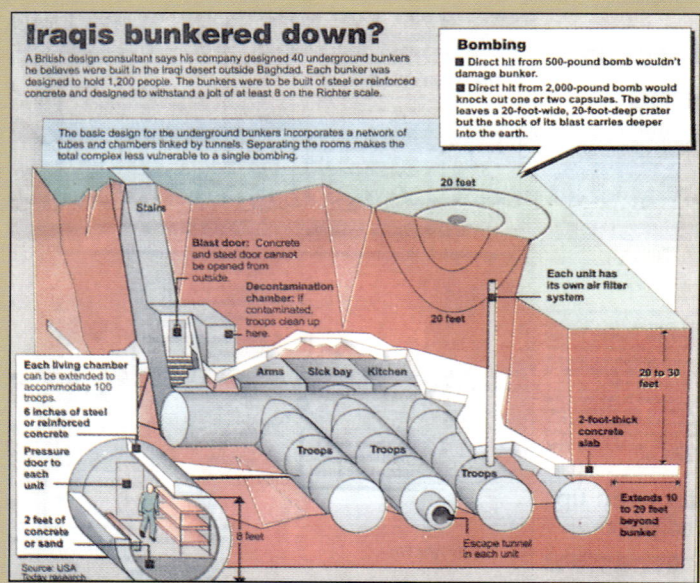

56 THE BEST OF NEWSPAPER DESIGN

BREAKING NEWS: EDITOR'S CHOICE
The Washington Times
Michael Keating, AME News; Joseph Scopin, AME Design; James Fiedler, Director of Photography; Greg Groesch, Art Director; Paul Woodward, Artist; Henry Christopher, Artist

NEWS: FRONT PAGE
The Washington Times
Michael Keating, AME/News

ILLUSTRATION: COLOR
BRONZE
The Washington Times
John Kascht, Art Director, Designer & Illustrator

NEWS: FRONT PAGE
The Washington Times
Michael Keating, AME/News

NEWS: FRONT PAGE
The Washington Times
Michael Keating, AME/News

NEWS: LOCAL PAGE
BRONZE
The Washington Times
Don Renfroe, Deputy News Editor

THE PERSIAN GULF WAR

NEWS: FRONT PAGE
Detroit Free Press
Lee Yarosh, Designer

BREAKING NEWS: U.S. BOMBING OF IRAQ
BRONZE
Detroit Free Press
John Goecke, Design Director; Wayne Kamidoi, Designer; Ken McDonald, Designer; Sue Parker, Designer; Lee Yarosh, Designer; Chip Visci, AME; Graphics Staff

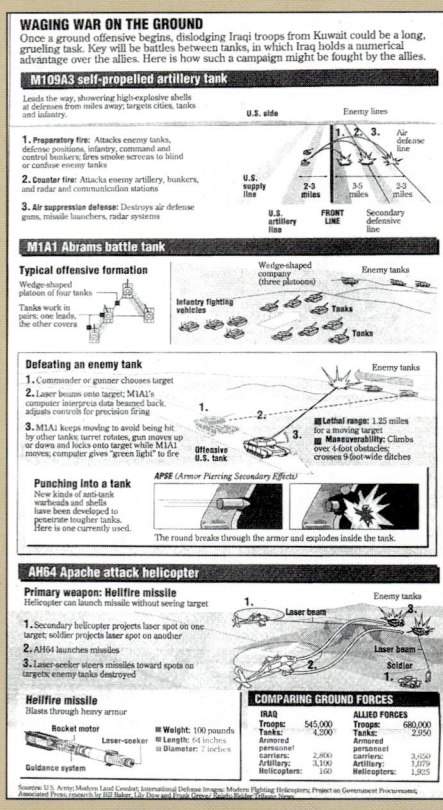

BREAKING NEWS: ALLIES GROUND WAR ATTACK
Detroit Free Press
John Groecke, Design Director; Wayne Kamidoi, Designer; Ken McDonald, Designer; Sue Parker, Designer; Lee Yarosh, Designer; Chip Visci, AME; Graphics Staff

BREAKING NEWS: IRAQ BOMBING OF ISRAEL
BRONZE
Detroit Free Press
John Goecke, Design Director; Wayne Kamidoi, Designer; Ken McDonald, Designer; Sue Parker, Designer; Lee Yarosh, Designer; Chip Visci, AME; Graphics Staff

BREAKING NEWS GRAPHIC: BLACK & WHITE
Detroit Free Press
Laura Varon Brown, Graphics Director; George Rorick, KRTN Graphics Director; Staff and KRTN Artists

PHOTOJOURNALISM: SPOT NEWS
SILVER
Detroit Free Press
David C. Turnley, Photographer

BREAKING NEWS GRAPHIC: BLACK & WHITE
Detroit Free Press
Bill Baker, KRTN Artist; Marty Westman, KRTN Artist; George Rorick, KRTN Graphics Director; Laura Varon Brown, Graphics Director

THIRTEENTH EDITION 59

THE PERSIAN GULF WAR

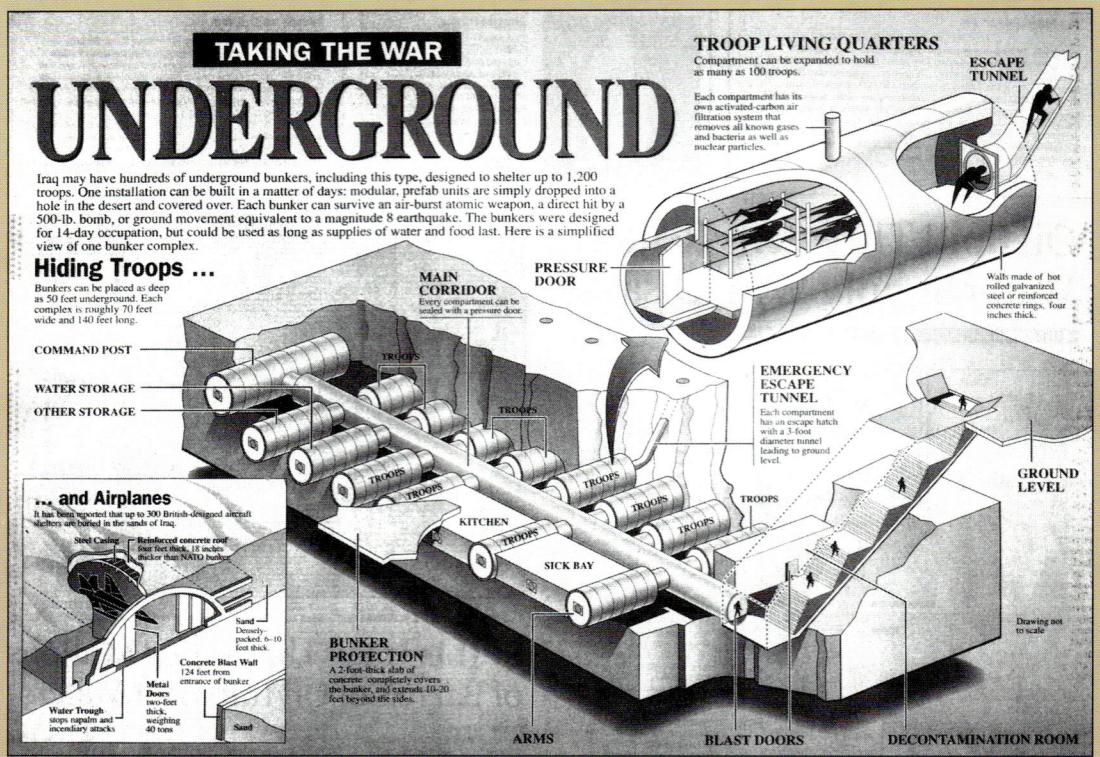

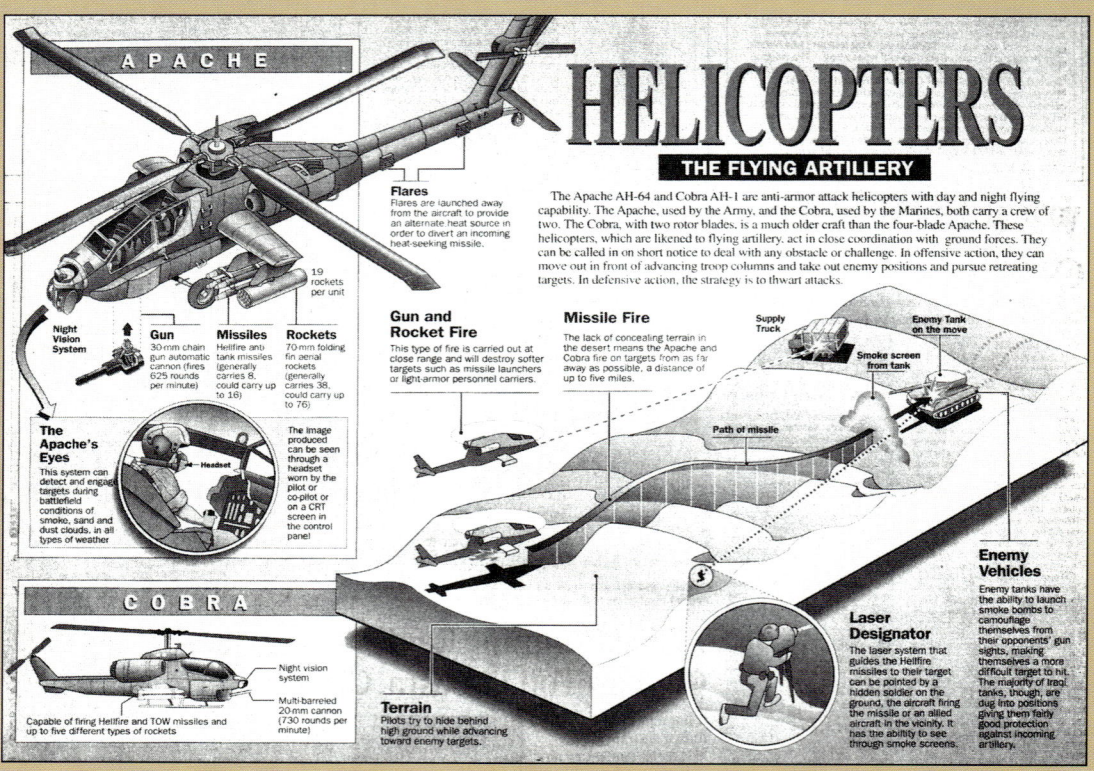

INFORMATIONAL GRAPHIC: BLACK & WHITE
SILVER & JSR
Los Angeles Times /
Orange County Edition
David Puckett, Illustrator & Researcher

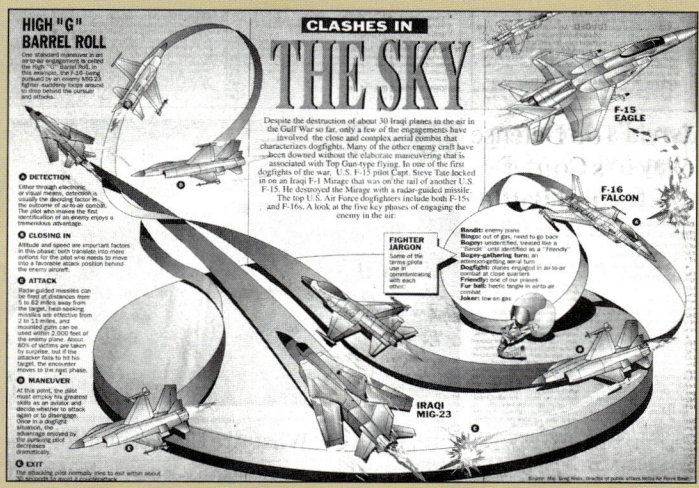

INFORMATIONAL GRAPHIC: BLACK & WHITE

BRONZE & JSR

Los Angeles Times

Bill Dunn, Art Director; James Owens, Illustrator & Designer

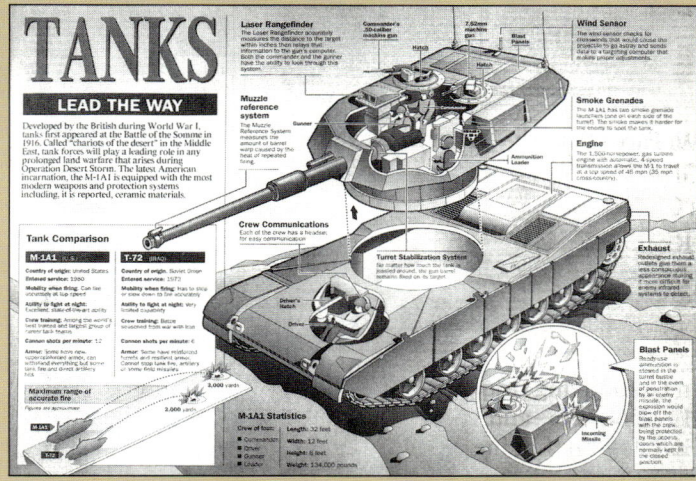

INFORMATIONAL GRAPHIC: BLACK & WHITE

BRONZE & JSR

Los Angeles Times / Orange County Edition

David Puckett, Illustrator & Researcher

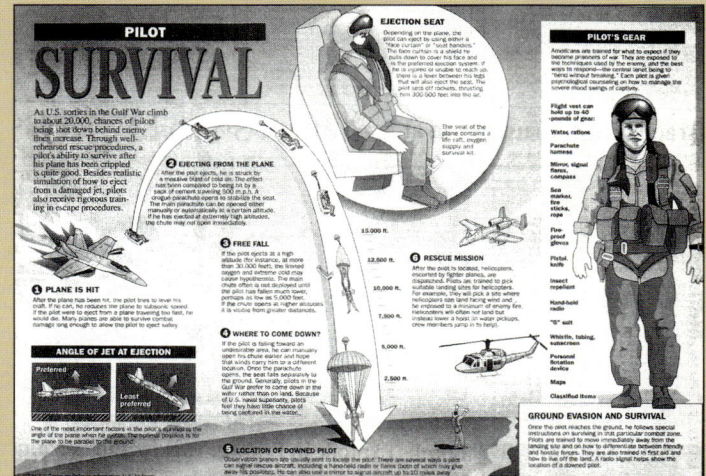

INFORMATIONAL GRAPHIC: BLACK & WHITE

BRONZE & JSR

Los Angeles Times

Bill Dunn, Art Director; James Owens, Illustrator & Designer

(ABOVE, MIDDLE)

BRONZE & JSR

Los Angeles Times

Bill Dunn, Art Director; Aners Ramberg, Illustrator & Designer

INFORMATIONAL GRAPHIC: BLACK & WHITE

BRONZE & JSR

Los Angeles Times / Orange County Edition

Dennis Lowe, Artist; Scott Brown, Writer

THIRTEENTH EDITION 61

THE PERSIAN GULF WAR

INFORMATIONAL GRAPHIC: BLACK & WHITE

Los Angeles Times / Orange County Edition

Scott Brown, Artist/Researcher; Lynette Johnson, Art Director

INFORMATIONAL GRAPHIC: BLACK & WHITE

Los Angeles Times / Orange County Edition

Scott Brown, Artist/Researcher

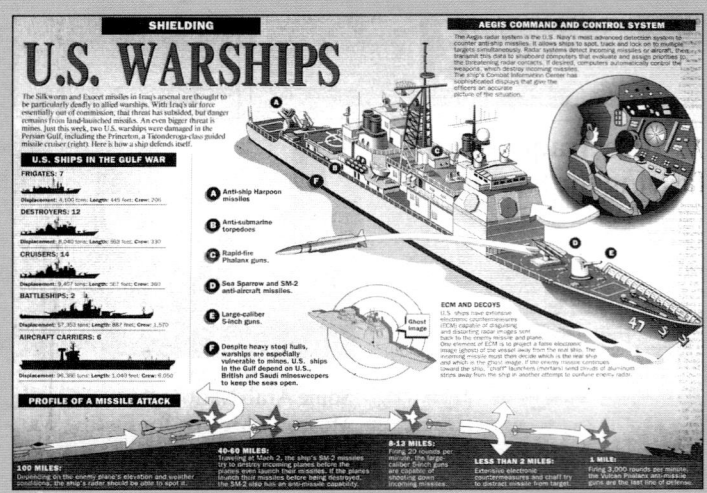

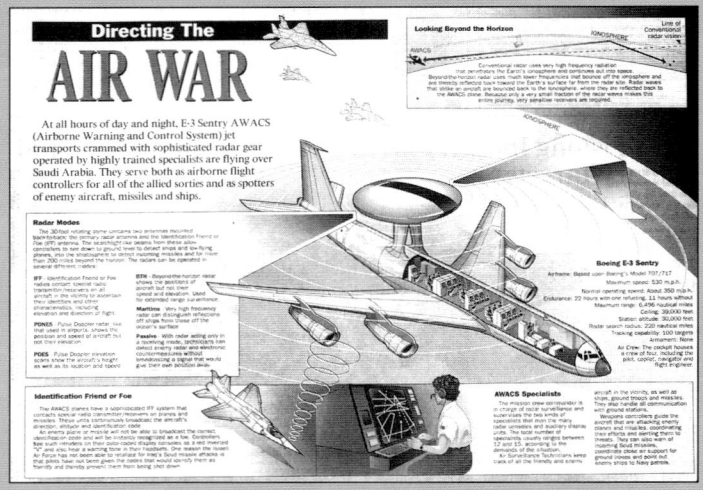

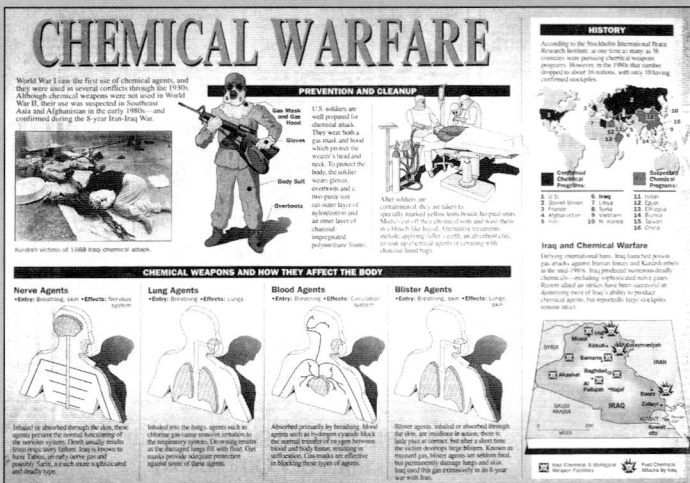

INFORMATIONAL GRAPHIC: BLACK & WHITE

Los Angeles Times / Orange County Edition

Dennis Lowe, Artist; Scott Brown, Writer

INFORMATIONAL GRAPHIC: BLACK & WHITE

Los Angeles Times

Anders Ramberg, Illustrator & Designer

(ABOVE, MIDDLE)

Los Angeles Times

Michael Hall, Illustrator

62 THE BEST OF NEWSPAPER DESIGN

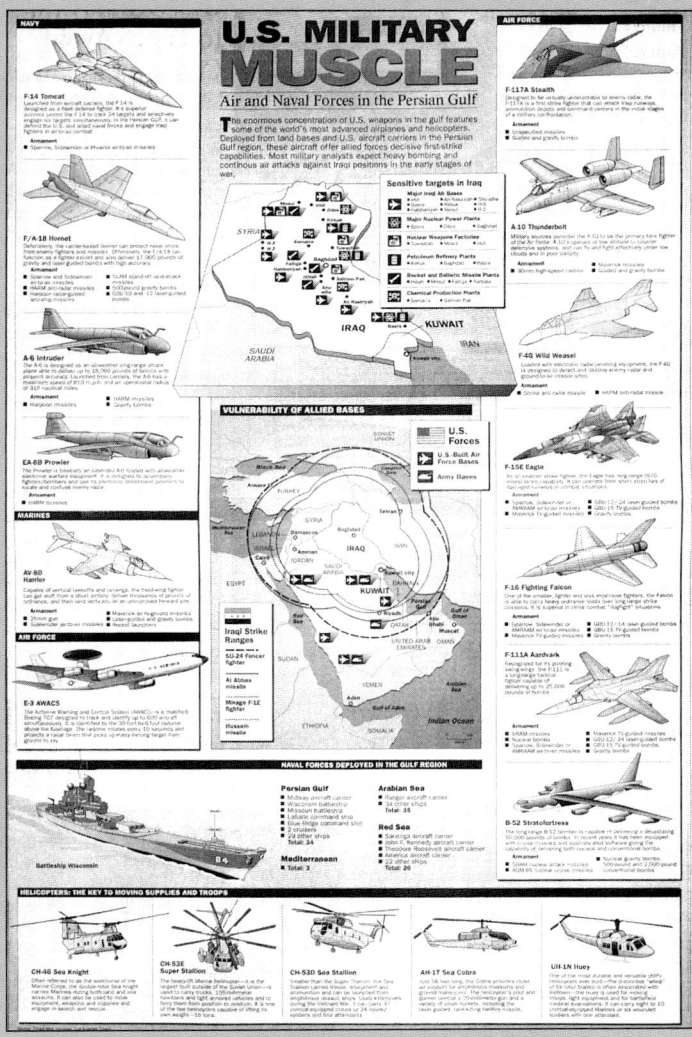

INFORMATIONAL GRAPHIC: BLACK & WHITE

Los Angeles Times

Bill Dunn, Art Director; Anders Ramberg, Artist; Sandy Kay, Artist; David Puckett, Artist; Juan Thomassie, Artist; Paul Gonzales, Artist; James Owens, Artist; Matt Moody, Artist

INFORMATIONAL GRAPHIC: BLACK & WHITE

Los Angeles Times

Sandy Kay, Illustrator

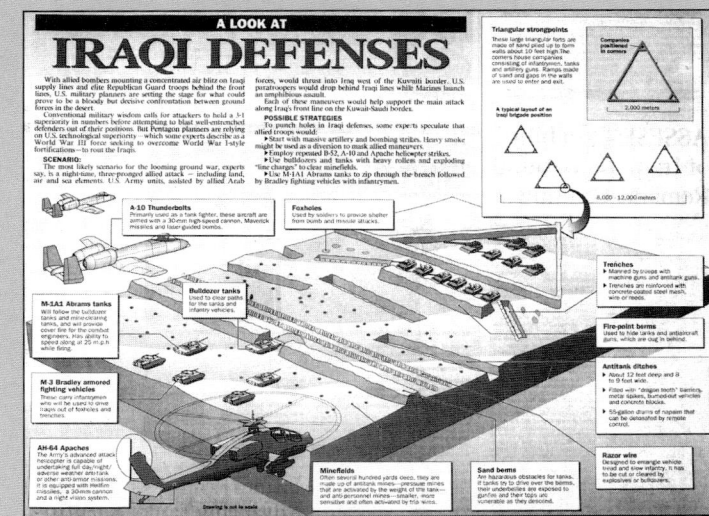

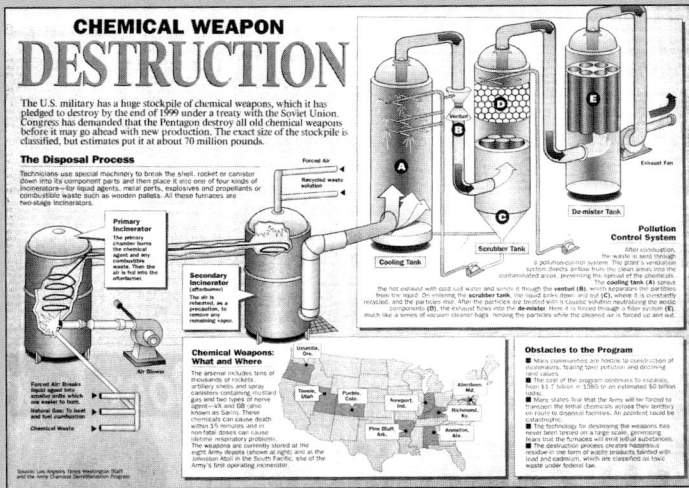

INFROMATIONAL GRAPHIC: BLACK & WHITE

Los Angeles Times

Patricia Mitchell, Artist; Victoria McCargar, Editor

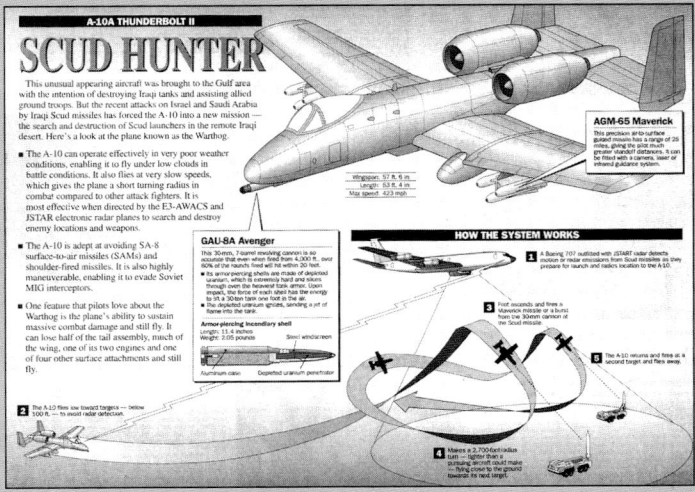

INFORMATIONAL GRAPHIC: BLACK & WHITE

Los Angeles Times

Juan Thomassie, Artist

THIRTEENTH EDITION 63

THE PERSIAN GULF WAR

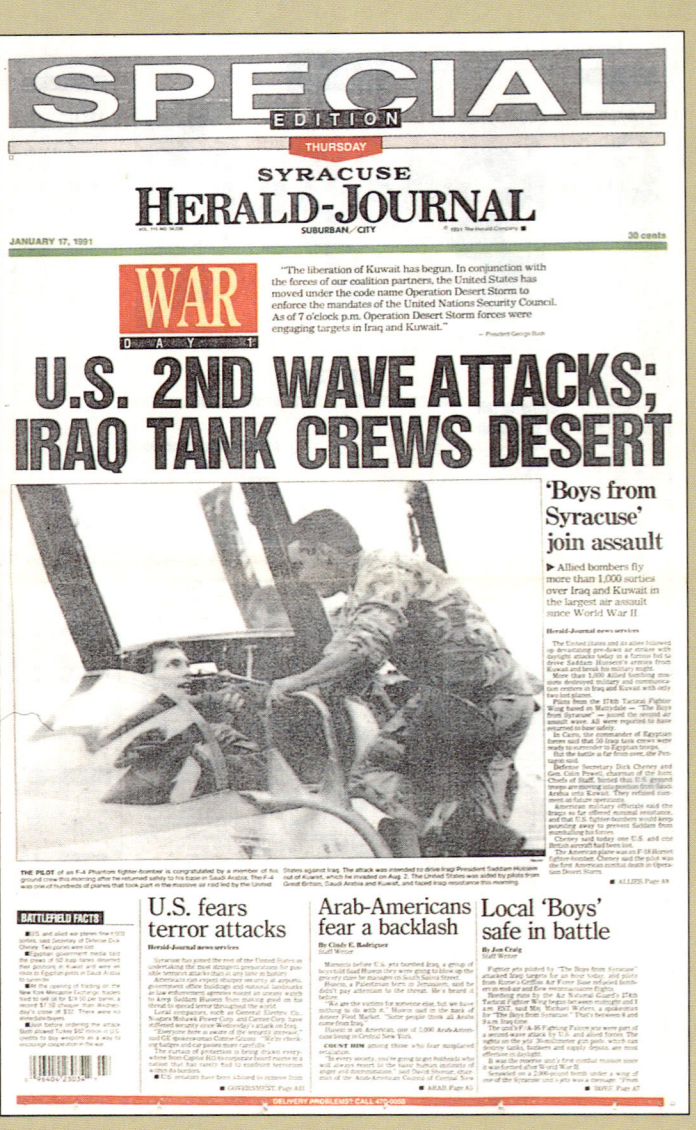

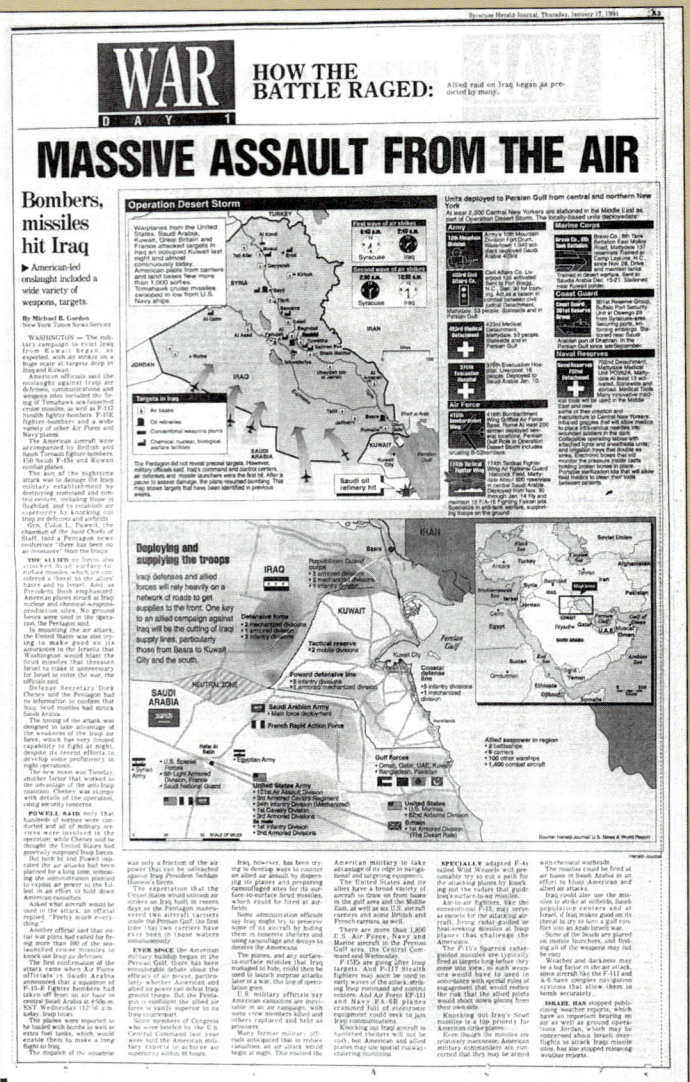

BREAKING NEWS: U.S. BOMBING OF IRAQ

SILVER

Syracuse Herald-Journal

Tim Atseff, Managing Editor

SPECIAL NEWS TOPIC: THE GULF WAR
Syracuse Herald-Journal
Tim Atseff, Managing Editor

BREAKING NEWS: ALLIES GROUND WAR ATTACK
BRONZE
Syracuse Herald-Journal
Tim Atseff, Managing Editor

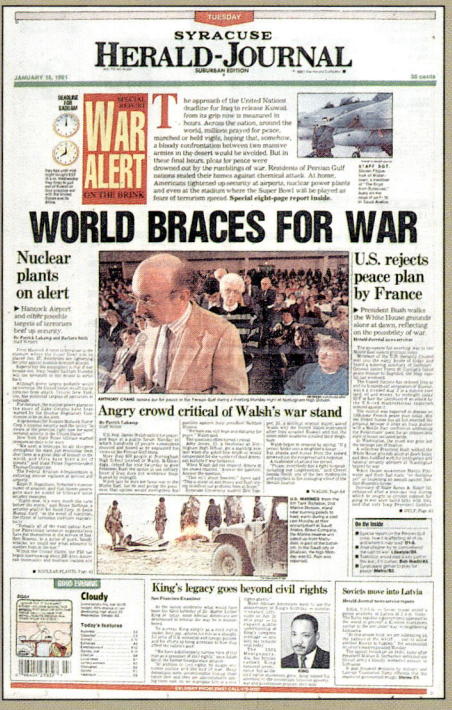

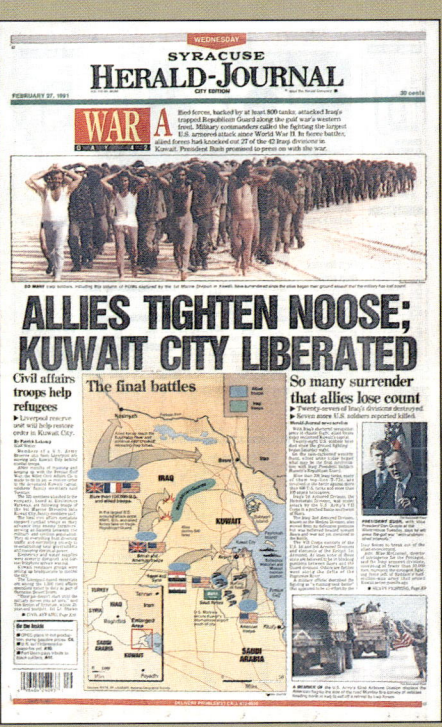

BREAKING NEWS: IRAQ BOMBING OF ISRAEL
Syracuse Herald-Journal
Tim Atseff, Managing Editor

SPECIAL NEWS TOPIC: THE GULF WAR
Syracuse Herald-Journal
Tim Atseff, Managing Editor

NEWS: FRONT PAGE
BRONZE
Syracuse Herald-Journal
Tim Atseff, Managing Editor

NEWS: FRONT PAGE
Syracuse Herald-Journal
Tim Atseff, Managing Editor

THIRTEENTH EDITION 65

THE PERSIAN GULF WAR

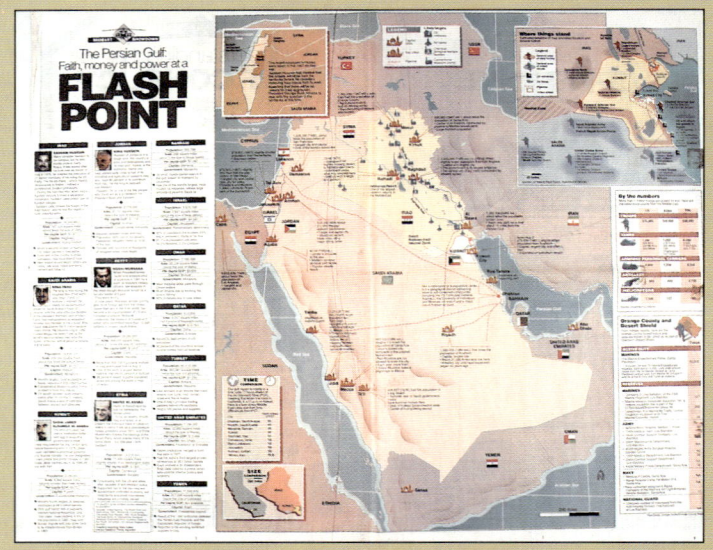

SPECIAL NEWS TOPIC: THE GULF WAR

SILVER

The Orange County Register
Santa Ana, CA

Kevin Byrne, News Editor/Design; John Fabris, Assistant News Editor/Design; Mark Yemma, Assistant News Editor/Design; Nanette Bisher, Art Director; Staff

BREAKING NEWS: IRAQ BOMBING OF ISRAEL
BRONZE
The Orange County Register
Kevin Byrne, News Editor/Design; John Fabris, Assistant News Editor/Design; Mark Yemma, Assistant News Editor/Design; Nanette Bisher, Art Director; Bernadette Finley, Assistant News Editor/Design; Staff Artist

NEWS: OTHER PAGE
The Orange County Register
Brenda Shoun, Designer; Staff

SPECIAL NEWS TOPIC: THE GULF WAR
Newsday
Jeff Massaro, Art Director & Designer; Bob Brandt, Managing Editor; Peter Bengelsdorf, Exec. News Editor

NEWS: FRONT PAGE
BRONZE
Newsday
Jeff Massaro, Art Director & Designer; Bob Brandt, Managing Editor; Peter Bengelsdorf, Exec. News Editor

THE PERSIAN GULF WAR

BREAKING NEWS: U.S. BOMBING OF IRAQ

SILVER

The Wichita Eagle
Staff

BREAKING NEWS: ALLIES GROUND WAR ATTACK
The Wichita Eagle
Staff

SPECIAL NEWS TOPICS: THE GULF WAR
The Wichita Eagle
Staff

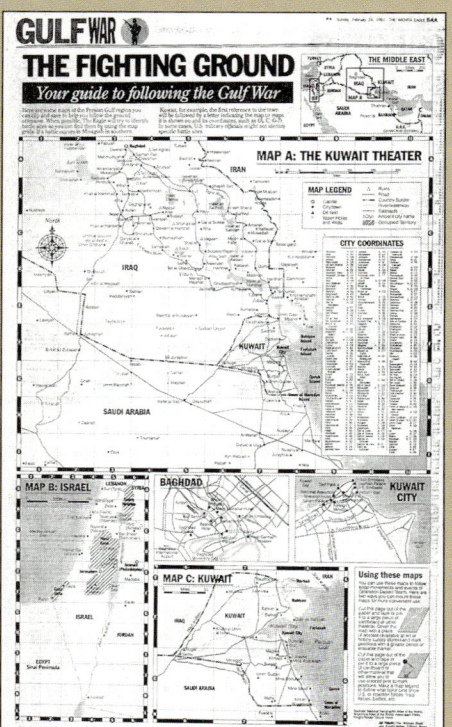

SPECIAL NEWS TOPIC: THE GULF WAR
The Christian Science Monitor
Boston, MA
Staff

BREAKING NEWS: U.S. BOMBING OF IRAQ
Times Advocate
Escondido, CA

Tom Spain, Designer

BREAKING NEWS: IRAQ BOMBING OF ISRAEL
The Post-Standard
Syracuse, NY

Staff

NEWS: FRONT PAGE
BRONZE
Dayton Daily News
John Thomson, AME Graphics; Ken Canfield, Executive News Editor; Frank Pauer, Designer

THIRTEENTH EDITION 69

THE PERSIAN GULF WAR

NEWS: FRONT PAGE
El Sol
Madrid, Spain
Juan Varela, Chief Editor; Staff

BREAKING NEWS: IRAQ BOMBING OF ISRAEL
El Sol
Juan Varela, Chief Editor; Staff

SPECIAL NEWS TOPIC: THE GULF WAR
El Sol
Juan Varela, Chief Editor; Luis Meson, Graphics; Staff

BREAKING NEWS: U.S. BOMBING OF IRAQ
The Seattle Times
Greg Rasa, News Page Designer

INFORMATIONAL GRAPHIC: COLOR
The Seattle Times
Rob Kemp, Designer & Artist; Christine Cox, Artist; Bo Hok Cline, Artist; Lisa Remillard, Artist; Celeste Ericson, Art Director; Kathleen Triesch Saul, Editor; Elizabeth Rhodes, Reporter

BREAKING NEWS: END OF GULF WAR
El Sol
Juan Varela, Chief Editor

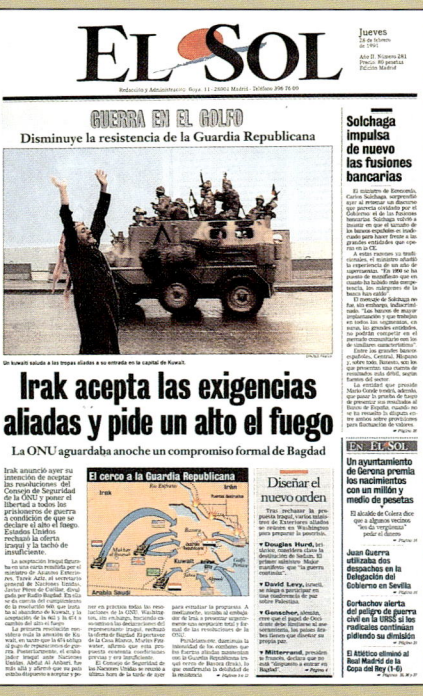

NEWS: FRONT PAGE
The Albuquerque Tribune
Mike Davis, Lead Designer; Gerald Cox, Assistant Designer; Richard Hindley, Wire Editor

PHOTOJOURNALISM: DESIGN
The Virginian-Pilot / Ledger-Star
Norfolk, VA
Alex Burrows, Chief Designer & Photo Editor; Bob Lynn, AME Graphics; Brian Stallcop, Designer & Photo Editor; Pat Thomas, A1 Layout

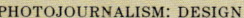

SPECIAL SECTION: WITH ADS
Lexington Herald-Leader
Jim Jennings, Assistant Managing Editor/Graphics; Malcolm Stallons, Design Desk Chief; Dean Holt, Designer; Molly Swisher, Artist

NEWS: FRONT PAGE
The Record
Hackensack, NJ
Dennis McCulley, Graphics Director; Bob Townsend, Designer; Steve Hockstein, Photographer; Linda Cataffo, Photographer; John Decker, Photographer; Peter Monsees, Photographer

BREAKING NEWS: EDITOR'S CHOICE
The Aberdeen American News
Staff

THIRTEENTH EDITION 71

THE PERSIAN GULF WAR

NEWS: INSIDE PAGE
Army Times
Carolyn Hax, News Editor

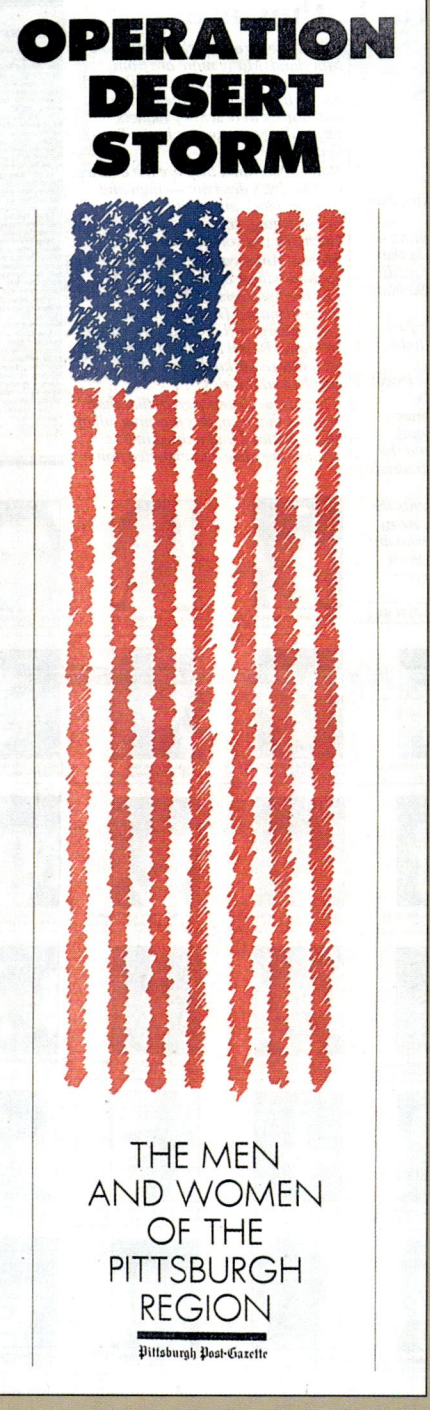

SPECIAL SECTION: COVER
Pittsburgh Post-Gazette
Anita Dufalla, Art Director & Illustrator;
Christopher Pett-Ridge, AME

NEWS: INSIDE PAGE
The Palm Beach Post
Jan Tuckwood, Assoc. Editor

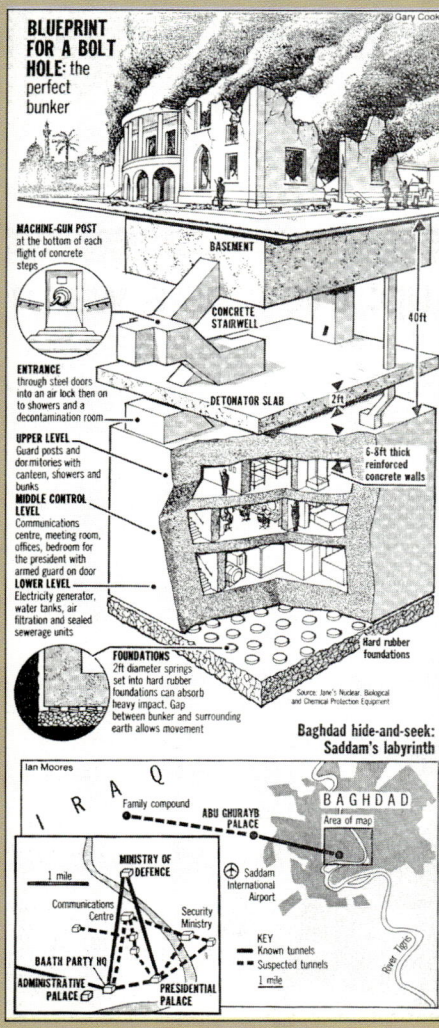

BREAKING NEWS GRAPHIC: BLACK & WHITE
The Sunday Times
London, England

Gary Cook, Illustrator & Designer

BREAKING NEWS GRAPHIC: BLACK & WHITE
The Times

Geoffrey Sims, Graphics Artist; John Lawson, Graphics Artist

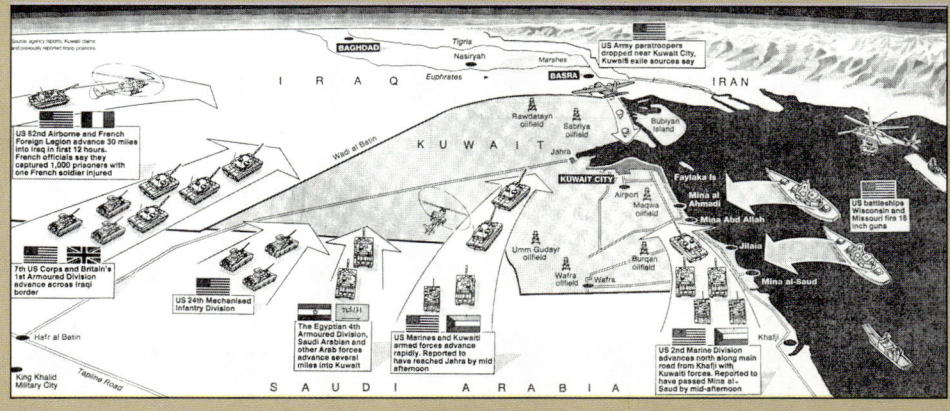

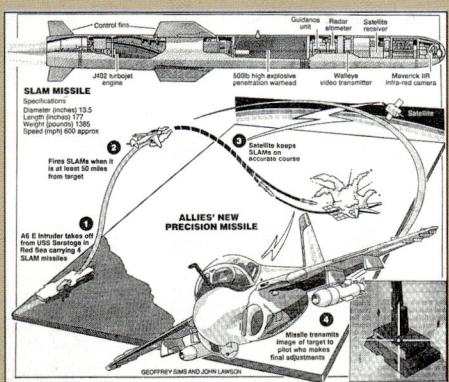

BREAKING NEWS GRAPHIC: BLACK & WHITE
The Times

John Lawson, Graphics Artist; Geoffrey Sims, Graphics Artist

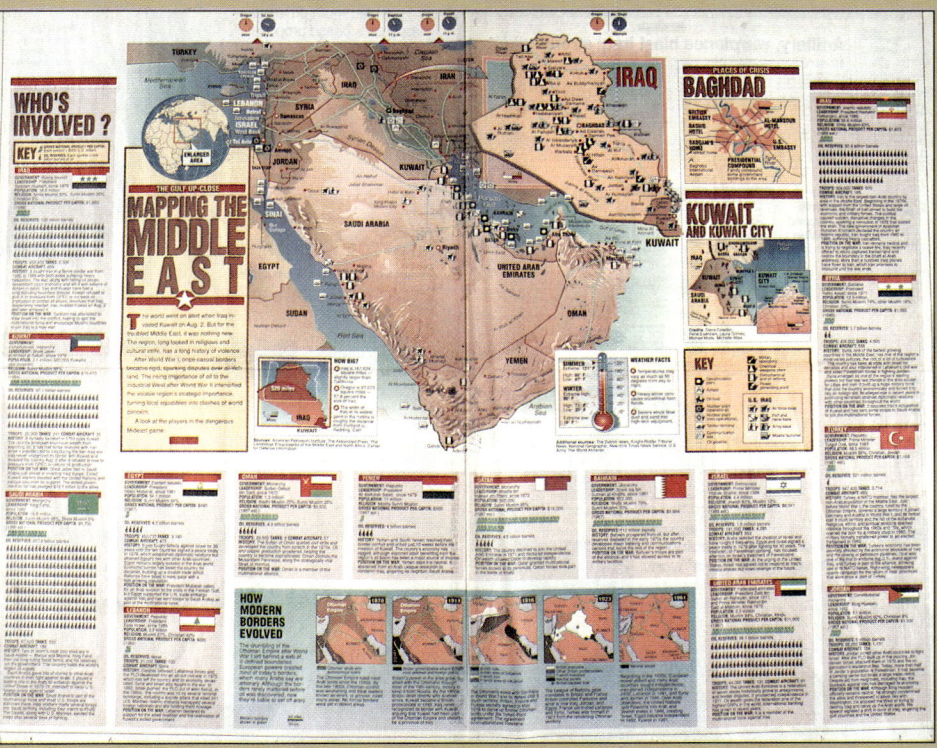

BREAKING NEWS GRAPHIC: COLOR
The Oregonian

Michelle Wise, Assistant Graphics Director; Steve Cowden, Graphics Artist; Rene Eisenbart, Graphics Artist; Michael Mode, Graphics Artist; Laura Grimes, Copy Editor

THIRTEENTH EDITION 73

THE PERSIAN GULF WAR

BREAKING NEWS GRAPHIC: COLOR

The Virginian-Pilot / Ledger-Star
Norfolk, VA

Bill Pitzer, Illustrator

BREAKING NEWS GRAPHIC: BLACK & WHITE

La Vanguardia
Barcelona, Spain

Carlos Perez de Rozas, Art Director; Rosa Mundet, Art Director Assistant; Jordi Paris, Senior Infographic Designer; Angels Soler, Infographic Designer; Sandra Villar, Infographic Designer; Rosa Maria Anechina, Infographic Designer; Josep Ramos, Infographic Designer; Jordi Bague, Infographic Designer; Rafael Salas, Infographic Designer

BREAKING NEWS GRAPHIC: COLOR

La Vanguardia

Carlos Perez de Rozas, Art Director; Rosa Mundet, Art Director Asst.; Jordi Paris, Senior Infographic Designer; Angels Soler, Infographic Designer; Sandra Villar, Infographic Designer; Rosa Maria Anechina, Infographic Designer; Josep Ramos, Infographic Designer; Jordi Bague, Infographic Designer; Rafael Salas, Infographic Designer

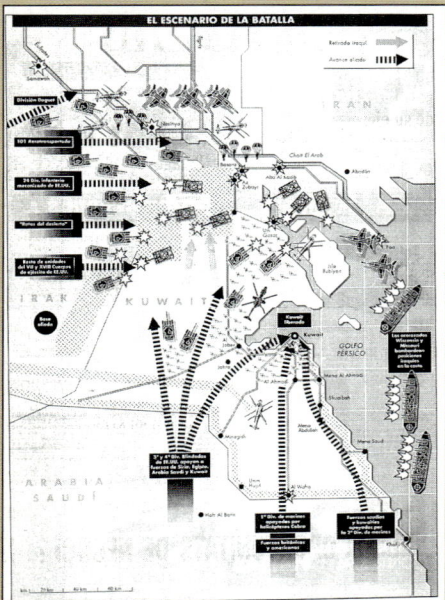
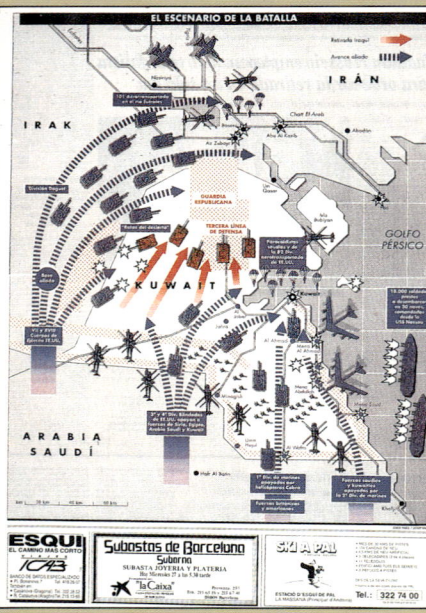
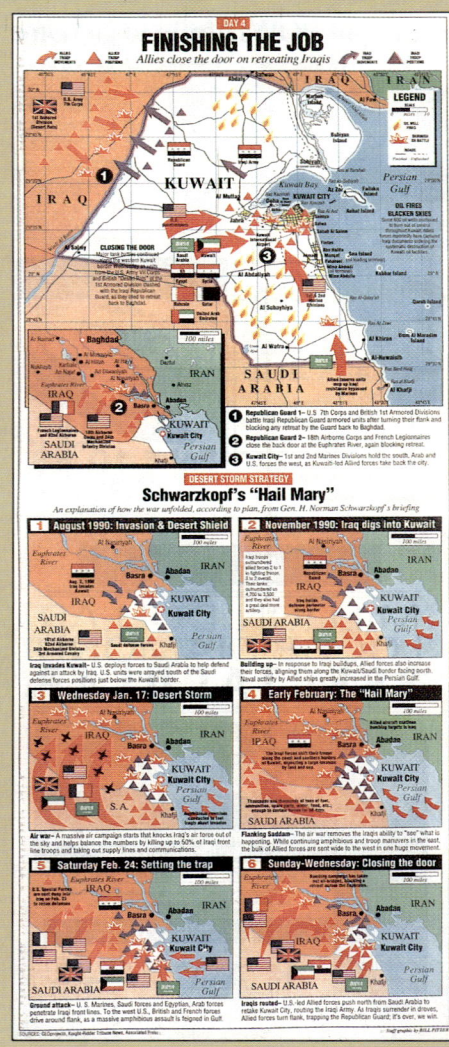
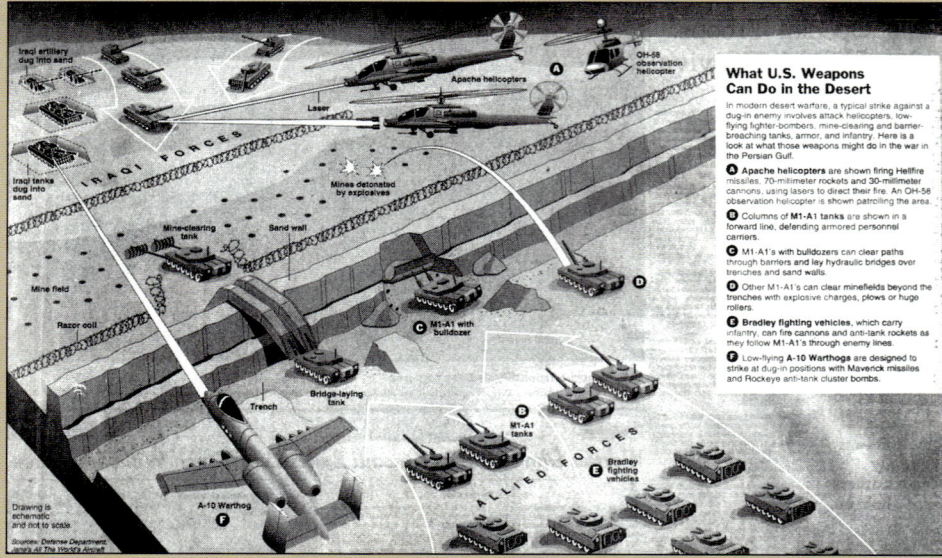

BREAKING NEWS GRAPHIC: BLACK & WHITE

The New York Times

Megan Jaegerman, Designer, Illustrator, Researcher; Keith Bradsher, Researcher; Margaret O'Connor, Art Director; Hank Iken, Illustrator; Rich Meislin, Graphics Editor; Tom Bodkin, Design Director

BREAKING NEWS GRAPHIC: COLOR

The Times-Picayune

James Zisk, Infographic Artist; Michael Jantze, Infographic Artist; Kurt Mutchler, Graphics Editor

INFORMATIONAL GRAPHIC: BLACK & WHITE
San Francisco Chronicle
Steve Outing, Graphics Editor; William Cone, Illustrator; Steve Kearsley, Illustrator; Kristine Strawser, Illustrator; Scott Wilson, Researcher

BREAKING NEWS GRAPHIC: COLOR
San Francisco Examiner
Kelly Frankeny, Graphics Editor

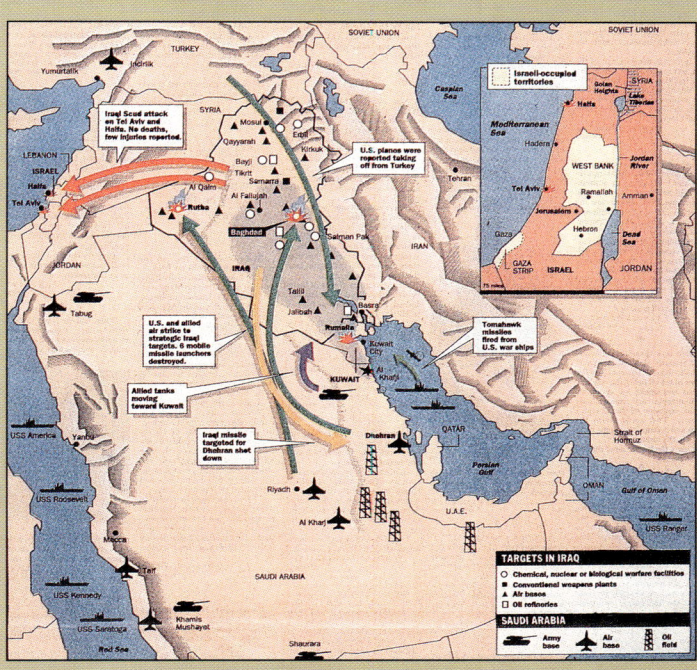

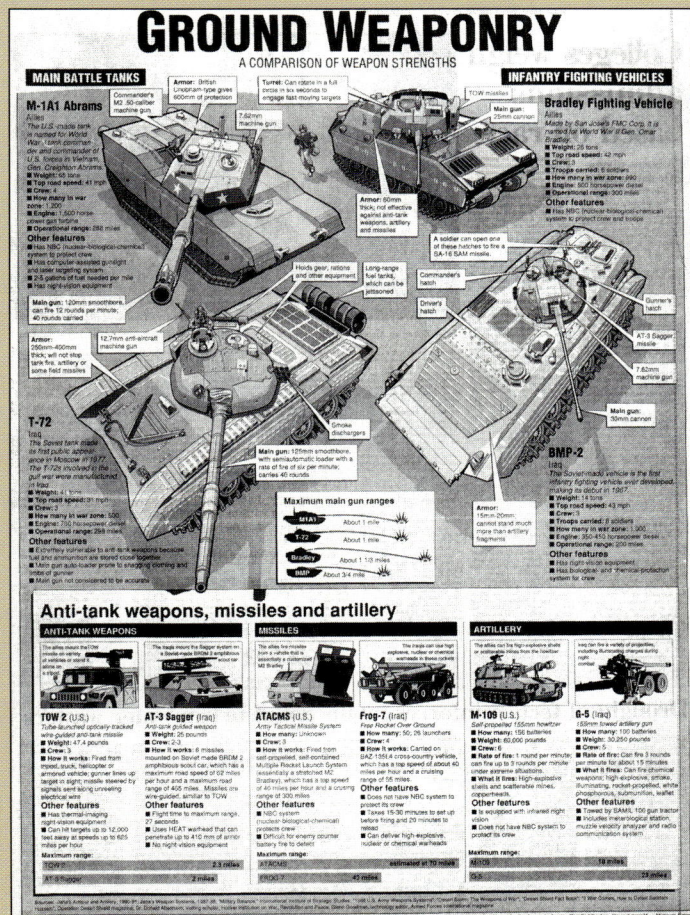

INFORMATIONAL GRAPHIC: COLOR
El Mundo
Madrid, Spain

Ulises Culebro, Illustrator; Mario Tascon, Infographics Director; Jeff Goertzen, Art Consultant

INFORMATIONAL GRAPHIC: BLACK & WHITE
San Jose Mercury News
Ron Coddington, Artist; Jenny Anderson, Artist; Doug Griswold, Artist; Maggie Hirsch, Reporter; Bob Reynolds, Art Director

THIRTEENTH EDITION 75

THE PERSIAN GULF WAR

THE GROUND WAR

Behind the lines in the Persian Gulf

Photography and text by David Leeson

A few hours before the Persian Gulf ground war was to begin, the mood of the Marine unit I was with changed from coarse laughter to whispers and long silences. The red evening sky was turning purple, then charcoal blue, as soldiers began assembling for an impromptu church service.

A young Marine lance corporal shyly approached a sergeant who was helping to prepare for Catholic service and asked if he could take Communion.

"Are you Catholic?" the sergeant asked.

The Marine, who couldn't have been older than 19, looked at the dust on his boots and then into the experience-worn face of the sergeant. "No," he said after a pause.

"I'm sorry, you can't take Communion," the sergeant told him.

"OK," the Marine said as a slight furrow appeared on his forehead. "Can I watch?"

His fear was as evident as his shyness, but he seemed content to (text continued on page 14)

Tanks move through a light rain across the Kuwait desert on the first day of the ground war.

Combat engineers in the First Marine Division's Ripper task force wear their gas masks and chemical protection suits after an alert was given prior to their assaults on the Kuwait International Airport. Sun filtering through wind-blown sand and smoke from oil fires gave an orange cast to the scene.

PHOTOJOURNALISM: FEATURE

SILVER

The Dallas Morning News

David Leeson, Photographer

These AK-47 assault rifles were among the thousands of Iraqi weapons confiscated during the ground war. They were later buried in the sand.

Sgt. Kevin O'Hora of Allendale, N.J., a Marine reservist with a light infantry unit, escorts two Iraqi prisoners across the desert. Sgt. O'Hora is a New Jersey police officer.

PHOTOJOURNALISM: PHOTO-STORY

SILVER

The Boston Globe Magazine

Lucy Bartholomay, Art Director, Photo Editor & Designer; Stan Grossfeld, Photo Editor; Sadayuki Mikami/AP, Photographer

THE PERSIAN GULF WAR

MAGAZINES: TWO OR MORE PAGES
SILVER
The New York Times Magazine
Janet Foelich, Art Director & Designer; Sebastiao Salgado, Photographer; Kathy Ryan, Photo Editor; Tom Bodkin, Design Director

PHOTOJOURNALISM: PHOTO-STORY
The Philadelphia Inquirer Magazine
Bert Fox, Art Director & Designer; Jessica Helfand, Design Director; Todd Buchanan, Photographer; Tom Gralish, Photo Editor; T.A. Frail, Writer

CHAPTER FOUR

IN THIS CHAPTER:

**Judges'
Special
Recognition**

The Boston Globe,
for feature page design.

Features

FEATURES Entertainment • Lifestyle Sections

BRONZE

The Washington Times
Joseph Scopin, Art Director; John Kascht, Art Director & Designer; Paul Watts, Designer

The Washington Times
Joseph Scopin, Art Director; John Kascht, Art Director & Designer; Paul Watts, Designer

The Washington Times
Joseph Scopin, Art Director; John Kascht, Art Director & Designer; Paul Watts, Designer

The Miami Herald
Herman Vega, Editorial Designer Illustrator; Emily Hathaway, Weekend Editor; Glenda Wolin, Assistant Features Desk Chief; Rhonda Prast, Features Design Editor; Juan Lopez, Staff Intern; Randy Stano, Director of Editorial Art & Design; Tony Krzczuk, Weekend Editor/Broward

The Toronto Star
Kam Wai Yu, Designer; Pat McCormick, Editor

(LIFESTYLE SECTION)

The Washington Times
Joseph Scopin, Art Director; Paul Watts, Designer; Charmaine Roberts, Designer

Fashion • Science • Other Sections

(FASHION SECTION)
The Dallas Morning News
Bob Shema, Designer; Lee Ann Bandy, Designer; Colleen Kelly, Designer

(SCIENCE SETION)
Detroit Free Press
Claire Innes, Designer; Deborah Withey, Design Director

La Vanguardia
Barcelona, Spain

Carlos Perez de Rozas, Art Director; Rosa Mundet, Art Director Assistant; Ferran Grau, Senior Designer; Monica Caparros, Designer; Anna Belil, Designer; Carol Tellez, Designer; Joan Corbera, Designer

(OTHER SECTION)
The Christian Science Monitor
Boston, MA

Staff

Goteborgs-Posten
Gothenburg, Sweden

Eleonor Ekstrom-Frisk, Designer; Karin Johansson, Designer; Ulf Johanson, Designer; Mats Widebrant, Designer

THIRTEENTH EDITION 81

FEATURES Other Section

BRONZE
The New York Times

Steven Heller, Art Director & Designer; Tom Bodkin, Design Director; Becky Sinkler, Editor

The Oregonian

Nancy Fullwiler, Designer; Michelle Wise, Art Director; Tim Lee, Illustrator

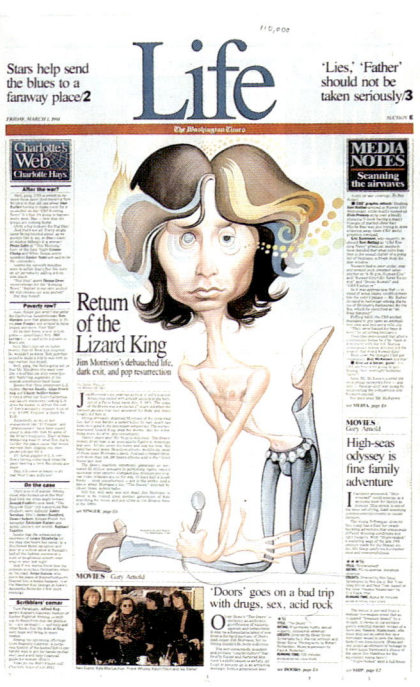

BRONZE
The Washington Times

Joseph Scopin, Art Director; Dolores Motichka, Art Director & Designer; Paul Watts, Designer

SILVER

Goteborgs-Posten
Gothenburg, Sweden

Mats Widebrant, Designer; Ulf Sveningson, Illustrator

FEATURES Opinion Page

Anchorage Daily News
Galie Jean-Louis, Art Director, Designer & Illustrator,

Berlingske Tidende
Copenhagen, Denmark

Gregers Jensen, Designer

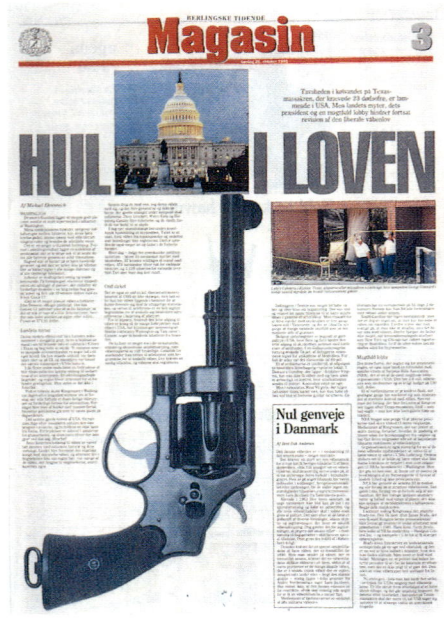

The Globe and Mail
Toronto, ON, Canada

Eric Nelson, Art Director & Designer; Sarah Murdoch, Editor

Detroit Free Press
Wayne Kamidoi, Designer; Alfred T. Kamajian, Illustrator

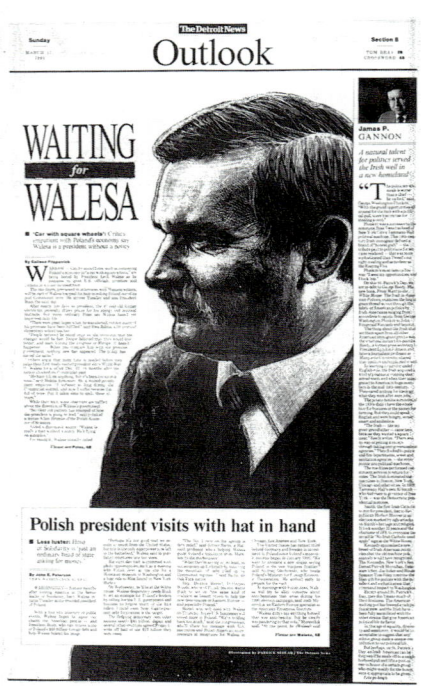

The Detroit News
Patrick Sedlar, Artist; Felix Grabowski, Graphics Director

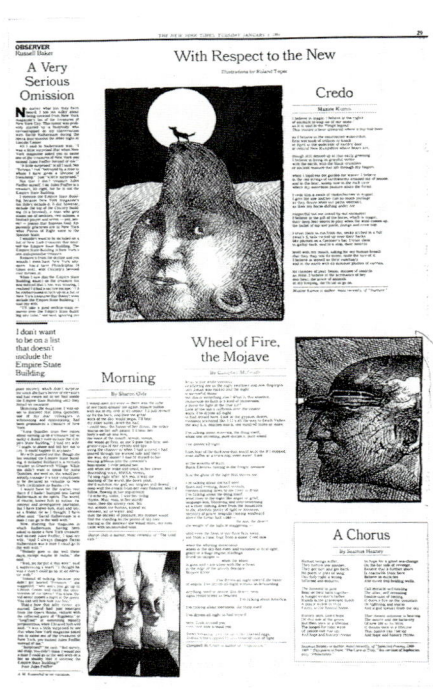

The New York Times
Michael Valenti, Art Director & Designer; Tom Bodkin, Design Director; Roland Topor, Illustrator

BRONZE

El Mundo
Madrid, Spain

Ricardo Martinez, Illustration Editor

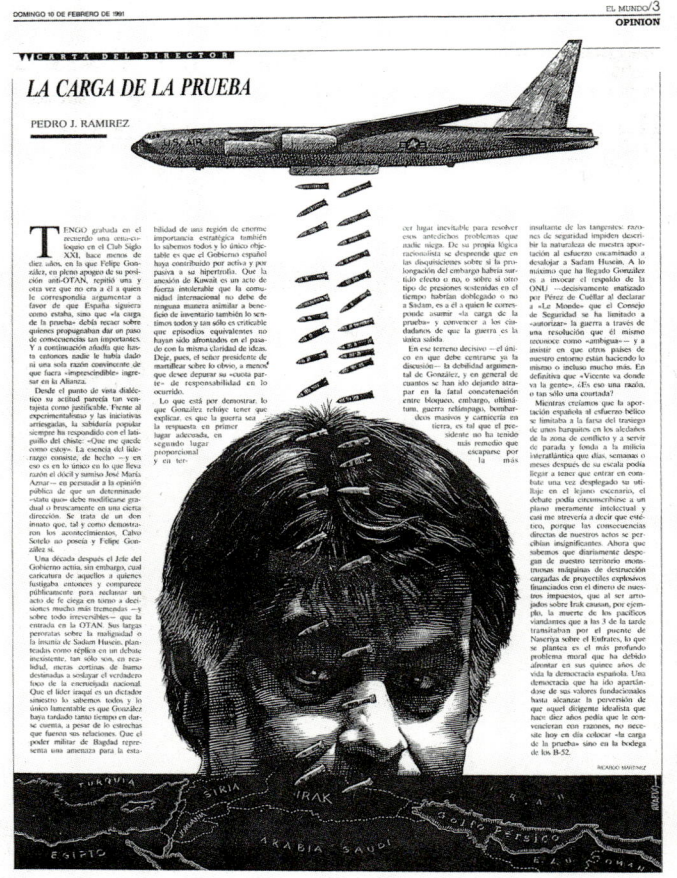

El Mundo

Ricardo Martinez, Illustration Editor

El Mundo

Ricardo Martinez, Illustration Editor

El Mundo

Ricardo Martinez, Illustration Editor

FEATURES Opinion Page

JSR

The Boston Globe

Nancy Lynn Goldberg, Art Director; Cynthia Hoffman, Editorial Designer; David H. Cowles, Illustrator

BRONZE

The Miami Herald

Patterson Clark, Editorial Artist; Randy Stano, Director of Editorial Art & Design; Rich Bard, Viewpoint Section Editor

The Washington Post

Peter Hoey, Designer; Michael Keegan, Art Director; Various Illustrators

Lifestyle Page

The Detroit News
Wes Bausmith, Art Director, Designer & Illustrator

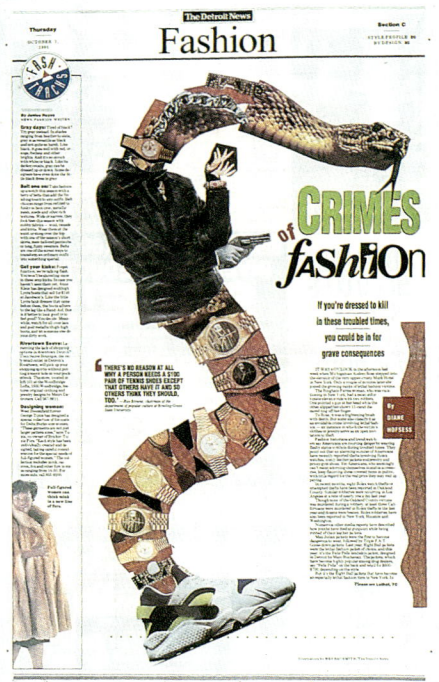

The Detroit News
Patrick Sedlar, Art Director, Designer & Illustrator

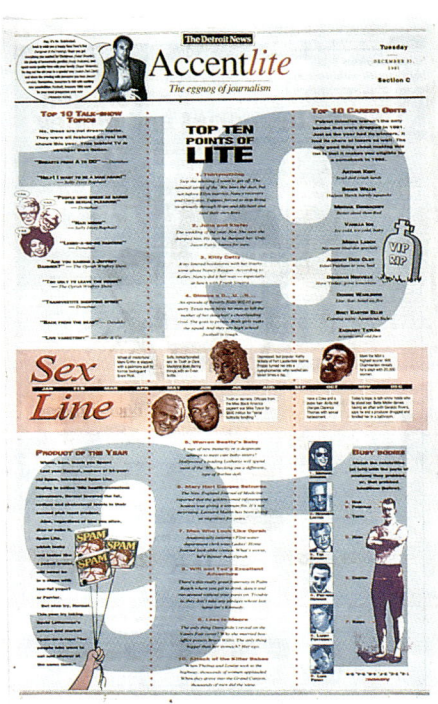

El Nuevo Dia
San Juan, PR

Jose L. Diaz de Villegas, Sr., Art Director, Designer & Illustrator

The Detroit News
Patrick Sedlar, Art Director, Designer & Illustrator

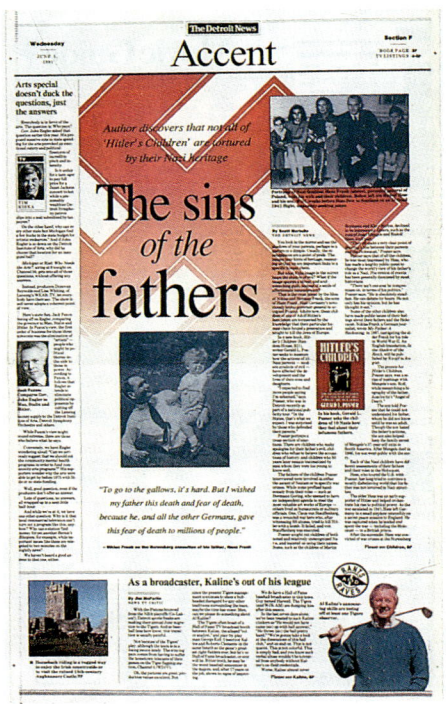

The Detroit News
Patrick Sedlar, Illustrator & Designer; Wes Bausmith, Art Director

El Nuevo Dia
Jose L. Diaz de Villegas, Sr., Art Director & Designer; Jose L. Diaz de Villegas, Jr., Illustrator

THIRTEENTH EDITION 87

FEATURES — Lifestyle Page

BRONZE

Chicago Tribune

Theresa Shechter, Art Director; John Twohey, Editor; Ron Grossman, Editor; Bill Hogan, Photographer

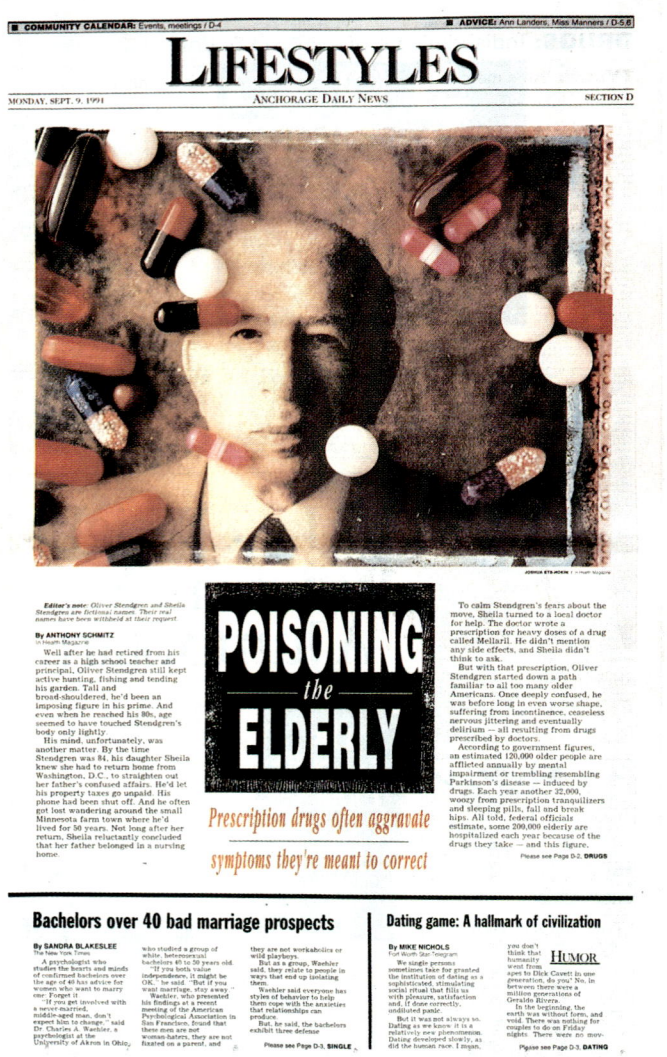

BRONZE

Anchorage Daily News

Pete Spino, Art Director & Designer; Joshua Ets-Hokin, Photographer

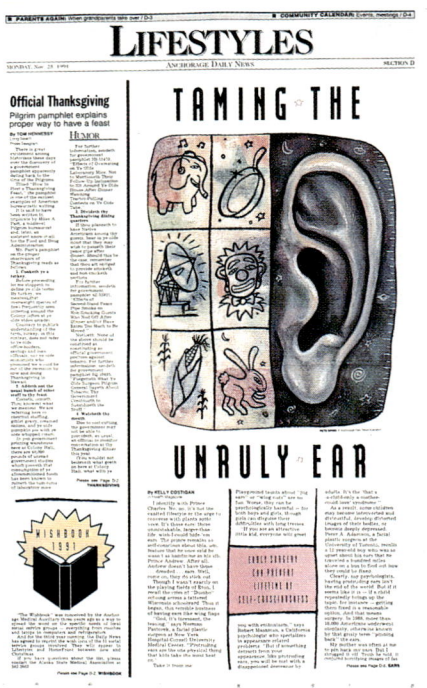

Anchorage Daily News

Pete Spino, Art Director, Designer & Illustrator

88 THE BEST OF NEWSPAPER DESIGN

Anchorage Daily News

Pete Spino, Art Director & Designer; Joel Nakamura, Illustrator

Anchorage Daily News

Pete Spino, Art Director & Designer; Anthony Russo, Illustrator

The New York Times

Richard Aloisio, Art Director & Designer; Tom Bodkin, Design Director; Robin Jareaux, Illustrator

Anchorage Daily News

Pete Spino, Art Director & Designer; William Duke, Photographer

Anchorage Daily News

Pete Spino, Illustrator & Designer; Galie Jean-Louis, Art Director

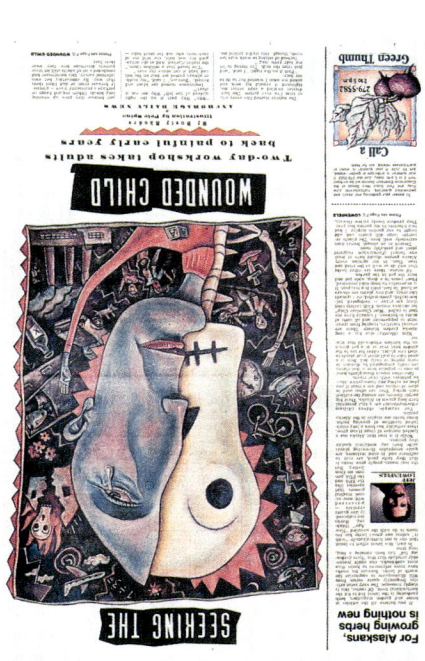

Anchorage Daily News

Pete Spino, Art Director and Designer

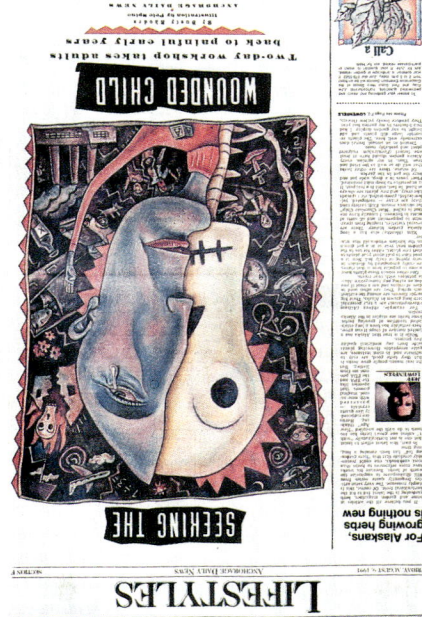

FEATURES Lifestyle Page

BRONZE

The Washington Times
John Kascht, Art Director & Designer

BRONZE

St. Louis Post-Dispatch
John Shew, Staff Artist; W. D. Kesler, Director of Photo Electronics

Novedades
Mexico City, Mexico
Claudio Rodríguez, Art Director; Juan Carlos Uría, Designer; Tony Scheffler, Researcher

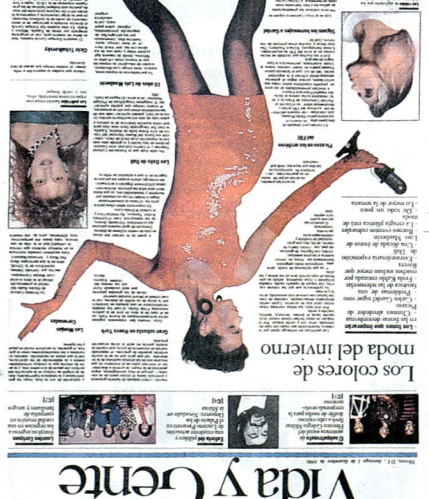

Lifestyle • Entertainment Pages

(ENTERTAINMENT PAGE)

JSR
The Boston Globe

Cynthia Hoffman, Art Director & Designer

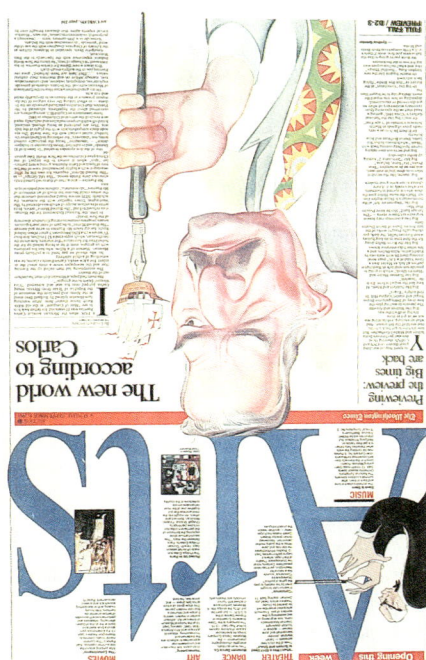

Detroit Free Press

Steve Anderson, Art Director & Designer; David H. Cowles, Illustrator; Deborah Withey, Design Director

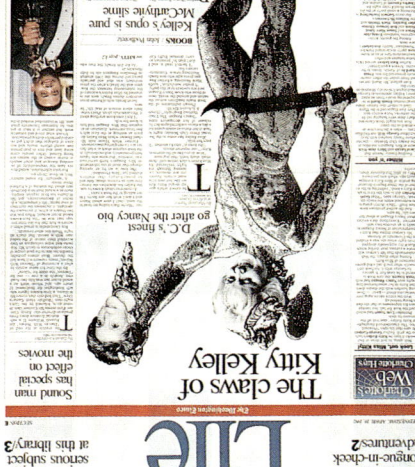

Detroit Free Press

Steve Anderson, Art Director & Designer; Philip Burke, Illustrator; Deborah Withey, Design Director

The Washington Times

John Kascht, Art Director, Designer & Illustrator

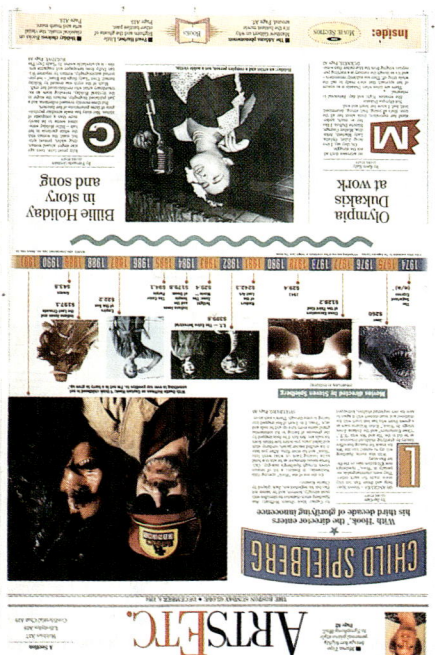

The Washington Times

Dolores Motichka, Art Director & Designer

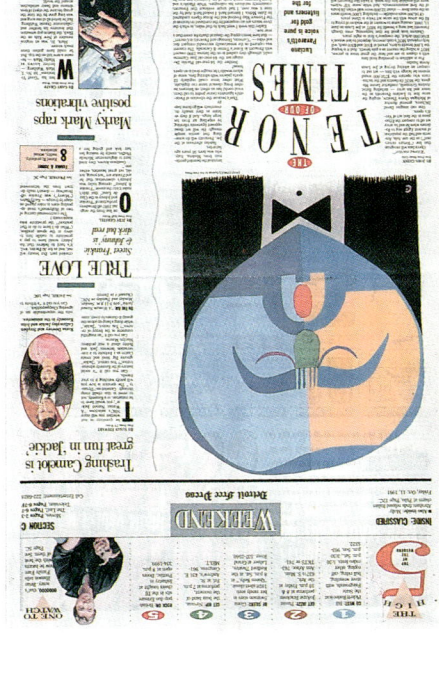

Pittsburgh Post-Gazette

John Kaplan, Photographer & Designer; Anita Dufalla, Art Director; Christopher Pett-Ridge, AME Graphics

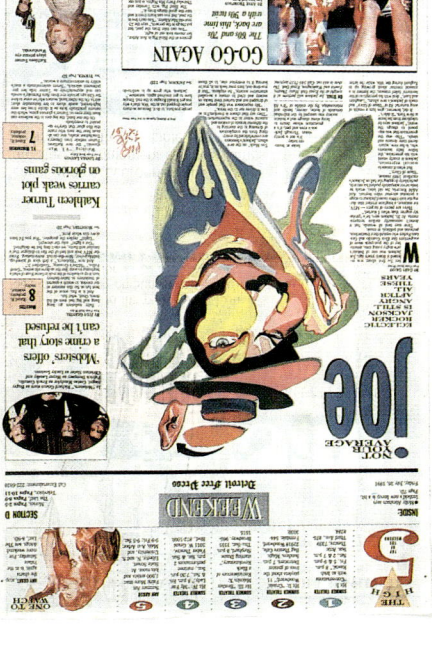

FEATURES Entertainment Page

SILVER

The New York Times

Genevieve Williams, Art Director & Designer; Tom Bodkin, Design Director; Sara Schwartz, Illustrator

The New York Times

Nancy Kent, Art Director & Designer; Tom Bodkin, Design Director

Los Angeles Times

Phil Waters, Art Director & Illustrator; John Lindsay, Editor

Los Angeles Times

Tracy Crowe, Art Director; Tom Trapnell, Design Director; John Lindsay, Editor; Philip Burke, Illustrator

The New York Times

Linda Brewer, Art Director & Designer; Tom Bodkin, Design Director; Alison Seiffer, Illustrator & Photographer

The Sun
Lowell, MA

Mitchell J. Hayes, Art Director & Designer; Tim Lewis, Illustrator; Carol McQuaid, Editor

NRC Handelsblad
Amsterdam, Netherlands

W. Van Zoetendaal, Art Director & Designer

THIRTEENTH EDITION 93

FEATURES Entertainment Page

Anchorage Daily News
Galie Jean-Louis, Art Director, Designer, Photo Editor & Illustrator

Anchorage Daily News
Galie Jean-Louis, Art Director, Designer & Photo Editor; Michael Biondo, Photographer

Anchorage Daily News
Galie Jean-Louis, Art Director, Designer & Photo Editor; The Douglas Brothers

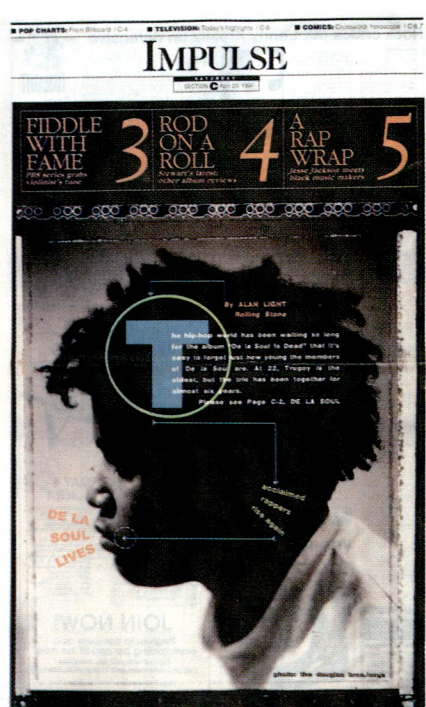

Anchorage Daily News
Galie Jean-Louis, Art Director, Designer & Illustrator

Anchorage Daily News
Dee Boyles, Designer & Illustrator

Anchorage Daily News
Galie Jean-Louis, Art Director & Designer

94 THE BEST OF NEWSPAPER DESIGN

Anchorage Daily News
Pete Spino, Illustrator & Designer; Galie Jean-Louis, Art Director

The Toronto Star
Kam Wai Yu, Designer; Pat McCormick, Editor

The Toronto Star
Kam Wai Yu, Designer; Pat McCormick, Editor

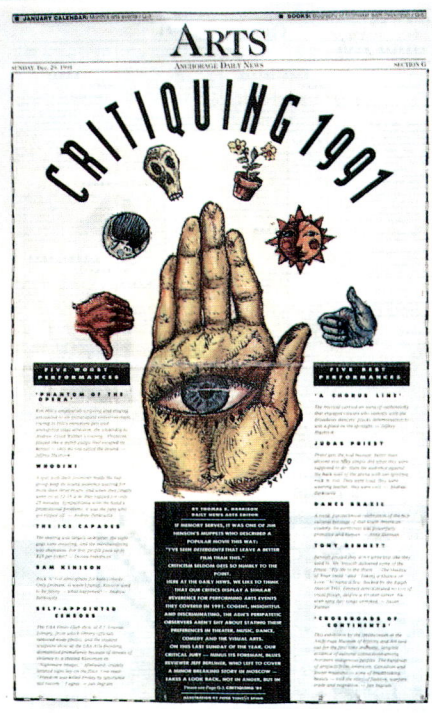

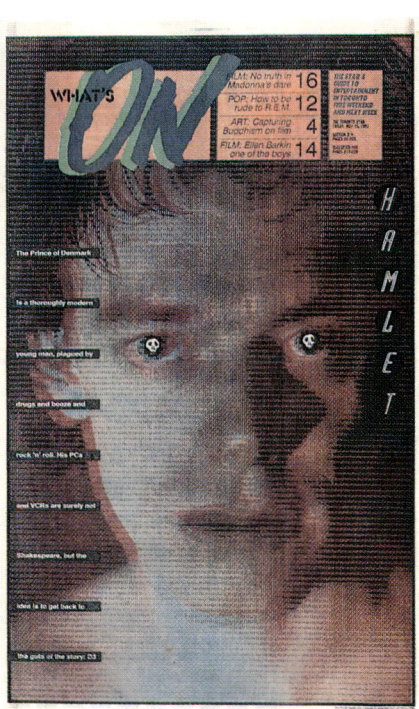

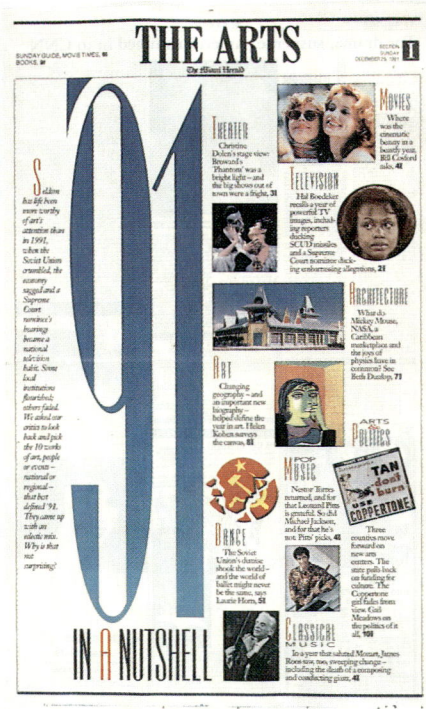
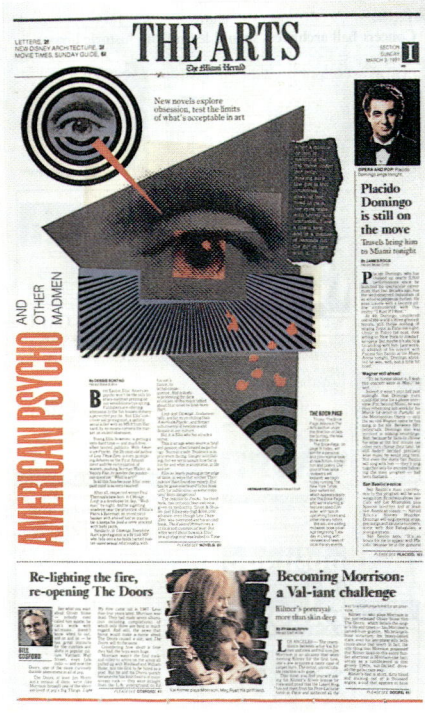

El Nuevo Herald
Miami, FL
Nuri Ducassi, Art Director & Designer; Olga Connor, Editor

The Miami Herald
Herman Vega, Editorial Design Illustrator; Steve Sonsky, Feature Editor; Randy Stano, Art Director; Rhonda Prast, Director of Editorial Art & Design

The Miami Herald
Herman Vega, Editorial Design Illustrator; Rhonda Prast, Features Design Editor; Steve Sonsky, Features Editor; Randy Stano, Director of Editorial Art & Design

FEATURES Entertainment • Food Pages

(ENTERTAINMENT PAGE)
The Washington Post
Michael Keegan, AME/News Art; Carol Porter, Art Director & Designer; Stephen Turk, Illustrator; Rich Leiby, Editor

Anchorage Daily News
Dee Boyles, Illustrator & Designer

The Dallas Morning News
Lee Ann Bandy, Designer

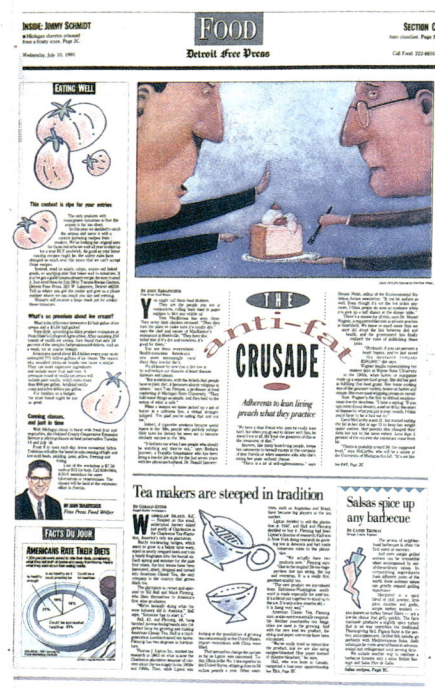

Detroit Free Press
Claire Innes, Art Director & Designer; David Cutler, Illustrator; Deborah Withey, Design Director

The Detroit News
Glenda Sinnamon, Designer; Joni Levy Liberman, Illustrator; Wes Bausmith, Art Director

Los Angeles Times
Tracy Crowe, Art Director; Tom Trapnell, Design Director; Ruth Reichl, Editor; Minnie Bernardino, Food Stylist; Donna Deane, Food Stylist; Steve Dykes, Photographer; Michael Edwards, Photographer

Food Page

JSR

The Boston Globe

Lynn Staley, Art Director; Julia Talcott, Illustrator; Yunghi Kim, Photographer

JSR

The Boston Globe

Aldona Charlton, Designer; Heidi Stevens, Illustrator; Eric Roth, Photographer; Michelle McDonald, Photographer

JSR

The Boston Globe

Sheri G. Lee, Art Director, Illustrator & Designer; Neil C. Pinchin, InfoGraphics Designer; Jo´se Ortega, Illustrator

JSR

The Boston Globe

Lynn Staley, Art Director; Tim Carroll, Illustrator

JSR

The Boston Globe

Sheri G. Lee, Art Director & Designer; John Blanding, Photographer; Sheryl Julian, Stylist

JSR

The Boston Globe

Aldona Charlton, Designer; Yunghi Kim, Photographer

THIRTEENTH EDITION 97

FEATURES Food Page

BRONZE

Saint Paul Pioneer Press

Ellen Simonson, Art Director & Designer; Kate Brennan-Hall, Illustrator

BRONZE

The Washington Post

Micheal Keegan, AME/News Art; Carol Porter, Art Director & Designer; Tim Clark, Illustrator

The Times-Picayune

Beth Aguillard, Designer; Julia Nead, Photo Stylist; Kathy Anderson, Photographer

Food • Fashion Pages

The Miami Herald
Rhonda Prast, Features Design Editor; Christian Potter Drury, Illustrator; Felicia Gressette, Food Editor

The Virginian-Pilot / Ledger-Star
Norfolk, VA

Janet Shaughnessy, Staff Artist

(FASHION PAGE)
Fort Worth Star-Telegram
Meda Kessler, Design Director; Ralph Lauer, Photographer

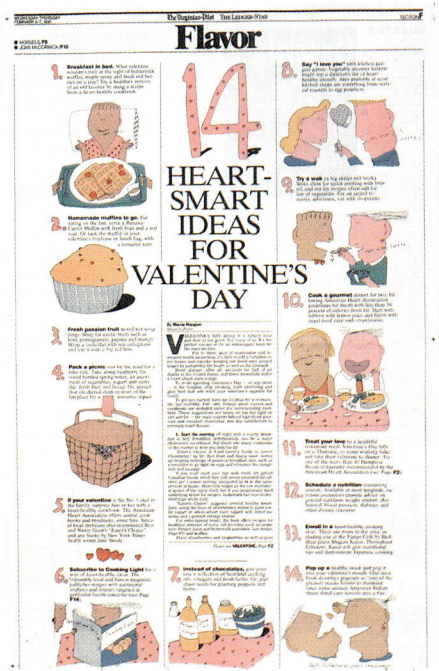

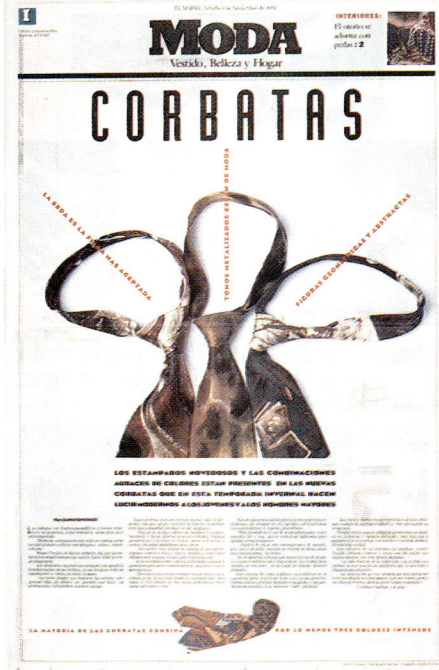
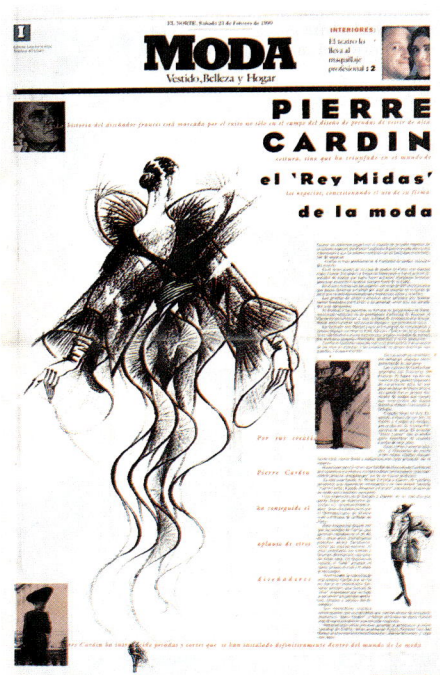

El Norte
Monterrey, Mexico

Raul Braulio Martinez, Designer; Estudio El Norte, Photographer

El Norte
Raul Braulio Martinez, Designer

Goteborgs-Posten
Gothenburg, Sweden

Mats Widebrant, Designer; Ulf Sveningson, Illustrator

THIRTEENTH EDITION 99

FEATURES Fashion Page

BRONZE

The Dallas Morning News

Bob Shema, Designer; Evans Caglage, Photographer

BRONZE

The Dallas Morning News

Bob Shema, Designer; Evans Caglage, Photographer

The Dallas Morning News

Bob Shema, Designer; Evans Caglage, Photographer

The Dallas Morning News
Bob Shema, Designer; Evans Caglage, Photographer

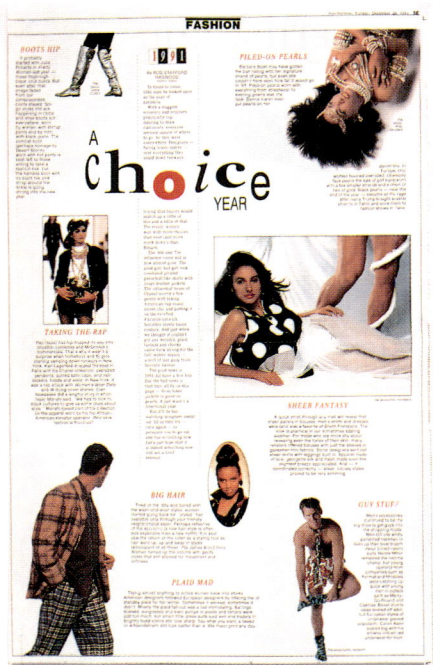

Sun-Sentinel
Fort Lauderdale, FL

Greg Carannante, Designer

BRONZE

The Gazette
Montreal, PQ, Canada

Gayle Grin, Designer; Mats Gustafson, Illustrator; Iona Monahan, Fashion Editor; Dave Yates, Editor

The Gazette
Gayle Grin, Designer; Linda Mason, Photographer; Iona Monahan, Fashion Editor; Dave Yates, Editor

FEATURES Fashion Page

BRONZE
The Columbus Dispatch
Scott Minister, Art Director & Designer

The Arizona Republic
Carolyn Rickerd, Designer; Patti Valdez, Art Director; Phil Hennessy, Graphics Coordinator; Jacques Barbey, Photographer; Howard I. Finberg, AME Graphics; Joe Coleman, Director of Photography; Anne M. Spitza, Writer; Amy Carlile, Features Editor

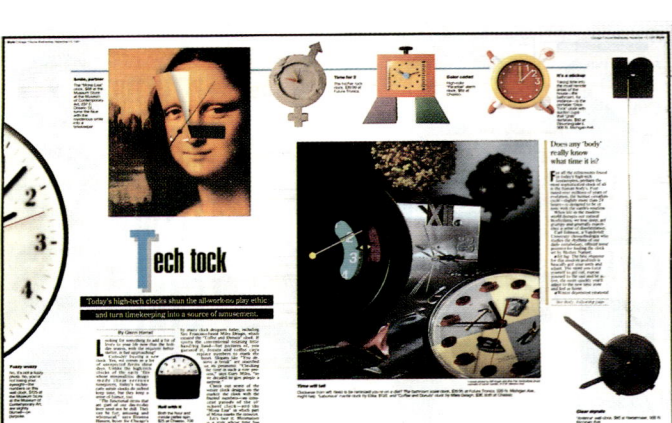

Chicago Tribune
David Syrek, Art Director; Bill Hogan, Photographer

Chicago Tribune
David Syrek, Art Director; Bob Fila, Photographer

Home Page

The Columbus Dispatch

Scott Minister, Art Director & Designer

The Columbus Dispatch

Robin Chenoweth, Designer; Scott Minister, Art Director; Jeff Hinckley, Photographer

The Columbus Dispatch

Scott Minister, Art Director & Designer

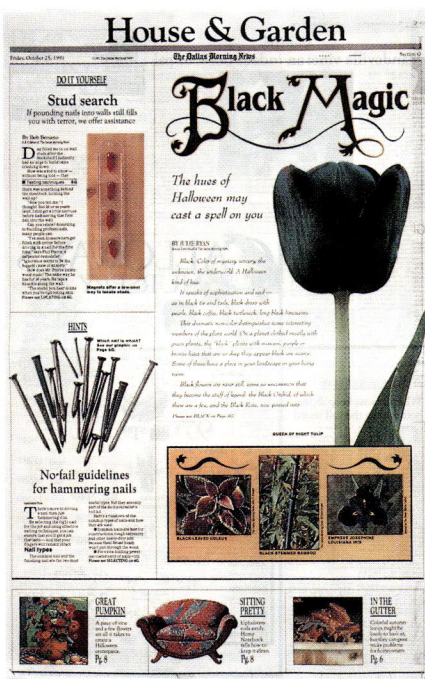

The Dallas Morning News

Karen Davis, Illustrator & Designer; Ed Kohorst, Art Director

The Dallas Morning News

Marilyn Glaser, Designer; Lamberto Alvarez, Illustrator

Detroit Free Press

Claire Innes, Art Director & Designer; John Green, Illustrator; Deborah Withey, Design Director

THIRTEENTH EDITION 103

FEATURES Home Page

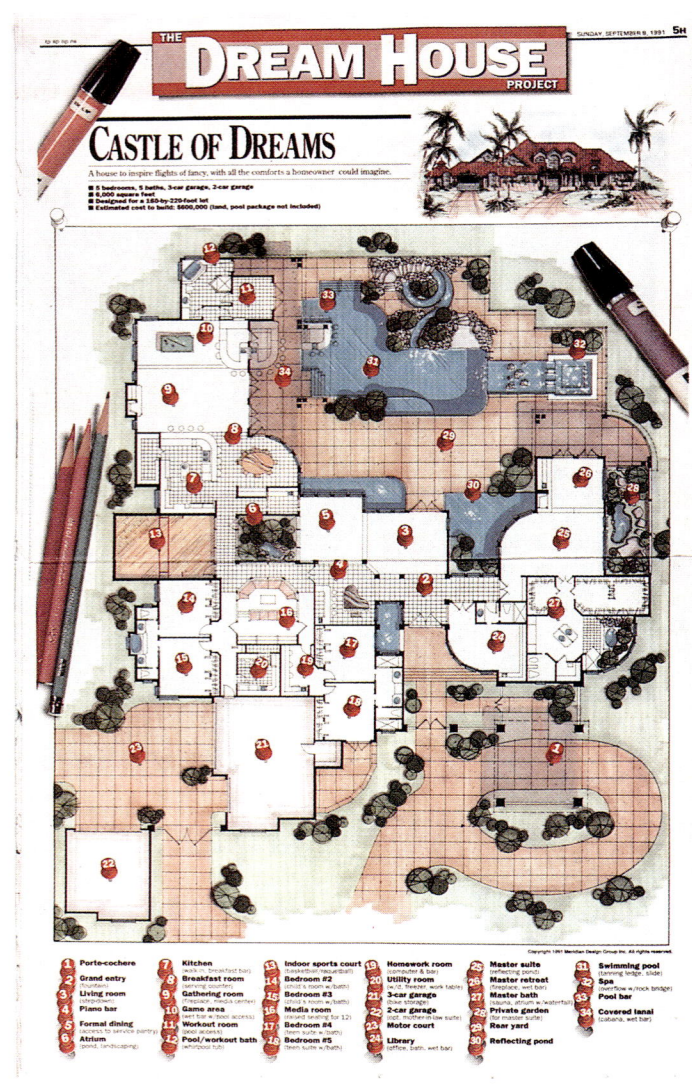

BRONZE & JSR

The Boston Globe

Aldona Charlton, Designer; Patrick Blackwell, Illustrator; Roxana Villa, Illustrator

BRONZE

St. Petersburg Times

Rick Holter, Designer; David Williams, Artist

The New York Times

Barbara Richer, Art Director & Designer; Tom Bodkin, Design Director; Cathie Bleck, Illustrator

Fort Worth Star-Telegram

Meda Kessler, Design Director

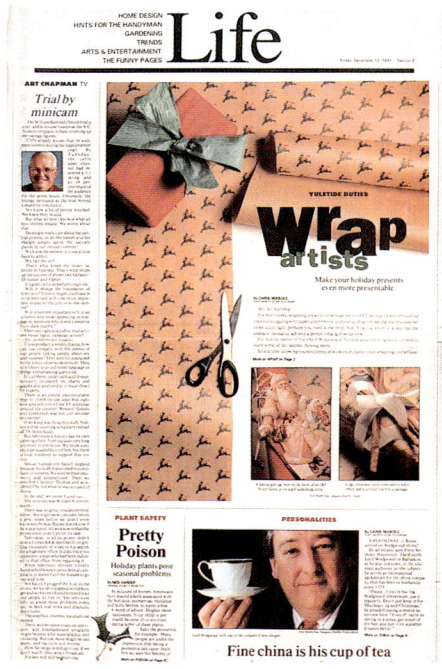

BRONZE

The Washington Times

Alexander Hunter, Art Director & Designer; Sharon Natoli, Photographer; Bert Gulait, Photographer

Fort Worth Star-Telegram

Meda Kessler, Design Director

The Star-Ledger
Newark, NJ

Bernadette Germain, Art Director; Chris Buckley, Designer; Nannette Finkel Rebach, Illustrator

FEATURES Home • Travel Pages

(HOME PAGE)
The Washington Post

Claudio Vazquez, Photographer; Kathy Legg, Art Director; Linda Hales, Editor

JSR
The Boston Globe

Jacqueline Berthet, Designer

JSR
The Boston Globe

Sheri G. Lee, Art Director & Designer; Shelley Rotner, Photographer; Robert Kasper, Illustrator

JSR
The Boston Globe

Jacqueline Berthet, Designer

JSR
The Boston Globe

Jacqueline Berthet, Designer

SILVER & JSR
The Boston Globe
Sheri G. Lee, Art Director & Designer; Thorina Rose, Illustrator

FEATURES Travel • Science Pages

The Hartford Courant
Patti Nelson, Art Director; Patricia Cousins, Illustrator

The San Diego Union
Shawn Vitt, Page Designer & Art Director; Jerry McClard, Photographer

San Francisco Examiner
Don McCartney, Designer; Kelly Frankeny, Graphics Editor; Joe Shoulak, Artist; Val Mina, Artist

JSR

The Boston Globe
Cynthia Daniels, Art Director & Designer; Neil C. Pinchin, Graphics Designer

JSR

The Boston Globe
Cynthia Daniels, Art Director & Designer; Neil C. Pinchin, Graphics Designer

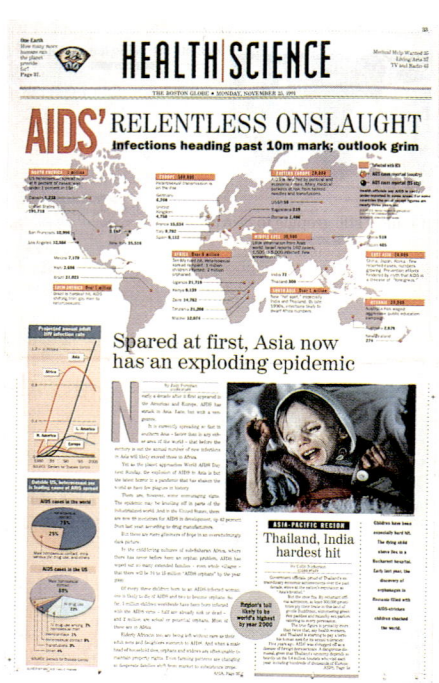

JSR

The Boston Globe
Cynthia Daniels, Art Director & Designer; Neil C. Pinchin, Graphic Designer

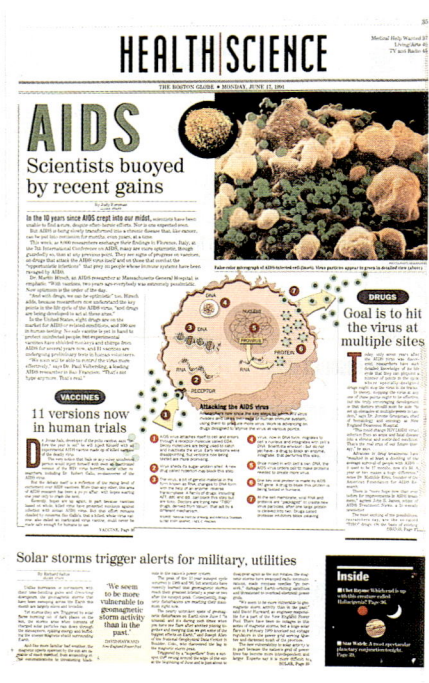

The New York Times

Nancy Sterngold, Art Director & Designer; Patricia J. Wynne, Illustrator; Tom Bodkin, Design Director

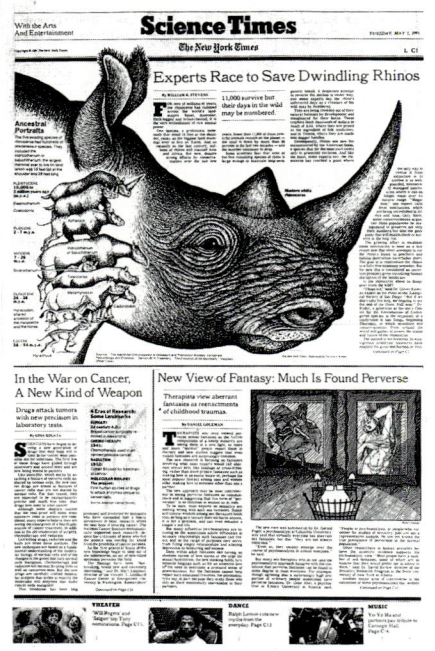

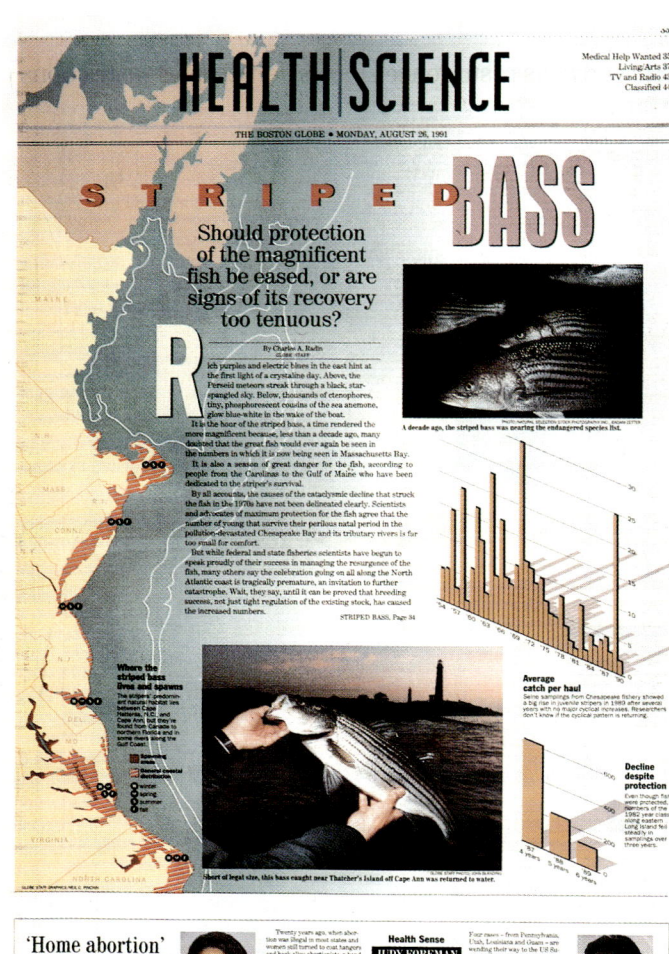

BRONZE & JSR
The Boston Globe

Cynthia Daniels, Art Director & Designer; Neil C. Pinchin, Graphics Designer

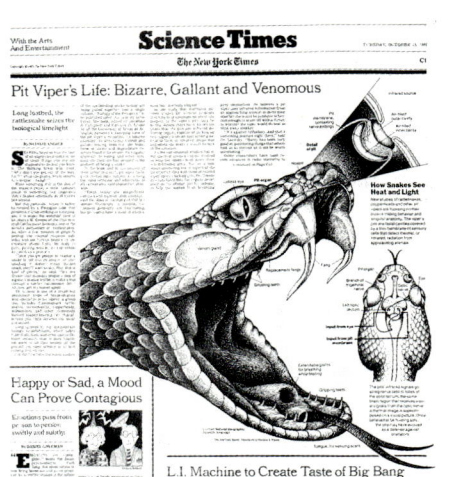

The New York Times

Nancy Sterngold, Art Director & Designer; Patricia J. Wynne, Illustrator; Megan Jaegerman, Graphic Artist; Tom Bodkin, Design Director

The New York Times

Nancy Sterngold, Art Director & Designer; Tom Bodkin, Design Director; Patricia J. Wynne, Illustrator

FEATURES Other Page

BRONZE

City Paper
Baltimore, MD

Mark Evans, Art Director; Peter Yuill, Illustrator

City Paper

Mark Evans, Art Director; Doug McDonough, Photographer

City Paper

Mark Evans, Art Director; Joseph Kohl, Photographer

Dagens Nyheter
Stockholm, Sweden

Hakan Ljung, Designer; Jan Romare, Illustrator

Edinburgh Evening News
Edinburgh, Scotland

Barbara Buchan, Author/Reporter; David Sim, Artist; Lucy Allsopp, Designer

BRONZE

Dagens Nyheter

Kerstin Wigstrand, Designer; Stina Eidem, Illustrator

El Nuevo Herald
Miami, FL

Nuri Ducassi, Illustrator & Designer; Silvia Licha, Editor

El Mundo

Carmelo Caderot, Art Director & Designer; Manuel de Miguel, Assistant Art Director; Antonio Benavidas, Illustrator

El Mundo
Madrid, Spain

Carmelo Caderot, Art Director & Designer; Manuel de Miguel, Asst. Art Director; Ulises Culebro, Illustrator

El Mundo

Carmelo Caderot, Art Director & Designer; Manuel de Miguel, Assistant Art Director

El Mundo

Carmelo Caderot, Art Director & Designer; Manuel de Miguel, Assistant Art Director

El Mundo

Carmelo Caderot, Art Director & Designer; Manuel de Miguel, Assistant Art Director; Samuel Velasco, Illustrator

El Mundo

Carmelo Caderot, Art Director & Designer; Manuel de Miguel, Assistant Art Director

El Mundo

Carmelo Caderot, Art Director & Designer; Manuel de Miguel, Asst. Art Director

St. Petersburg Times

Rick Holter, Designer

The Star-Ledger
Newark, NJ

Bernadette Germain, Art Director & Designer; David G. Klein, Illustrator

Reporter
Buffalo, NY

Rebecca Farnham, Art Director

FEATURES Other • Inside Pages

The Washington Times

John Kascht, Art Director & Designer

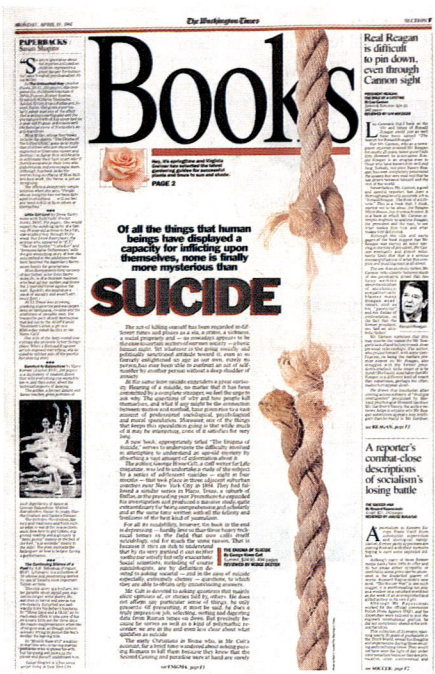

The Washington Times

John Kascht, Art Director, Designer & Illustrator

The Wall Street Journal Reports

Greg Leeds, Art Director; Joe Dizney, Designer; Brian Cronin, Illustrator; Alison Seiffer, Illustrator

(INSIDE PAGE)

Eastsideweek
Kirkland, WA

Sandra Schneider, Art Director; Jerry Gay, Photographer

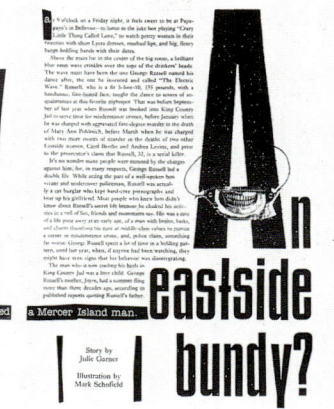

Eastsideweek

Sandra Schneider, Art Director; Mark Schofield, Illustrator

114 THE BEST OF NEWSPAPER DESIGN

CHAPTER FIVE

Magazines

MAGAZINES Overall Design

The Globe and Mail / West Magazine
Vancouver, BC, Canada

Susan Casey, Art Director; Paul Sullivan, Editor

Color Cover

GOLD

The Globe and Mail /
Toronto Magazine

Susan Casey, Creative Director; George Karabotsos, Art Director; Kathy Boake, Illustrator

MAGAZINES Color Cover

SILVER

The Globe and Mail /
Toronto Magazine

Susan Casey, Creative Director; George Karabotsos, Art Director; Mark Mainguy, Photographer; Marianne Lovink, Stylist

SILVER

The Globe and Mail / West Magazine
Vancouver, BC, Canada

Susan Casey, Creative Director; Robert Kopecky, Illustrator; Paul Sullivan, Editor

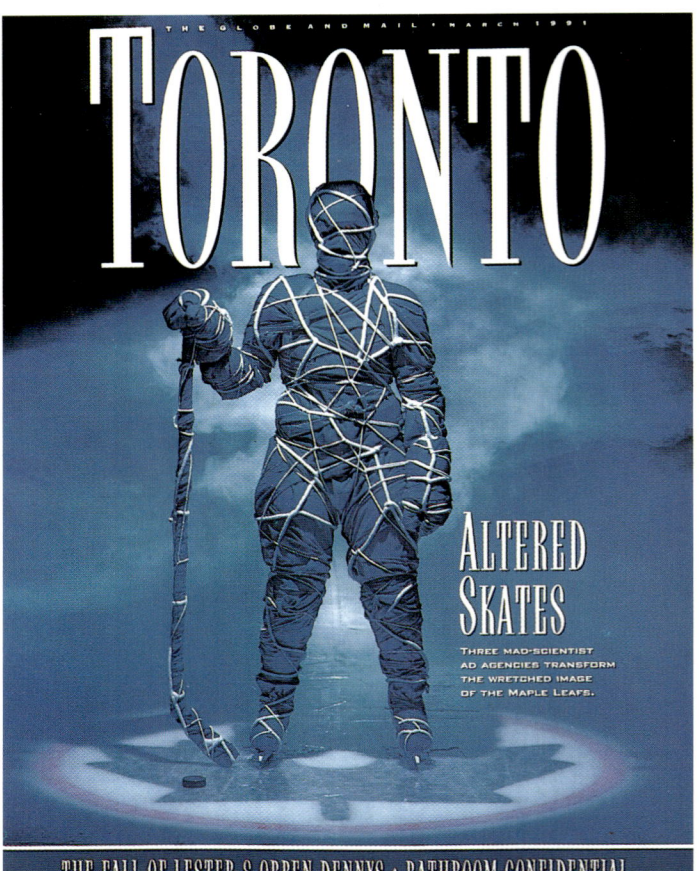

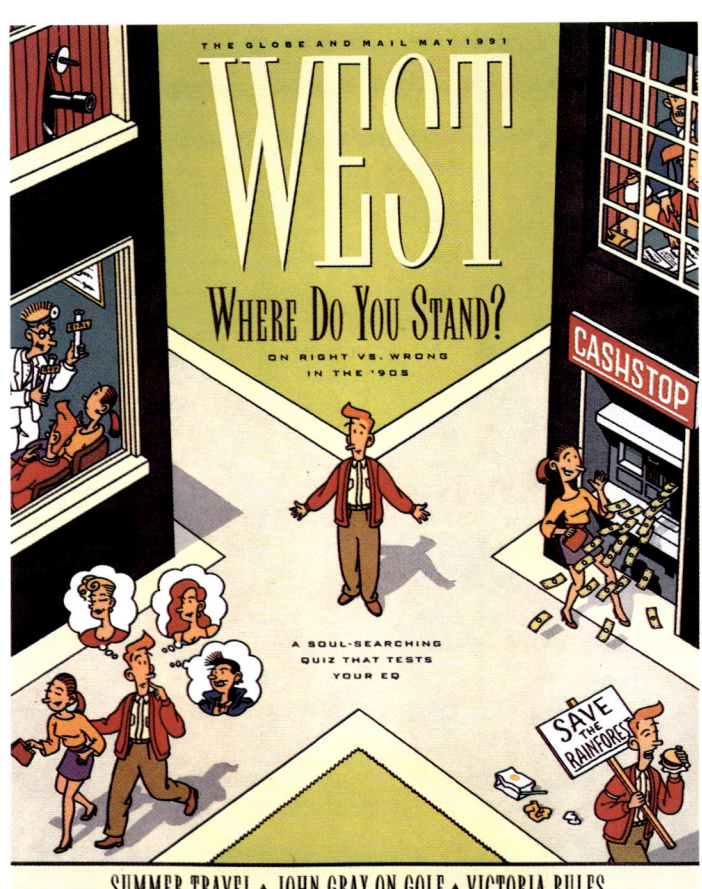

The Globe and Mail / West Magazine

Susan Casey, Art Director; Shelley Youngblut, Editor; Barry Blitt, Illustrator

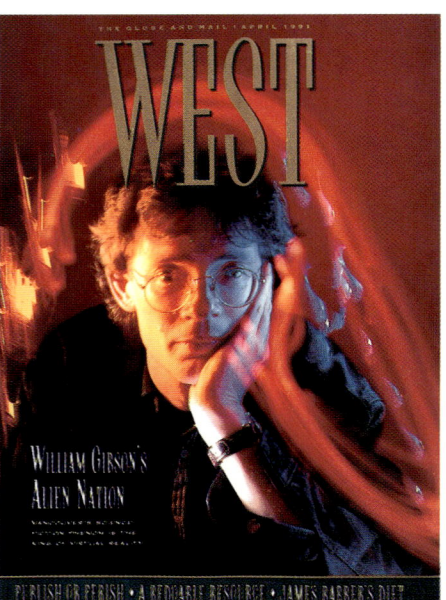

The Globe and Mail / West Magazine

Susan Casey, Art Director; Patrick Koslo, Photographer; Paul Sullivan, Editor

SILVER

El Mundo / Metropoli
Madrid, Spain

Carmelo Caderot, Art Director; Ulises Culebro, Illustrator & Designer

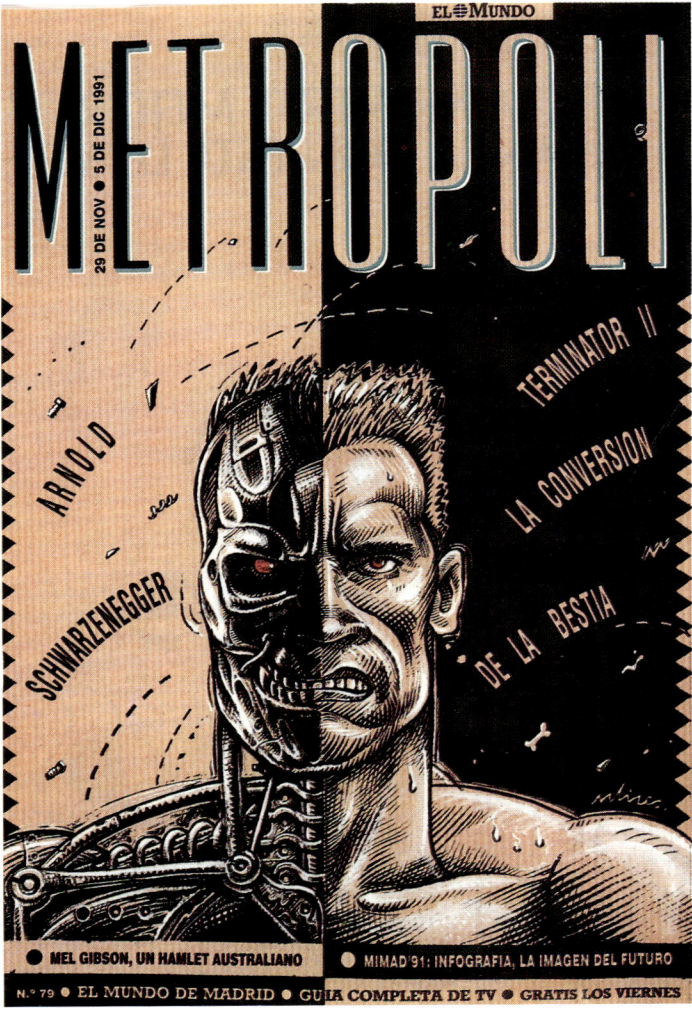

BRONZE

The Orlando Sentinel / Florida Magazine

Santa Choplin, Design Director; John Ceballos, Illustrator

El Sol
Madrid, Spain

Juan Varela, Editor In Chief; Rodrigo Sanchez, Design Chief; Miguel Gonzalez, Photo Chief; Amparo Redondo, Designer; Cristina Marti, Designer

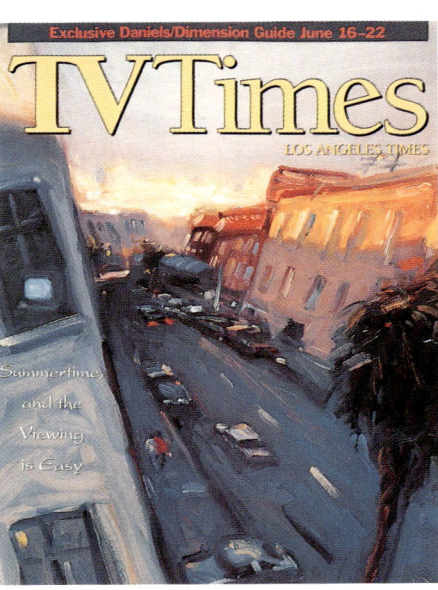

Los Angeles Times / TV Times

Phil Waters, Art Director; Sherry Stern, Editor; James Stigg, Illustrator

The Providence Sunday Journal

Mick Cochran, Art Director; Susan Huntemann, Designer; Thea Breite, Photo Editor; Rachel Ritchie, Photographer

THIRTEENTH EDITION 119

MAGAZINES Color Cover

BRONZE

The New York Times Magazine

Janet Froelich, Art Director; Kandy Littrell, Designer; Charles Burns, Illustrator; Tom Bodkin, Design Director

The New York Times Magazine

Janet Froelich, Art Director; Kandy Littrell, Designer; Timothy Greenfield-Sanders, Photographer; Kathy Ryan, Photo Editor; Tom Bodkin, Design Director

The New York Times Magazine

Janet Froelich, Art Director; Kandy Littrell, Designer; Michael O'Neill, Photographer; Kathy Ryan, Photo Editor; Tom Bodkin, Design Director

The New York Times Magazine

Janet Froelich, Art Director; Kandy Littrell, Designer; Mary Ellen Mark, Photographer; Kathy Ryan, Photo Editor; Tom Bodkin, Design Director

The Boston Globe Magazine

Lucy Bartholomay, Art Director & Designer

The Boston Globe Magazine

Lucy Bartholomay, Art Director & Designer; Theo Rudnak, Illustrator

The Boston Globe Magazine

Lucy Bartholomay, Art Director & Designer; Terry Allen, Illustrator

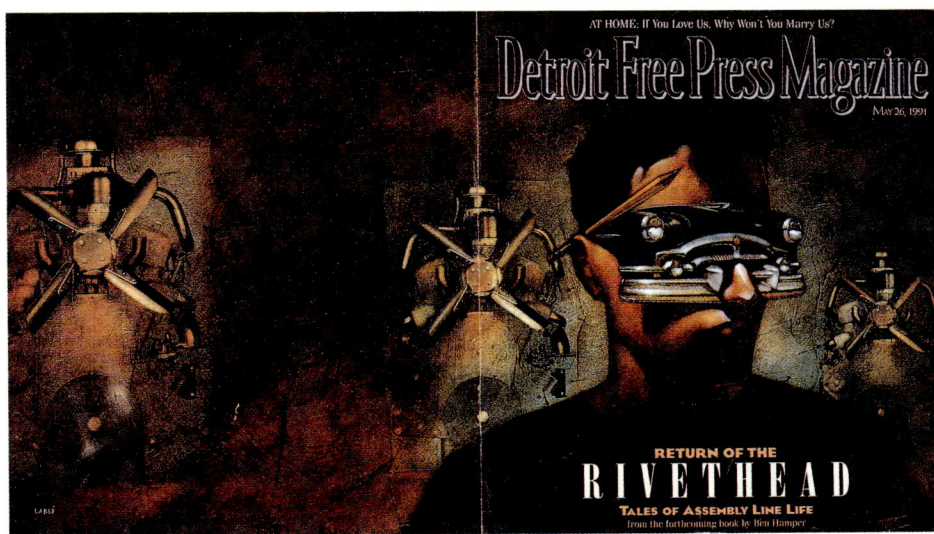

Detroit Free Press Magazine

Andrew Hartley, Art Director & Designer; John Labbe, Illustrator; Deborah Withey, Design Director

The Hartford Courant / Northeast Magazine

David Kendrick, Art Director & Designer; Henrik Drescher, Illustrator

MAGAZINES Color Cover

BRONZE

The Washington Post Magazine

Richard Baker, Art Director & Designer; Anita Kunz, Illustrator

The Washington Post Magazine

Richard Baker, Art Director & Designer; Oberto Gili, Photographer; Deborah Needleman, Photo Editor

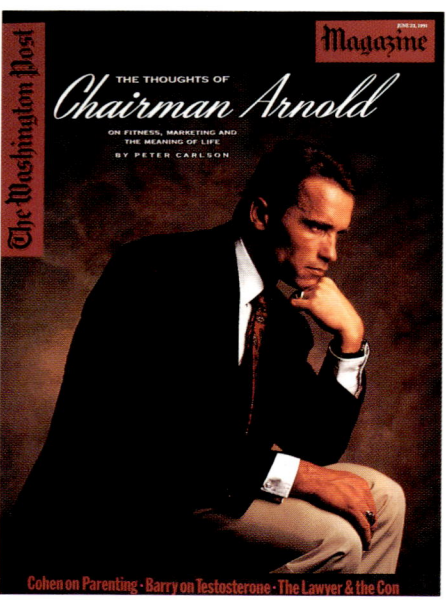

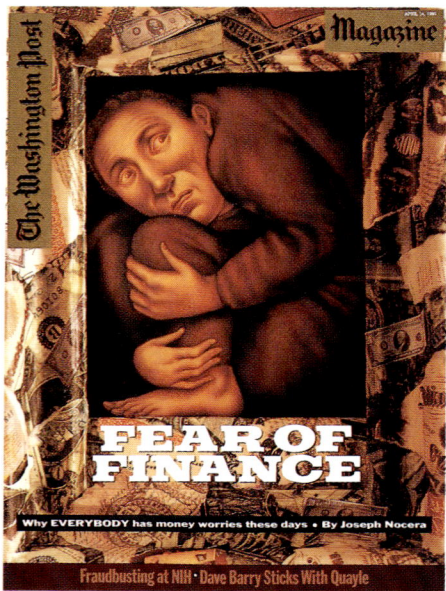

The Washington Post Magazine

Kelly Doe, Deputy Art Director & Designer; Richard Baker, Art Director; Janet Wolley, Illustrator

The Washington Post Magazine

Richard Baker, Art Director & Designer; Tom Wolff, Photographer; Deborah Needleman, Photo Editor

The Washington Post Magazine

Richard Baker, Art Director & Designer; Anita Kunz, Illustrator

Black & White Cover • Special Section

SILVER

El Sol
Madrid, Spain

Juan Varela, Editor in Chief; Rodrigo Sanchez, Design Chief; Miguel Gonzalez, Photo Chief; Ricardo Salvador, Illustration Chief; Anparo Redondo, Designer; Cristina Darti, Designer; Dan Winters, Photographer

SILVER

The Philadelphia Inquirer Magazine

Bert Fox, Art Director; Jessica Helfand, Design Director; William Sloan, Illustrator; Jessica Helfand, Designer

(SPECIAL SECTION)

The Boston Globe Magazine

Lucy Bartholomay, Art Director & Designer; Marty Blake, Illustrator; James Yang, Illustrator; Thomas Kerr, Illustrator; Scott Menchin, Illustrator; Yunghi Kim, Photographer; Neil C. Pinchin, Infographics Artist

MAGAZINES: Two or More Pages

SILVER
The New York Times Magazine

Janet Froelich, Art Director & Designer; Sheila Metzner, Photographer; Tom Bodkin, Design Director

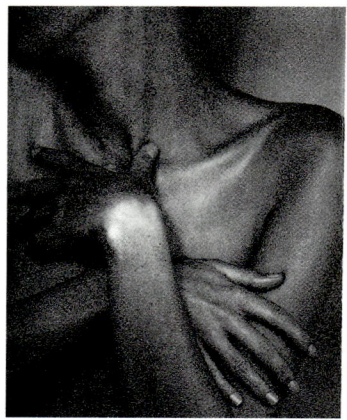

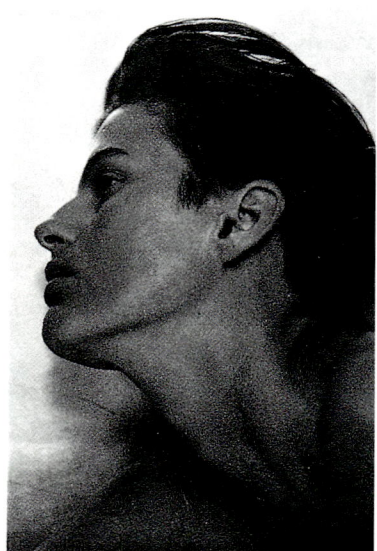

Cosmetics companies have a new obsession with body parts. Six writers do a little obsessing of their own.

BODY LANGUAGE

Photographs by Sheila Metzner

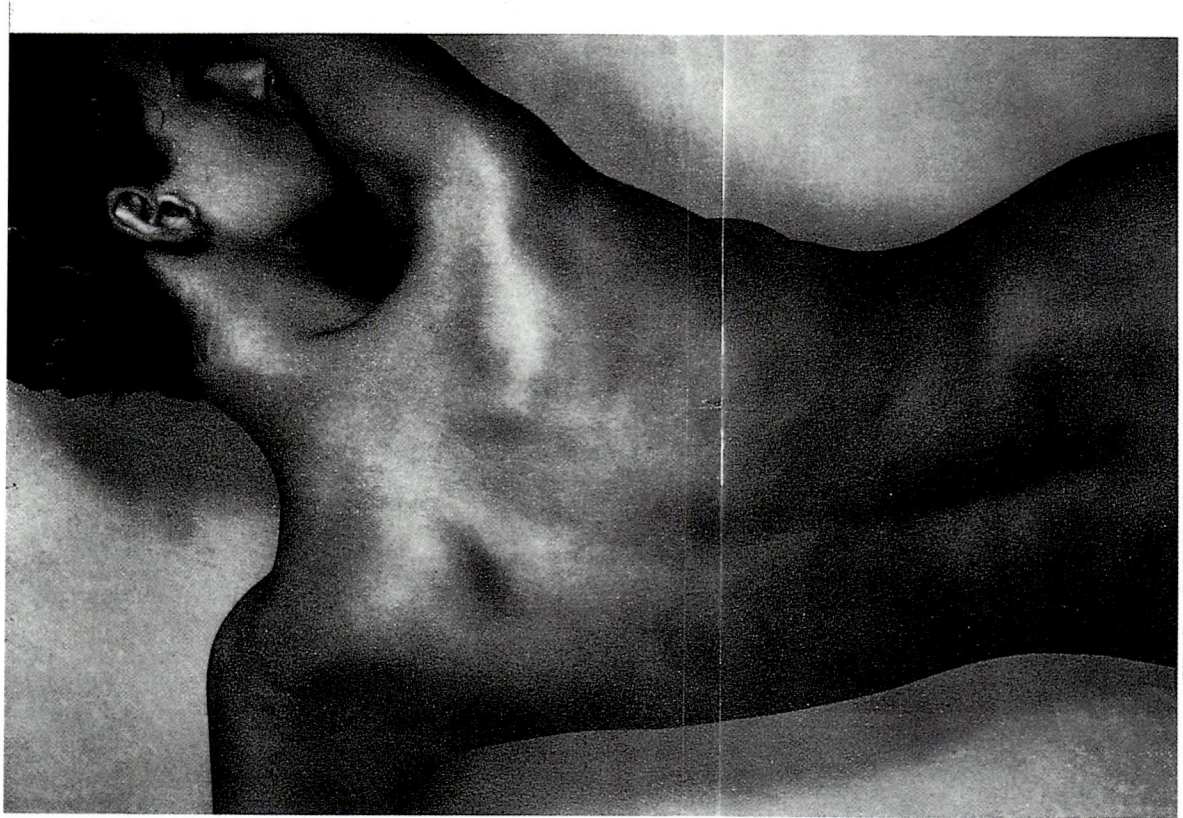

SILVER

The New York Times Magazine

Janet Froelich, Art Director & Designer; Henrik Drescher, Illustrator; Blair Drawson, Illustrator; Michael Bartalos, Illustrator; Amy Guip, Illustrator; Janet Woolley, Illustrator; Marshall Arisman, Illustrator; Brian Cronin, Illustrator; Tom Bodkin, Design Director

MAGAZINES: Two or More Pages

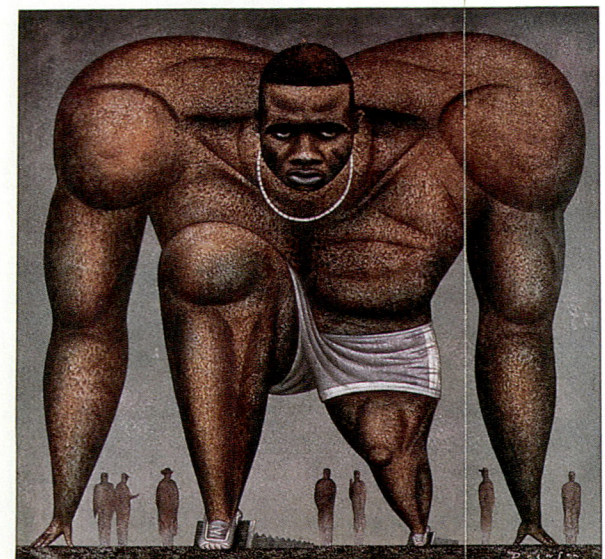

BRONZE

The Globe and Mail / Toronto Magazine

Susan Casey, Creative Director; George Karabotsos, Art Director; Blair Drawson, Illustrator

BRONZE

The Washington Post Magazine

Richard Baker, Art Director & Designer; Brian Cronin, Illustrator

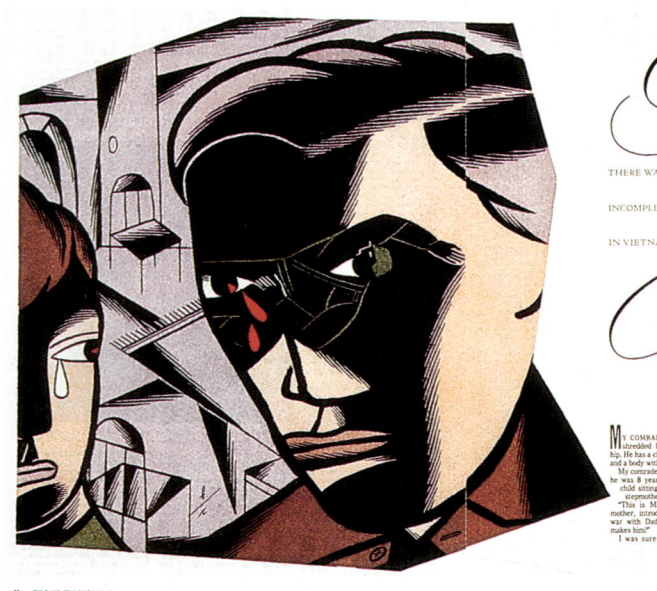

The Boston Globe Magazine

Lucy Bartholomay, Art Director & Designer; Annie Leibovitz, Photographer

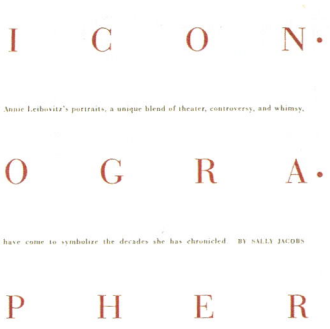

The Boston Globe Magazine

Lucy Bartholomay, Art Director & Designer; Brian Cronin, Illustrator

126 THE BEST OF NEWSPAPER DESIGN

The New York Times Magazine

Janet Froelich, Art Director; Kandy Littrell, Designer; Josef Astor, Photographer; Tom Bodkin, Design Director

The New York Times Magazine

Janet Froelich, Art Director & Designer; Michel Comte, Photographer; Tom Bodkin, Design Director

The New York Times Magazine

Janet Froelich, Art Director; Kandy Littrell, Designer; Karen Kuehn, Photographer; Tom Bodkin, Design Director; Kathy Ryan, Design Director

The New York Times Magazine

Janet Froelich, Art Director; Kathi Rota, Designer; Josh Gosfield, Illustrator; Tom Bodkin, Design Director

THIRTEENTH EDITION 127

MAGAZINES Single Page

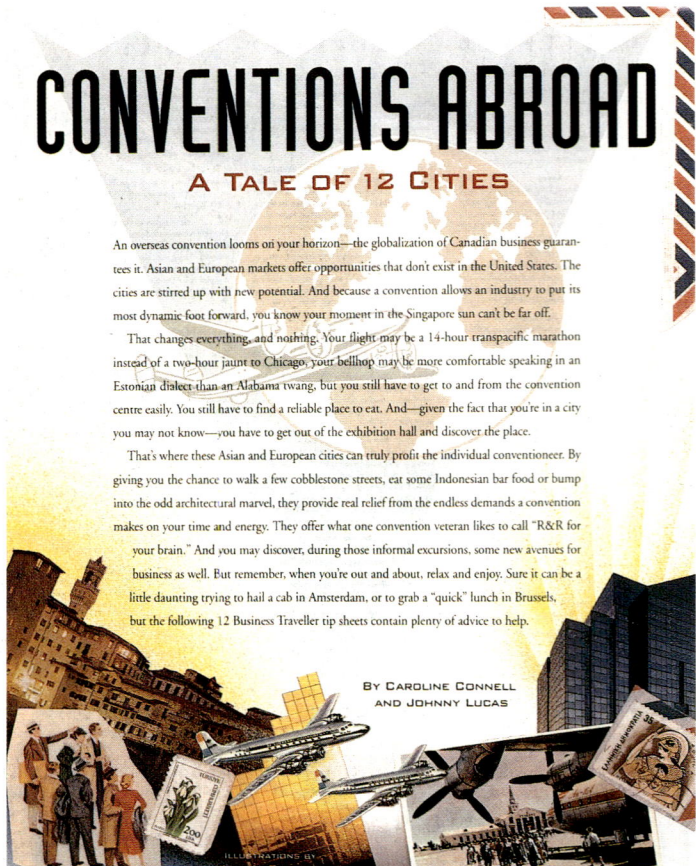

BRONZE

The Globe and Mail / Business Traveller Magazine
Toronto, ON, Canada

George Karabotsos, Art Director; Kevin N. Ghiglione, Illustrator

The Boston Globe Magazine

Lucy Bartholomay, Art Director & Designer

The Globe and Mail / Toronto Magazine

Susan Casey, Creative Director; George Karabotsos, Art Director; Edward Gajdel, Photographer

CHAPTER SIX

Special Sections

Invaders Threaten Island Wildlife

ECOTOURISM
SURVIVAL OF THE GALAPAGOS

Photos by Melanie Stetson Freeman, staff photographer

By David Holmstrom
Staff writer of The Christian Science Monitor

GALAPAGOS ISLANDS, ECUADOR

NOTE TO READERS
Our "Points of the Compass" feature, usually found on these pages, will return next week.

SILVER

The Christian Science Monitor
Boston, MA

Melanie Stetson Greeman, Photographer & Photo Editor; John Van Pelt, Designer

SILVER

La Vanguardia
Barcelona, Spain

Carlos Perez de Rozas, Art Director; Rosa Mundet, Art Director Asst.; Ferran Grau, Senior Designer; Joan Corbera, Designer

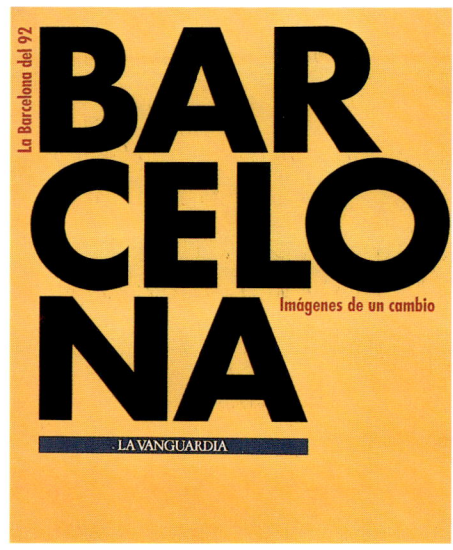

SPECIAL SECTIONS — Single Subject Series

SILVER
The Oregonian
Steve Cowden, Artist; Mark Wigginton, Art Director

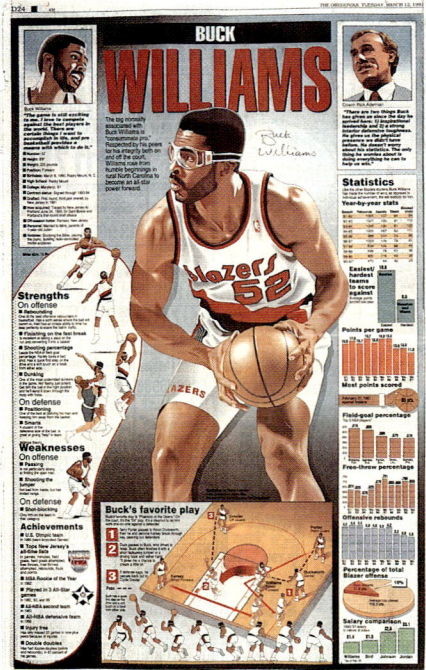

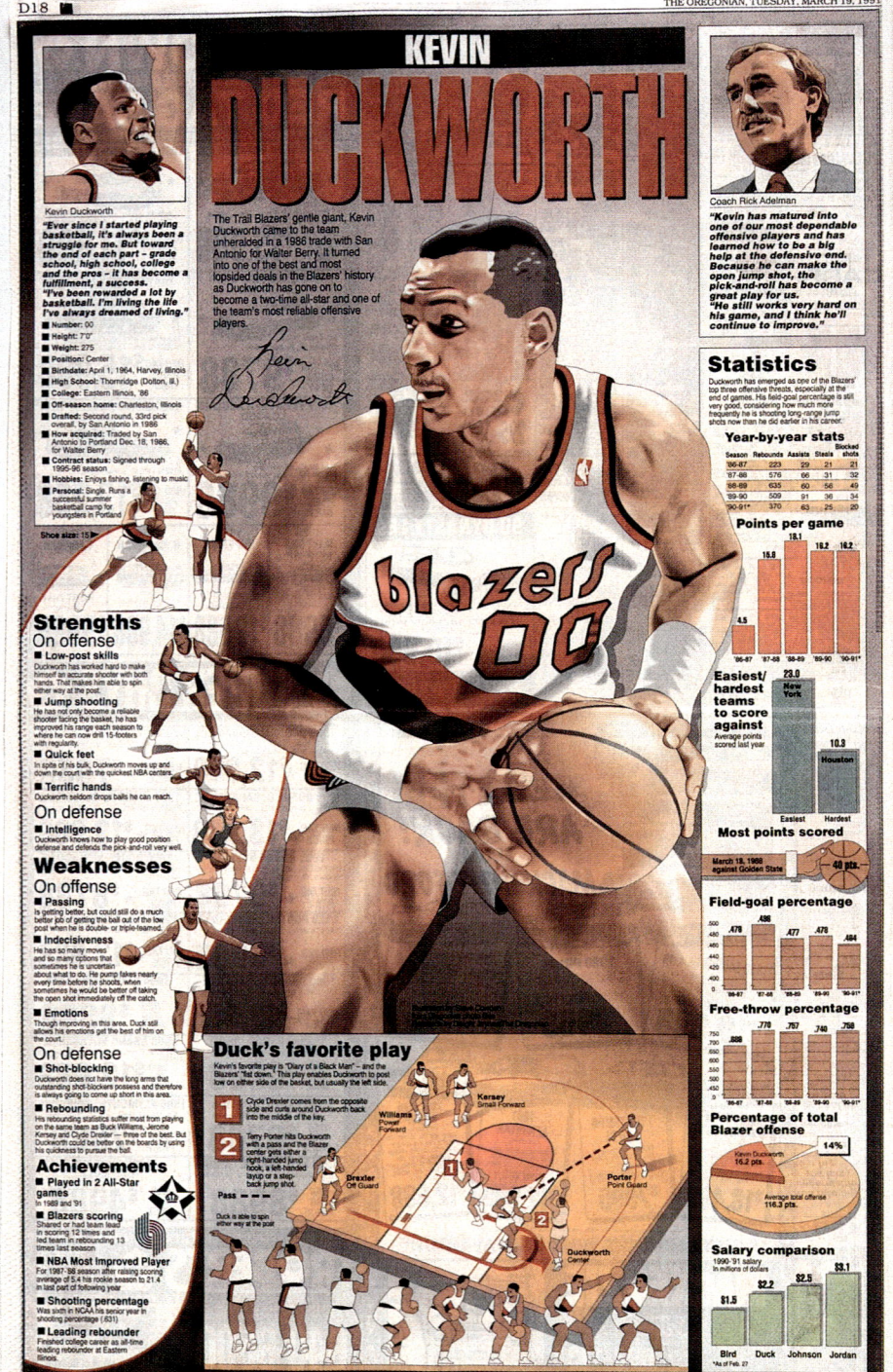

BRONZE
St. Petersburg Times

Rick Holter, Designer; Maurice Rivenbark, Photographer; Thomas French, Writer

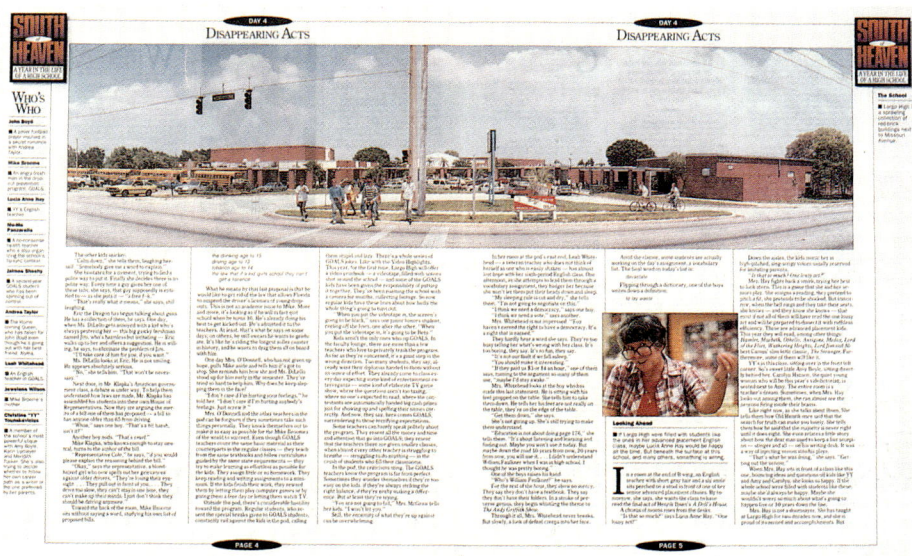

BRONZE
The Detroit News

Dale Peskin, AME; Nancy Hanus, Assistant News Editor; Dierck Casselman, AME Graphics/Design; Robert Graham, Graphics Artist

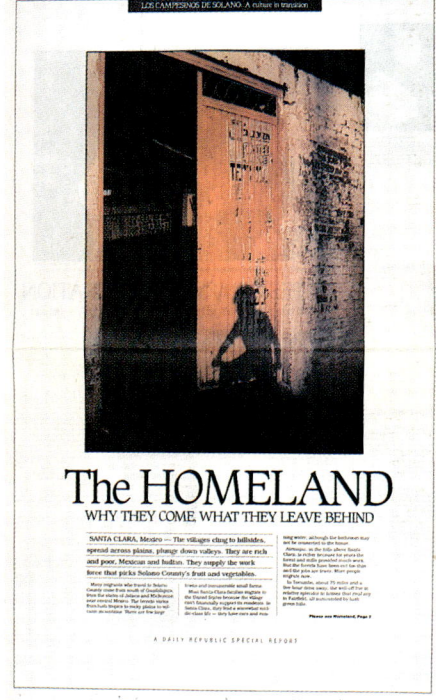

Daily Republic
Fairfield, CA

Colleen Lanchester, Art Director & Designer; Mona Reeder, Photographer; Gary Goldsmith, Photographer; Michael Coleman, Photographer

THIRTEENTH EDITION 133

SPECIAL SECTIONS Single Subject Series

The Christian Science Monitor
Boston, MA

Guy Stuart, Designer; Robert Harbison, Photographer

The Denver Post

Vince Bzdek, News Editor; Blair Hamill, Artist; Brian Brainerd, Photographer

The Christian Science Monitor

John Van Pelt, Designer & Graphics Artist; Shirley Horn, Graphics Artist; Guy Stuart, Graphics Artist

The Christian Science Monitor

Shirley Horn, Graphics Artist; John Van Pelt, Designer; Paul Kitagaki, Photographer; Stuart Silverstone, Graphic Research

The Albuquerque Tribune

Lara Edge, Designer; Jeff Neumann, Graphics Artist; Randall K. Roberts, Graphics Editor

Anchorage Daily News

Richard J. Murphy, Photo Editor & Designer; Mike Campbell, AME & Designer; Erik Hill, Staff Photographer

Los Angeles Times

Steve Moore, News Editor & Designer; Tammy Lechner, Photographer; Al Seib, Photographer; J. Albert Diaz, Photographer; Patrick Downs, Photographer; Beverly Beyette, Staff Writer; Iris Schneider, Photo Editor; Karen Wada, View Section Editor

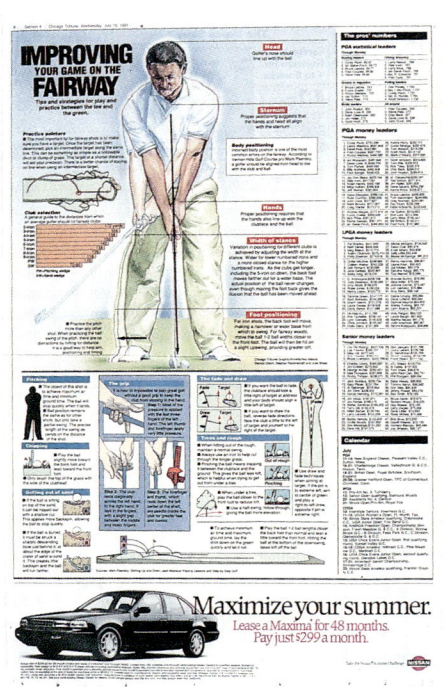

Saint Paul Pioneer Press
Staff

Chicago Tribune

Dennis Odom, Art Director & Illustrator; Stephen Ravenscraft, Illustrator & Researcher; Julie Sheer, Researcher; Annette Ney Meade, Researcher; Stephen Cvengros, Illustrations Editor

Gannett Suburban Newspapers
White Plains, NY

Monica Moses, Senior Design Editor

THIRTEENTH EDITION 135

SILVER

The Dallas Morning News

Karen Davis, Illustrator & Designer; Laura Stanton, Graphics; Ed Kohorst, Art Director; Erich Schiegel, Photographer

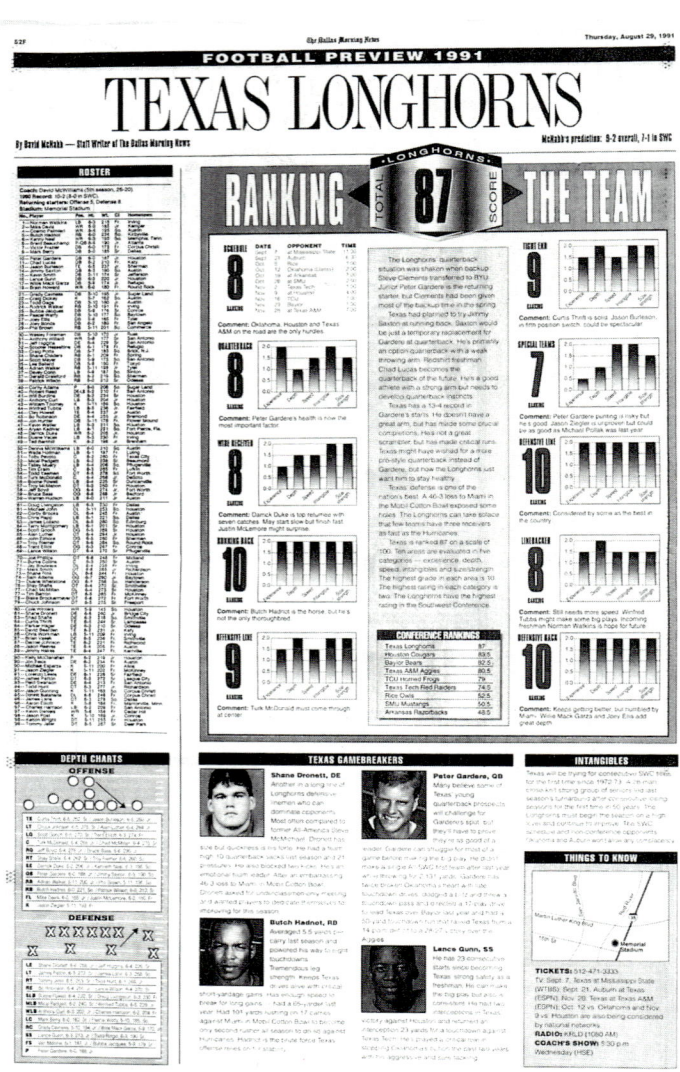

SILVER

The Wall Street Journal Reports

Greg Leeds, Design Director & Designer; Joe Dizney, Art Director & Designer

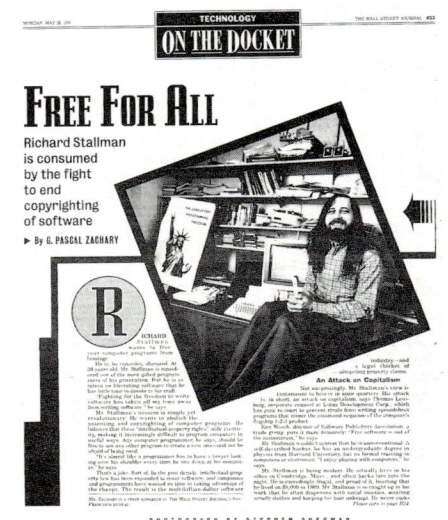

THIRTEENTH EDITION 137

SPECIAL SECTIONS With Ads

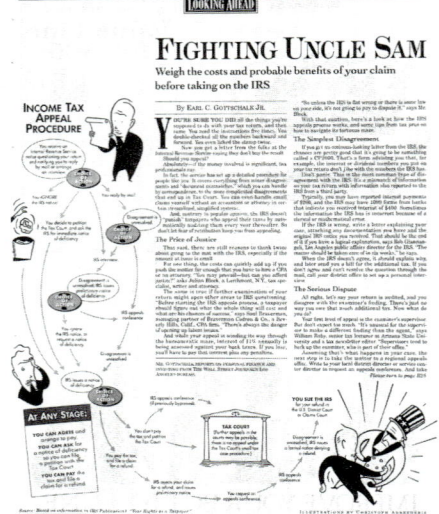

BRONZE
The Wall Street Journal Reports

Greg Leeds, Art Director & Designer; Joe Dizney, Art Director & Designer

BRONZE
The Virginian-Pilot / Ledger-Star
Norfolk, VA

Bill Pitzer, Illustrator & Designer; Alex Burrows, Picture Editor & Designer; Ed Power, Editor

The Boston Globe

Sheri G. Lee, Art Director & Designer; Daniel Pelavin, Illustrator; Neil C. Pinchin, Infographics Designer

Detroit Free Press

Claire Innes, Art Director, Designer & Illustrator; Deborah Withey, Design Director

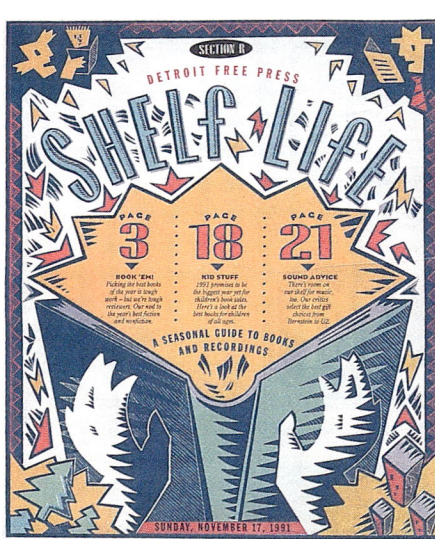

Patuxent Publishing Company / Holiday Entertaining '91
Columbia, MD

Claudia Lafuse, Art Director; John Workman, Design Coordinator; Donna Ellis, Editor; Claudia Lafuse, Illustrator

The Orange County Register
Santa Ana, CA

John Fabris, Asst. News Editor/Design; Nanette Bisher, Art Director; Michelle Cardon, Photo Editor

The Wall Street Journal Reports

Greg Leeds, Design Director & Designer; Joe Dizney, Art Director & Designer

The Wall Street Journal Reports

Greg Leeds, Design Director & Designer; Joe Dizney, Art Director & Designer

THIRTEENTH EDITION 139

SPECIAL SECTIONS | Without Ads • Cover

The Kansas City Star
Jean Moxam, AME Graphics/Design

The Spokesman-Review & Spokane Chronicle
Neal Pattison, AME & Designer; Scott Sines, Photo Editor & Designer; Kit King, Chief Photographer; Fred King, News Editor

The Miami Herald
Herman Vega, Section Designer; Wes Albers, Section Editor & Researcher; Rick Brownlee, Infographics Artist & Researcher; Hiram Henriquez, Infographics Artist; Woody Vondracek, Designer; Reggie Myers, Infographics Artist; Liz Donovan, Researcher; Martin Merzer, Writer and Researcher; Al Diaz, Photographer; Dennis Copeland, Director of Photography; Randy Stano, Director of Editorial Art & Design

(COVER)
Detroit Free Press
Deborah Withey, Art/Design Director & Illustrator; Steve Anderson, Designer

El Mundo
Madrid, Spain

Carmelo Caderot, Art Director & Designer; Manuel de Miguel, Asst. Art Director

The New York Times
Genevieve Williams, Art Director & Designer; Patrick Blackwell, Illustrator; Tom Bodkin, Design Director

Cover

The Detroit News
Dale Peskin, AME; Diane Weiss, Photographer

BRONZE

The New York Times
Barbara Richer, Art Director & Designer; Tom Bodkin, Design Director; Tim Lewis, Illustrator

The New York Times
Barbara Richer, Art Director & Designer; Cathie Bleck, Illustrator

THIRTEENTH EDITION 141

SPECIAL SECTIONS | Cover • Inside Page

GOLD

The Wall Street Journal Reports

Greg Leeds, Design Director & Designer; Wendy Wray, Illustrator

(INSIDE PAGE)

SILVER

The Wall Street Journal Reports

Greg Leeds, Art Director & Designer; David Gurman, Illustrator; Brian Callanan, Illustrator

The Wall Street Journal Reports

Greg Leeds, Art Director & Designer; Dennis Ortiz Lopez, Typographer

142 THE BEST OF NEWSPAPER DESIGN

Inside Page

BRONZE

The Wall Street Journal Reports

Joe Dizney, Art Director & Designer

The Wall Street Journal Reports

Joe Dizney, Art Director & Designer; Alison Seiffer, Illustrator

The Wall Street Journal Reports

Greg Leeds, Art Director & Designer; Christopher Bing, Illustrator

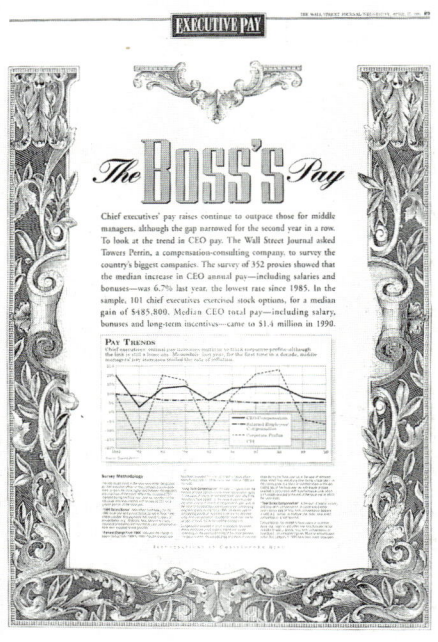

The Wall Street Journal Reports

Greg Leeds, Art Director & Designer; Robert De Michiell, Illustrator

THIRTEENTH EDITION 143

SPECIAL SECTIONS | Inside Page • Reprint

The Dallas Morning News

Ed Kohorst, Art Director; Laura Stanton, Illustrator & Designer

Chicago Tribune

Therese Shechter, Art Director; John Twohey, Editor; Ron Grossman, Editor; Bill Hogan, Photographer

Chicago Tribune

Theresa Shechter, Art Director; John Twohey, Editor; Ron Grossman, Editor; Bill Hogan, Photographer

(REPRINT)

Chicago Tribune

Tony Majeri, Creative Designer; Theresa Shechter, Art Director; Bob Condor, Editor; Tim Brokema, Picture Editor; Steven Bialer, Designer

144 THE BEST OF NEWSPAPER DESIGN

CHAPTER SEVEN

IN THIS CHAPTER:

Judges' Special Recognition

Dale Peskin of The Detroit News, for his portfolio of news pages.

The Globe and Mail, for its portfolio of covers from Toronto, Montreal and West magazines.

Design Portfolios

DESIGN PORTFOLIOS — News: 250,000 Plus

SILVER & JSR
The Detroit News
Dale Peskin, AME

The Detroit News

Dale Peskin, AME; Nancy Hanus, Assistant News Editor; Beth Valone, Assistant News Editor; Joe Gray, Assistant News Editor; Cathy Anderson, Assistant News Editor

Los Angeles Times

Ligaya Gritz, Art Director; Tom Trapnell, Design Director; Jon Thurber, News Editor; Dan Fisher, Section Editor

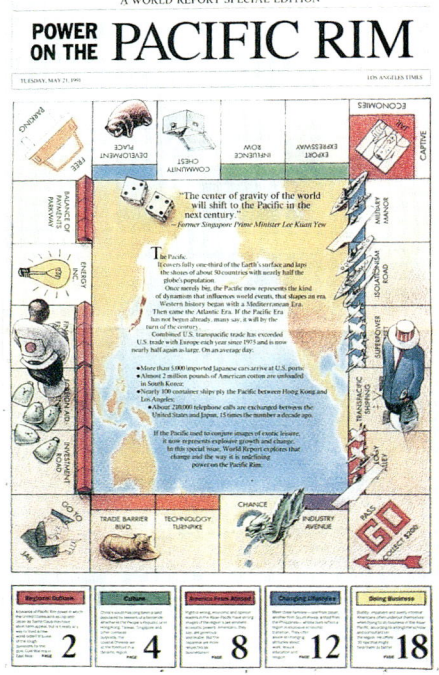

The Miami Herald

Ana Lense Larrauri, Editorial Artist; Jim Watters, Business Monday News Editor; Randy Stano, Director of Editorial Art & Design

THIRTEENTH EDITION 147

DESIGN PORTFOLIOS News: 250,000 Plus

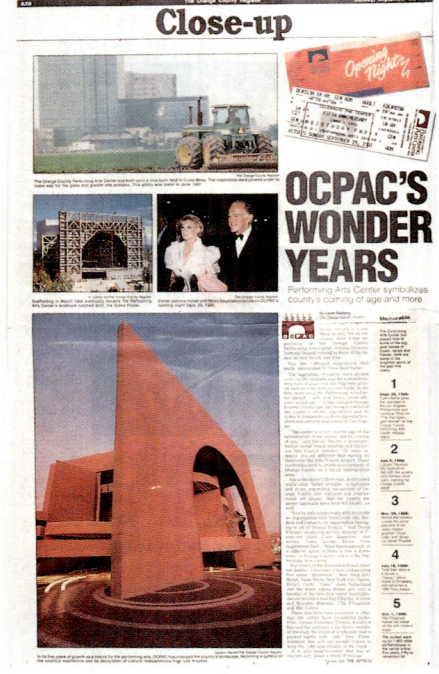

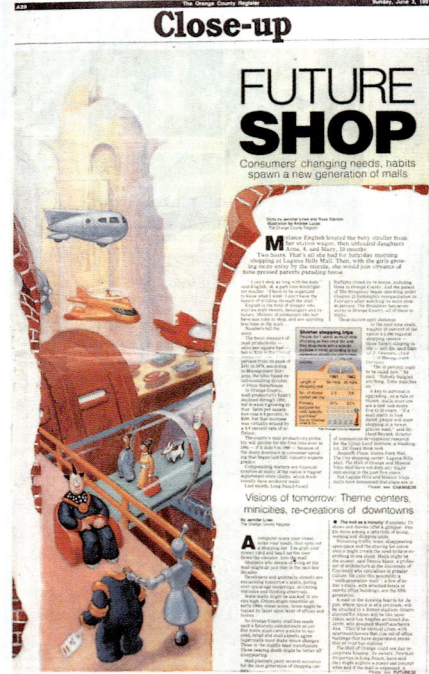

The Orange County Register
Santa Ana, CA

Brenda Shoun, Designer; Staff

The Providence Journal

Thea Breite, Designer & Picture Editor

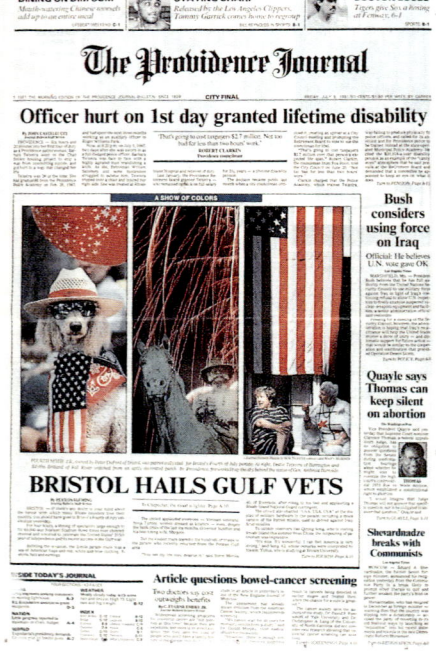

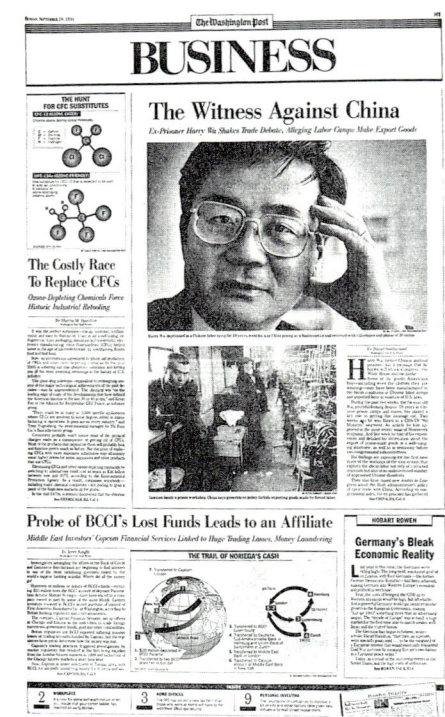

The Washington Post

Michael Keegan, AME/News Art; Carol Porter, Art Director & Designer; Javier Romero, Illustrator; David Cutler, Illustrator; Joe Ciardiello, Illustrator; Randall Enos, Illustrator; Tom Herzberg, Illustrator; Dick Furno, Cartographer; Carol Porter, Infographic Artist

News: 100,000–249,999

The Washington Times

George Kolb, Sports Layout Editor

BRONZE

The Washington Times

Michael Keating, AME/News

The Washington Times

Don Renfroe, Deputy News Editor

THIRTEENTH EDITION 149

DESIGN PORTFOLIOS   News: 100,000–249,999

The Washington Times
Joseph Scopin, Art Director; James Fiedler, Director of Photography; Paul Compton, Designer

Asbury Park Press
Tim Oliver, Designer

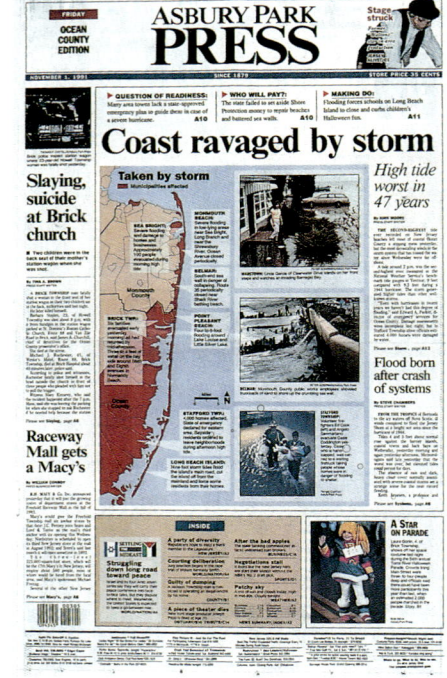

Gazette Telegraph
Colorado Springs, CO
David Demi-Smith, Designer

150   THE BEST OF NEWSPAPER DESIGN

News: 50,000-99,999

Lansing State Journal
Christopher J. Kozlowski, Design Editor

Syracuse Herald-Journal
Tim Atseff, Managing Editor

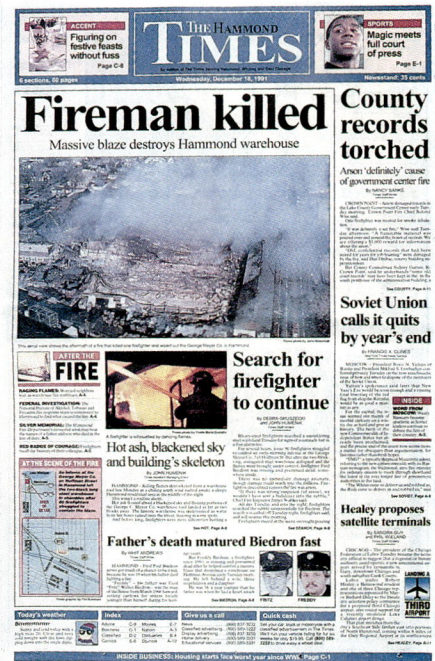

BRONZE

The Times
Munster, IN

John Humenik, AME Design; Craig Edwards, Page Designer; Theresa Badovich, Page Designer; Staff

THIRTEENTH EDITION 151

DESIGN PORTFOLIOS News: 25,000-49,999 • 9,999 or Less

Naples Daily News
Naples, FL

Vic DeRobertis, Designer

BRONZE
The News
Boca Raton, FL

Rick Press, News Editor & Designer

(9,999 OR LESS)

The Daily Journal
Wheaton, IL

Channon Seifert, Design Editor

152   THE BEST OF NEWSPAPER DESIGN

News: 10,000-24,999

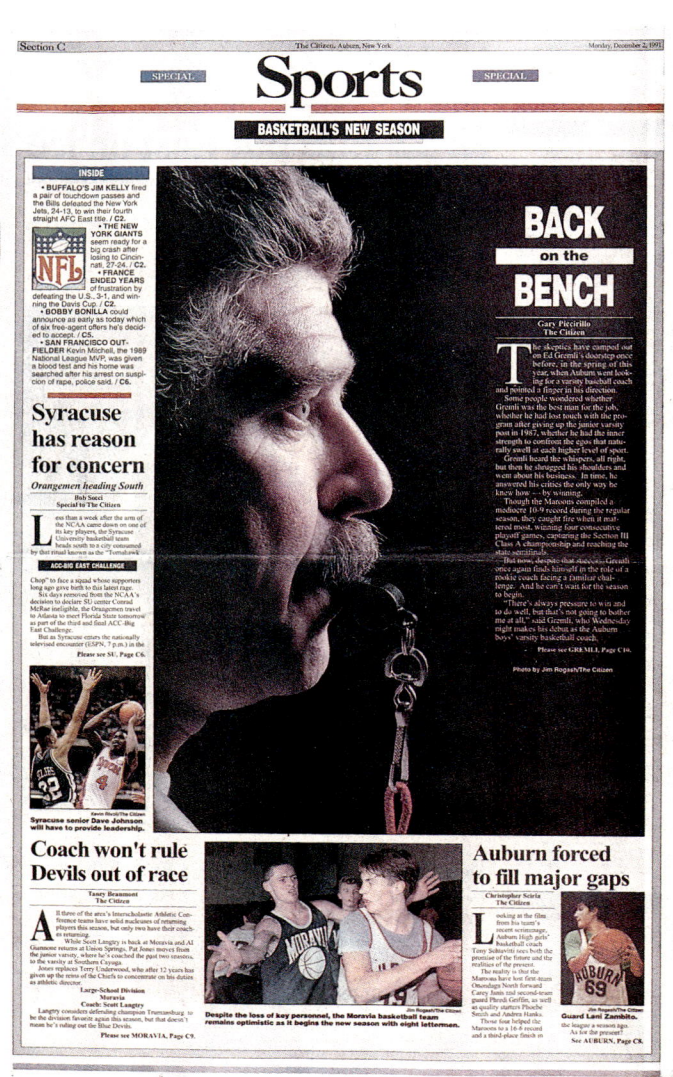

SILVER

The Citizen
Auburn, NY

Gary Piccirillo, Sports Editor & Designer

DESIGN PORTFOLIOS Features: 250,000 Plus

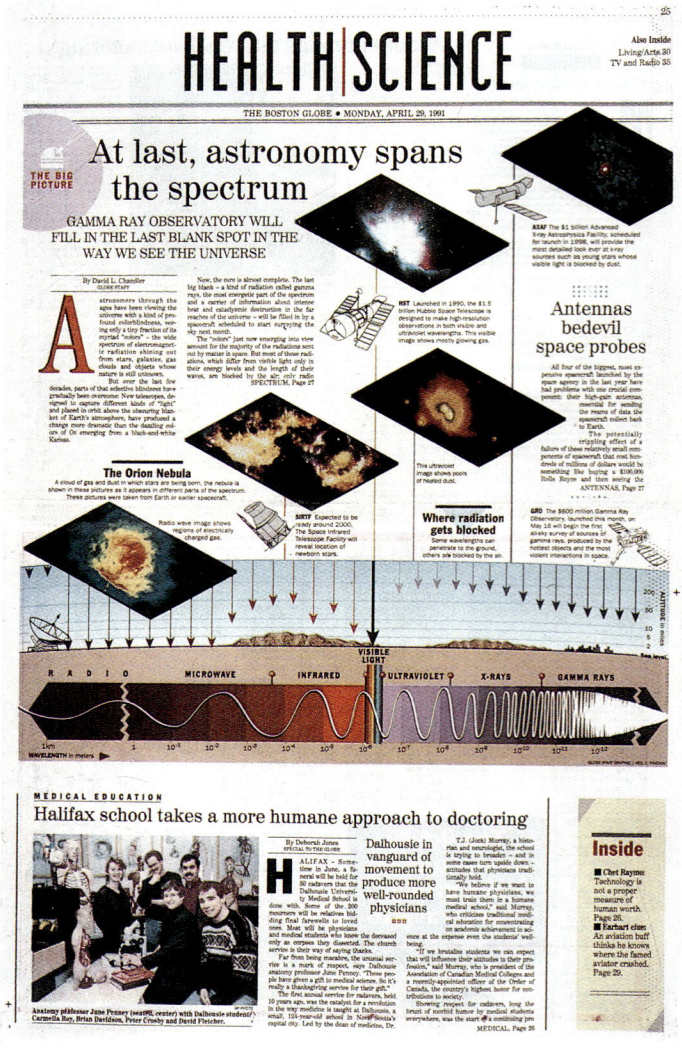

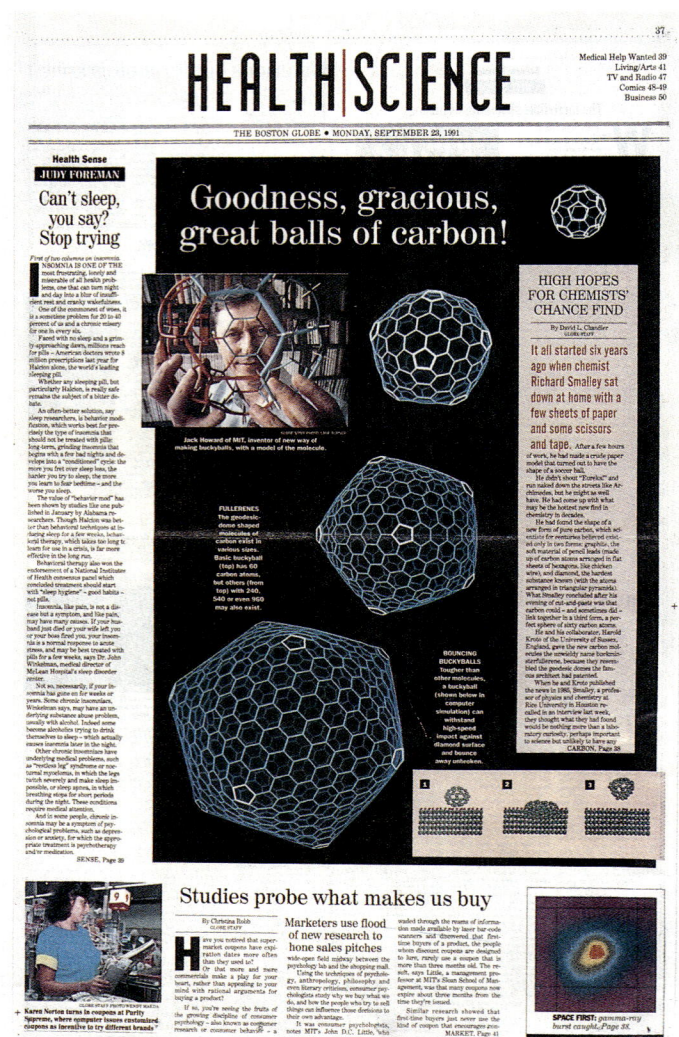

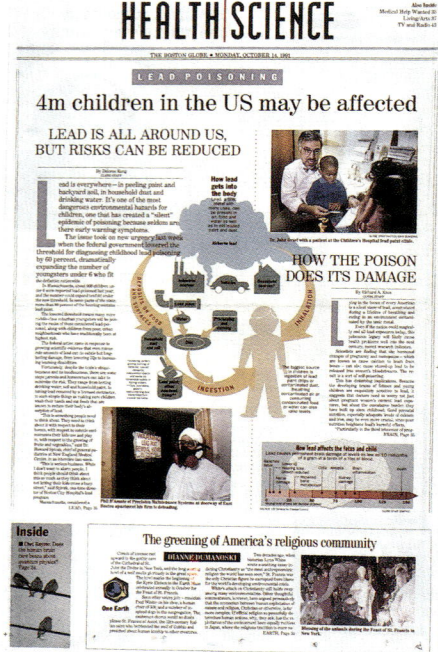

SILVER

The Boston Globe

Cynthia Daniels, Art Director & Designer; Neil C. Pinchin, Graphic Designer

154 THE BEST OF NEWSPAPER DESIGN

SILVER

The Wall Street Journal Reports

Greg Leeds, Art Director & Designer

DESIGN PORTFOLIOS   Features: 250,000 Plus

The Boston Globe Magazine
Sheri G. Lee, Art Director & Designer

The Boston Globe
Cynthia Hoffman, Art Director & Designer

The Dallas Morning News
Bob Shema, Designer; Evans Caglage, Photographer

156 THE BEST OF NEWSPAPER DESIGN

Detroit Free Press

Steve Anderson, Designer; Deborah Withey, Design Director

The Detroit News

Patrick Sedlar, Illustrator & Designer; Wes Bausmith, Art Director

The Globe and Mail
Toronto, ON, Canada

Eric Nelson, Art Director & Designer

THIRTEENTH EDITION 157

DESIGN PORTFOLIOS Features: 250,000 Plus

Goteborgs-Posten
Gothenburg, Sweden

Mats Widebrant, Designer

The Miami Herald

Herman Vega, Editorial Design Illustrator; Emily Hathaway, Weekend Editor; Glenda Wolin, Assistant Features Desk Chief; Randy Stano, Director of Editorial Art & Design; Tony Krzczuk, Weekend Editor/Broward

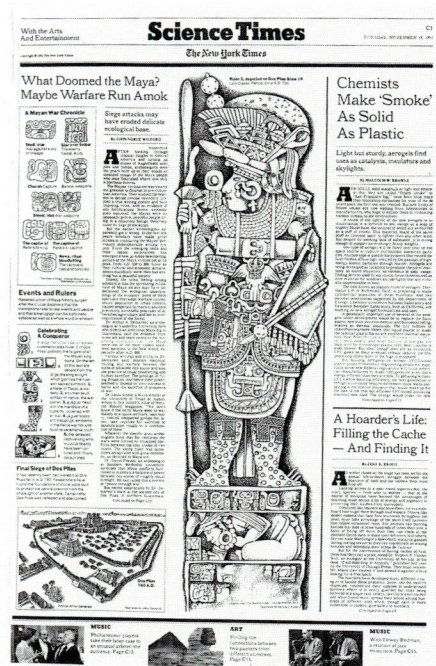

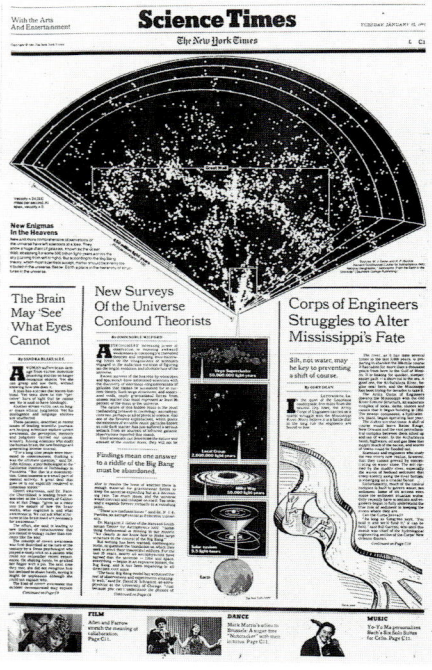

BRONZE
The New York Times

Nancy Sterngold, Art Director & Designer; Tom Bodkin, Design Director

158 THE BEST OF NEWSPAPER DESIGN

The Star-Ledger
Newark, NJ

Lisa Zollinger, Art Director & Designer; Steven Mark Needham, Photographer; Jerry McCrea, Photographer; Jim MacBride, Photographer; Nannette Finkel Rebach, Illustrator

The Toronto Star

Kam Wai Yu, Designer; Pat McCormick, Editor; Jeff Goode, Photographer

The Washington Post

Michael Keegan, Art Director; Marty Barrick, Designer; Larry McIntire, Illustrator; Jotto Seibold, Illustrator; Bonnie Timmons, Illustrator; David Ricceri, Illustrator; Roxana Villa, Illustrator; Nicholas Wilton, Illustrator; Gary Baseman, Illustrator

THIRTEENTH EDITION 159

DESIGN PORTFOLIOS   Features: 100,000-249,999

The Christian Science Monitor
Boston, MA

John Van Pelt, Designer

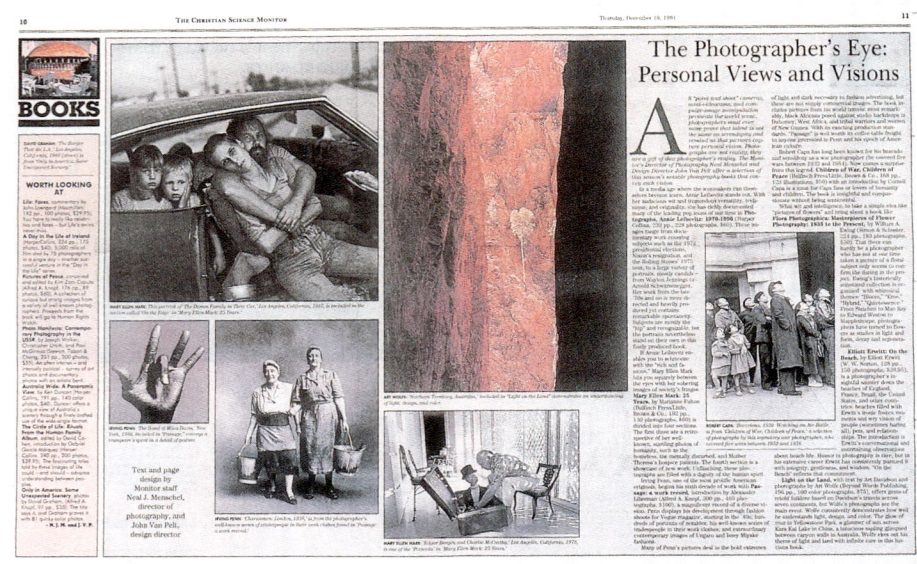

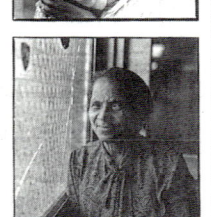

The Village Voice

Florian Bachleda, Senior Art Director; Steve Brodner, Illustrator; Robert Newman, Design Director

Features: 250,000 Plus • 100,000–249,999

BRONZE
The Washington Post

Michael Keegan, Art Director; Marty Barick, Designer; Whitney Sherman, Illustrator; Randall Enos, Illustrator; Christopher Vorlet, Illustrator; James Yang, Illustrator; Carol Guzy, Photographer; Lawrence Meyer, Editor

(100,000–249,999)
BRONZE
The Washington Times

John Kascht, Art Director, Designer & Illustrator

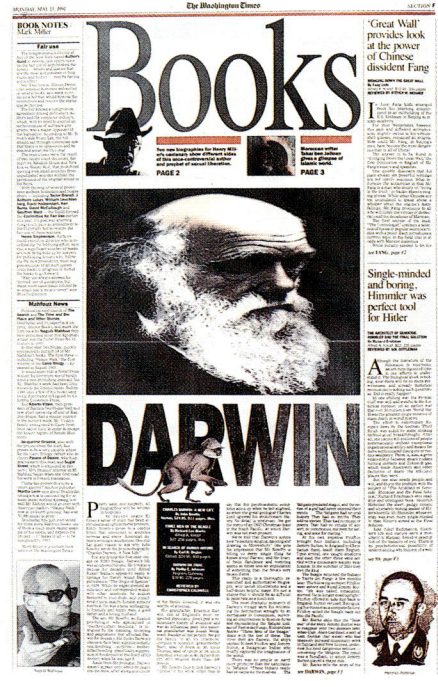

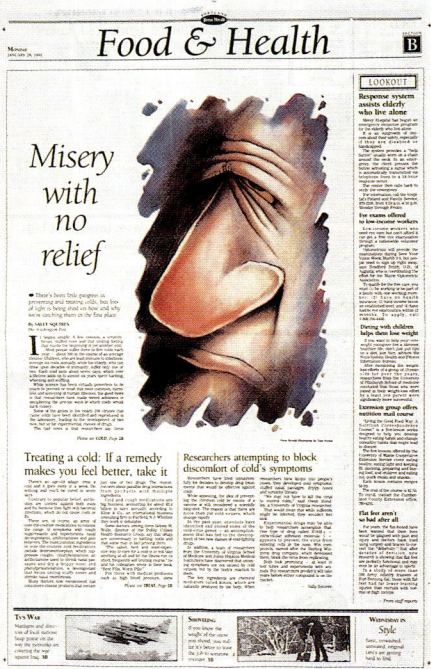

Portland Press Herald
Portland, ME

Andrea Philbrick, Design Editor; Rick Wakely, Designer; Tom Peyton, Illustrator; Don Asmussen, Illustrator; John Ewing, Photographer; Warren Watson, Managing Editor

THIRTEENTH EDITION 161

DESIGN PORTFOLIOS Features: 50,000-99,999

SILVER

Anchorage Daily News

Galie Jean-Louis, Art Director, Designer, Photo Editor, Photographer & Illustrator

Features: 50,000-99,999 • Magazine: 250,000 Plus

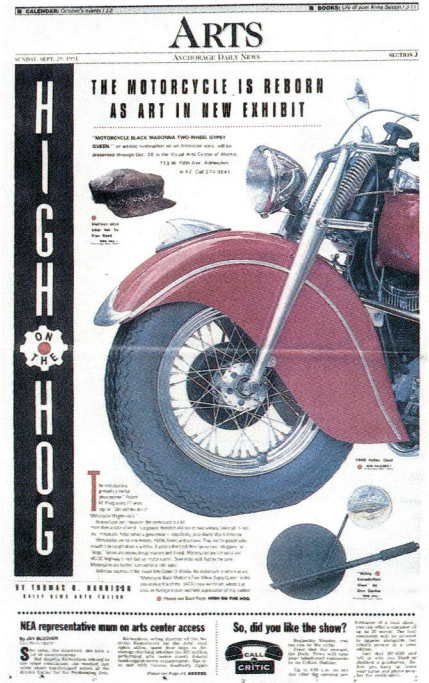

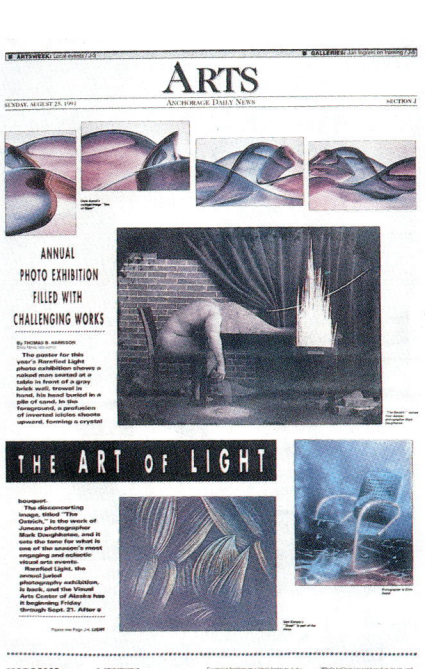

BRONZE

Anchorage Daily News

Pete Spino, Art Director, Designer & Illustrator

The Citizen
Auburn, NY

Kevin Rivoli, Photo Editor

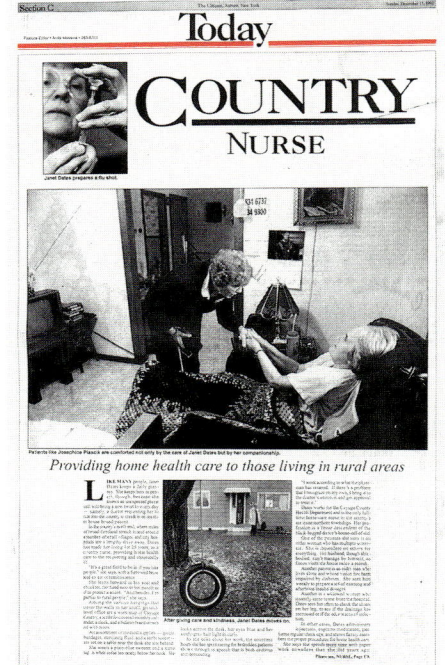

(MAGAZINE: 250,000 PLUS)

The Boston Globe Magazine

Lucy Bartholomay, Art Director & Designer; Theo Rudnak, Illustrator; Leonardo deVinci, Illustrator; Malcolm Tarlofsky, Illustrator; Terry Allen, Illustrator; Marty Blake, Illustrator

THIRTEENTH EDITION 163

DESIGN PORTFOLIOS Magazine: 250,000 Plus

BRONZE
Detroit Free Press Magazine

Andrew Hartley, Art Director & Designer; Deborah Withey, Design Director

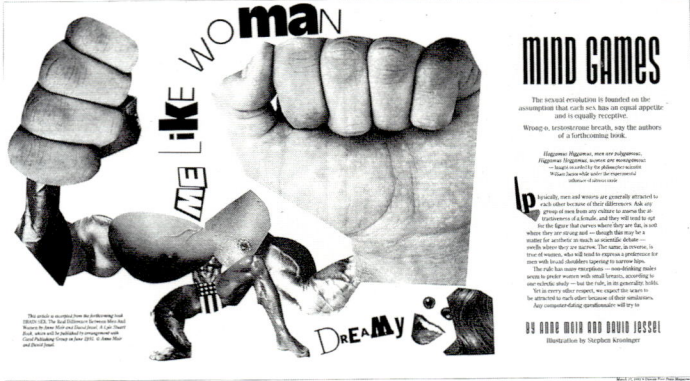

Detroit Free Press Magazine

Andrew Hartley, Art Director & Designer; Deborah Withey, Designer & Design Director

BRONZE
The Washington Post Magazine

Richard Baker, Art Director & Designer; Dan Winters, Photographer; Deborah Needleman, Photo Editor

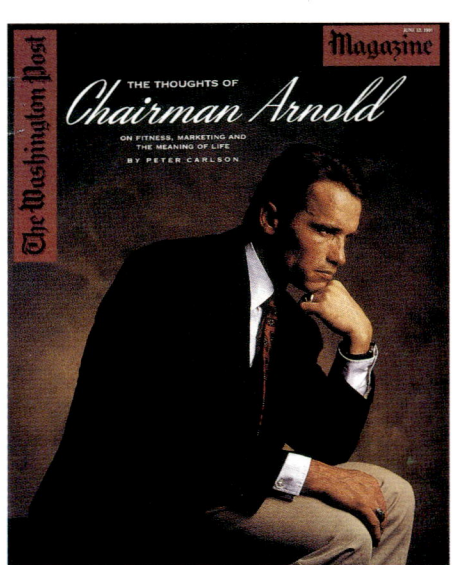
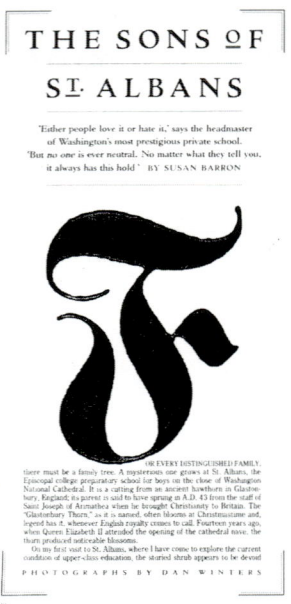

Magazine: 100,000-249,999

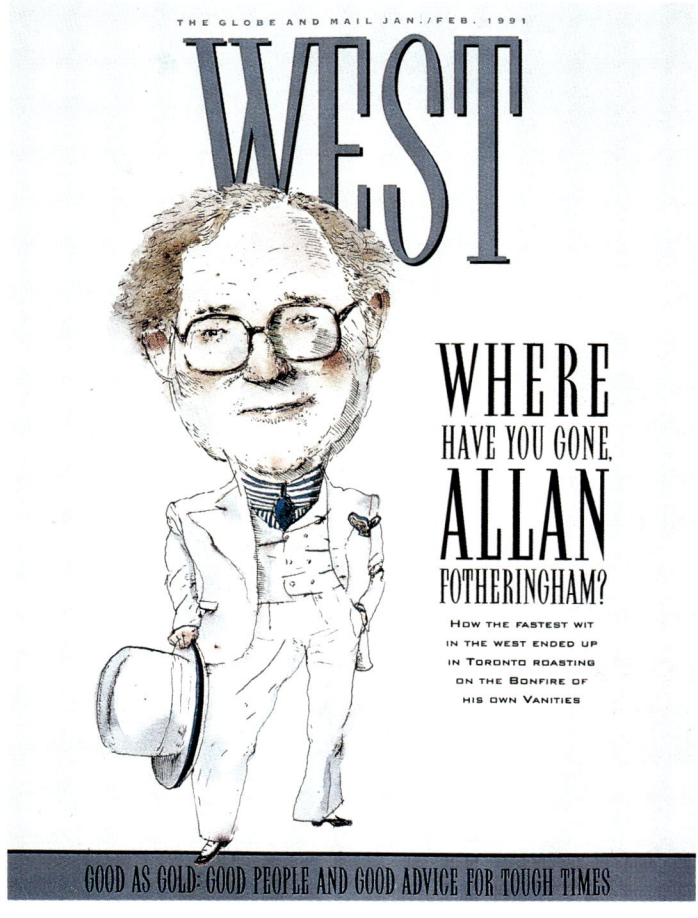

SILVER & JSR

The Globe and Mail / Magazine Network- West, Toronto, Montreal
Susan Casey, Art Director; Paul Sullivan, Editor; George Karabotsos, Designer; Christine Houde, Designer; Various Illustrators & Photographers

DESIGN PORTFOLIOS — Combination: 50,000-99,999 • Non-daily

The Sun
Lowell, MA

Mitchell J. Hayes, Art Director & Designer; Joni Levy-Liberman, Illustrator; David Haynes, Editor; Cromwell Schubarth, Editor; Carol McQuaid, Editor; Burton Morris, Illustrator; Christopher Bing, Illustrator; James Kraus, Illustrator; Deborah Drummond, Illustrator; Tim Lewis, Illustrator

(NON-DAILY)

The San Francisco Bay Guardian

Tracy Cox, Art Director & Designer; Lori Eanes, Photographer

166 THE BEST OF NEWSPAPER DESIGN

CHAPTER EIGHT

IN THIS CHAPTER:

Judges' Special Recognition

Kit King of the Spokesman-Review & Spokane Chronicle, for lifelong contribution to photojournalism. King died last year in a fishing accident.

Photojournalism

PHOTOJOURNALISM Spot News

SILVER
Contra Costa Times
Walnut Creek, CA

Karl Mondon, Photographer; Robert Casey, Design Director; Susan Pollard, Photo Editor

The Citizen
Auburn, NY

Kevin Rivoli, Photo Editor

BRONZE & JSR
The Spokesman-Review & Spokane Chronicle

Kit King, Chief Photographer; Scott Sines, Photo Editor & Designer; Neal Pattison, Editor & Designer; John Kafentzis, Editor; Vince Grippi, Graphics Editor; Molly Quinn, Graphics Artist

The New York Times Magazine

Mary Ellen Mark, Photographer; Janet Froelich, Art Director; Kandy Littrell, Designer; Kathy Ryan, Photo Editor; Tom Bodkin, Design Director

The Washington Post Magazine

Dan Winters, Photographer; Richard Baker, Art Director; Richard Baker, Designer

The Providence Journal

Rachel Ritchie, Photographer; Thea Breite, Picture Editor; Susan Huntemann, Designer

The Philadelphia Inquirer Magazine

David H. Well, Photographer; Bert Fox, Art Director; Jessica Helfand, Design Director; Tom Gralish, Photo Editor; Bert Fox, Designer

The Philadelphia Inquirer Magazine

Todd Buchanan, Photographer; Bert Fox, Art Director; Jessica Helfand, Design Director & Designer; Tom Gralish, Photo Editor

PHOTOJOURNALISM Feature

BRONZE

San Jose Mercury News / West Magazine

Joe Cavaretta, Photographer; Sandra Eisert, Art Director

The Providence Journal

Bob Thayer, Photographer; Thea Breite, Picture Editor; Wes Bausmith, Designer

The Boston Globe

Suzanne Kreiter, Photographer

Concord Monitor
Concord, NH

Dan Habib, Photographer

170 THE BEST OF NEWSPAPER DESIGN

Feature • Illustration

El Sol
Madrid, Spain

Juan Varela, Editor in Chief; Miguel Gonzalez, Photo Chief

Vagabond
Bromma, Sweden

Micke Berg/Mira, Photographer; Tommy Sundstrom, Art Director

Dagens Nyheter
Stockholm, Sweden

Susanne Walstrom, Photographer

(ILLUSTRATION)

The Dallas Morning News

Evans Caglage, Photographer

THIRTEENTH EDITION 171

PHOTOJOURNALISM Illustration

BRONZE

The New York Times Magazine

Raymond Meier, Photographer; Janet Froelich, Art Director & Designer; Tom Bodkin, Design Director

The New York Times Magazine

Michel Comte, Photographer; Janet Froelich, Art Director & Designer; Tom Bodkin, Design Director

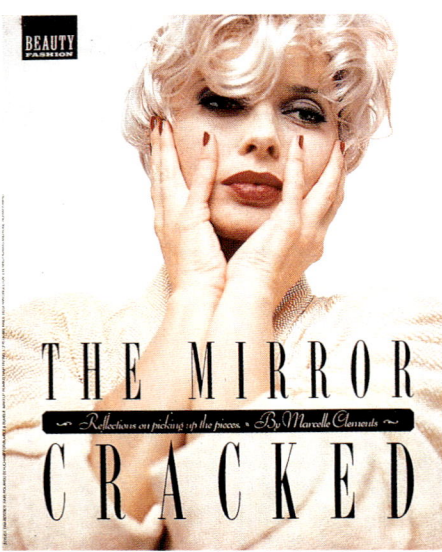

The Philadelphia Inquirer Magazine

Michael Bryant, Photographer; Bert Fox, Art Director; Jessica Helfand, Design Director

BRONZE

The New York Times Magazine

Josef Astor, Photographer; Janet Froelich, Art Director; Kandy Littrell, Designer; Tom Bodkin, Design Director

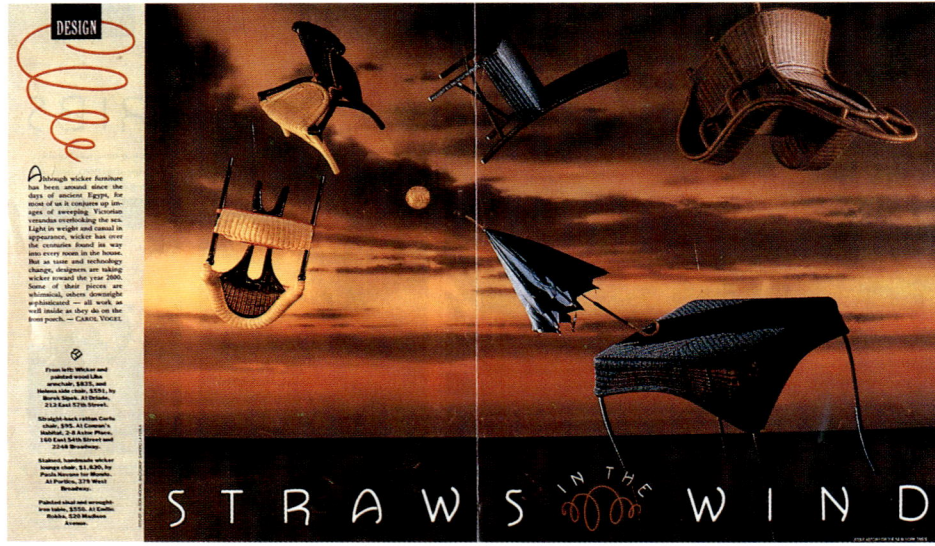

BRONZE

The New York Times Magazine

Sheila Metzner, Photographer; Janet Froelich, Art Director & Designer; Tom Bodkin, Design Director

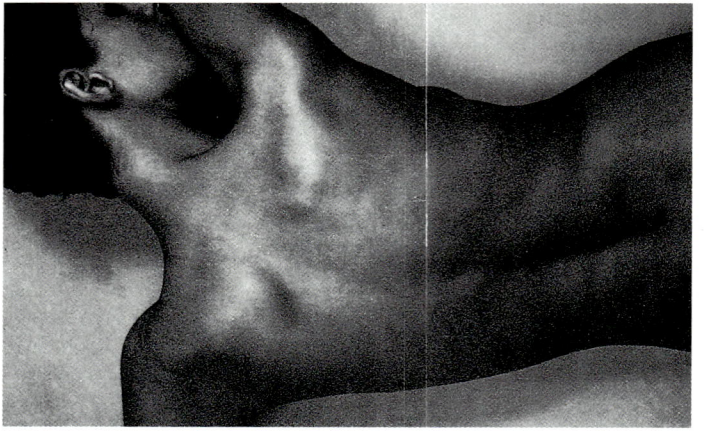

Illustration • Photo-story

(ILLUSTRATION)
BRONZE
InfoWorld
San Mateo, CA

Ben Barbante, Associate Art Director & Illustrator;
Ron Cioffi, Design Director

Detroit Free Press Magazine

Pauline Lubens, Photographer; Mike Smith, Photo Editor; Randy Miller, Photo Editor; Susan Tusa, Photo Editor; Andrew Hartley, Art Director & Designer; Deborah Withey, Design Director; Marcia Prouse, Photo Editor

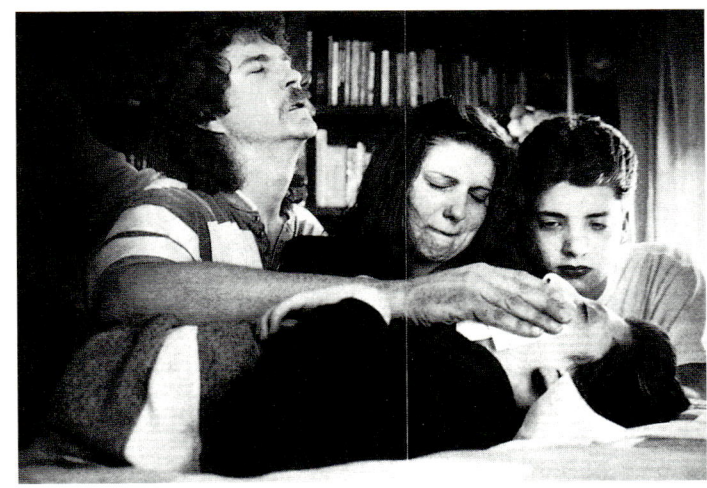

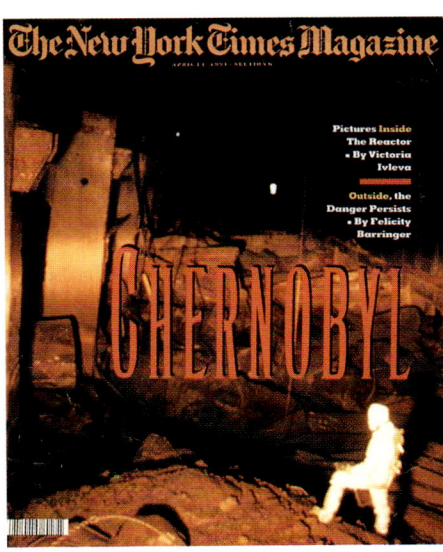

The New York Times Magazine

Gueorgui Pinkhassov, Photographer; Victoria Ivleva, Photographer; Janet Froelich, Art Director; Kandy Littrell, Designer; Kathy Ryan, Photo Editor; Tom Bodkin, Design Director

BRONZE
Detroit Free Press

David C. Turnley, Staff Photographer; Chris Magerl, Photo Editor; Marcia Prouse, Photo Editor; Mike Smith, Photo Editor; Susan Tusa, Photo Editor

THIRTEENTH EDITION 173

PHOTOJOURNALISM Photo-story

SILVER
The Providence Journal

Bob Thayer, Photographer; Anne Peters, Picture Editor; Susan Huntemann, Designer

AFFECTIONATE INFATUATION

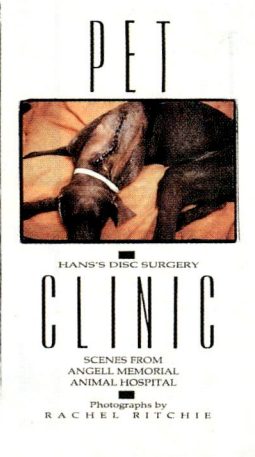

BRONZE

The Providence Journal

Rachel Ritchie, Photographer; Thea Breite, Picture Editor; Susan Huntemann, Designer

The Providence Journal

Bob Thayer, Photographer; Thea Breite, Picture Editor; Wes Bausmith, Designer

PHOTOJOURNALISM Photo-story

WRANGLING the REINDEER

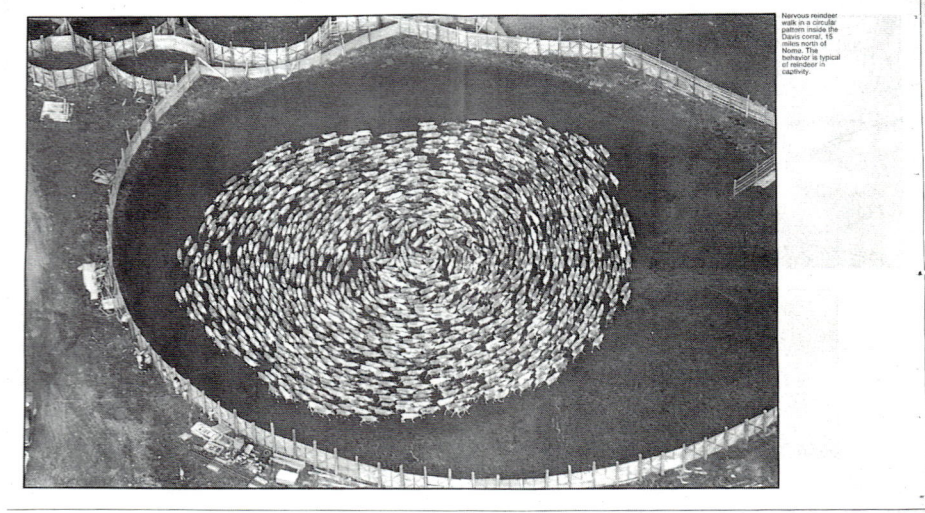

BRONZE

Anchorage Daily News

Charles Mason, Photographer; Richard J. Murphy, Photo Editor & Designer; Pamela Dunlap-Shohl, Cover Designer; Pam Dalgleish, Copy Editor

BRONZE

The Philadelphia Inquirer Magazine

Ed Kashi, Photographer; Bert Fox, Art Director & Designer; Jessica Helfand, Design Director; Tom Gralish, Photo Editor; Eric Mencher, Photographer; John Corr, Writer

176 THE BEST OF NEWSPAPER DESIGN

BRONZE

The Philadelphia Inquirer Magazine

Michael S. Wirtz, Photographer; Bert Fox, Art Director & Designer; Jessica Halfand, Design Director; Tom Gralish, Photo Editor; T. A. Frail, Writer

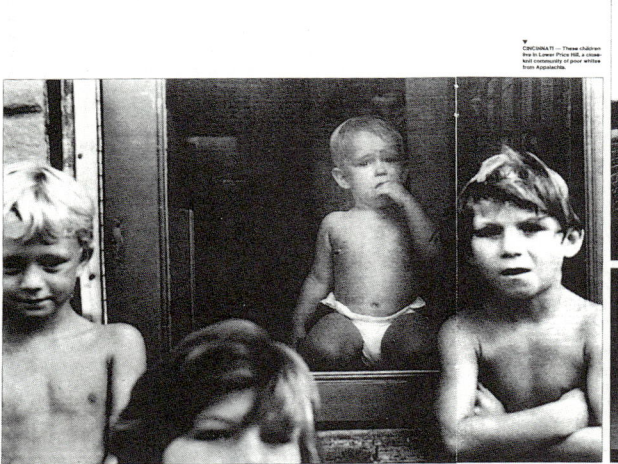

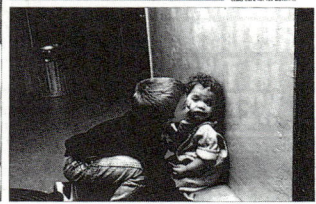

The Philadelphia Inquirer Magazine

Stephen Shames, Photographer; Bert Fox, Art Director & Designer; Jessica Helfand, Design Director; Tom Gralish, Photo Editor; Art Carey, Writer

The Dallas Morning News / Dallas Life Magazine

William Snyder, Photographer & Editor; Lesley Becker, Designer & Editor

THIRTEENTH EDITION 177

PHOTOJOURNALISM Photo-story

The Monterey Herald
John Kaplan, Photographer

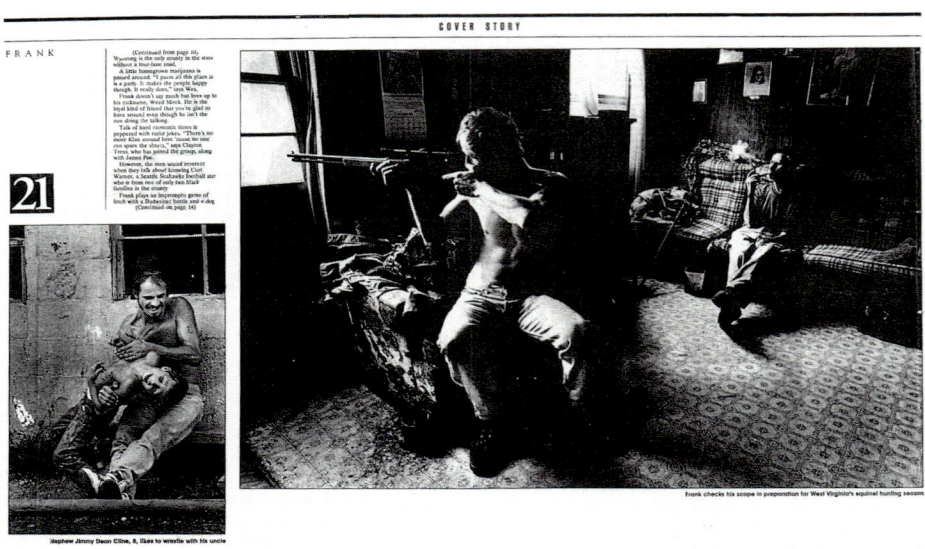

The Times-Leader
Wilkes-Barre, PA

Clark Van Orden, Photographer

The Anchorage Times
Mark Dolan, Photo Editor

Concord Monitor
Concord, NH

Dan Habib, Photographer

178 THE BEST OF NEWSPAPER DESIGN

Portfolio

SILVER
The Providence Journal

Bob Thayer, Photographer; Picture Editing & Design Staff

THIRTEENTH EDITION 179

PHOTOJOURNALISM Portfolio

BRONZE
The Sacramento Bee

Randy Pench, Photographer

BRONZE
The Philadelphia Inquirer Magazine

Michael S. Wirtz, Photographer; Bert Fox, Art Director & Designer; Jessica Helfand, Design Director & Designer; Tom Gralish, Photo Editor

180 THE BEST OF NEWSPAPER DESIGN

BRONZE & JSR
The Spokesman-Review & Spokane Chronicle
Kit King, Chief Photographer

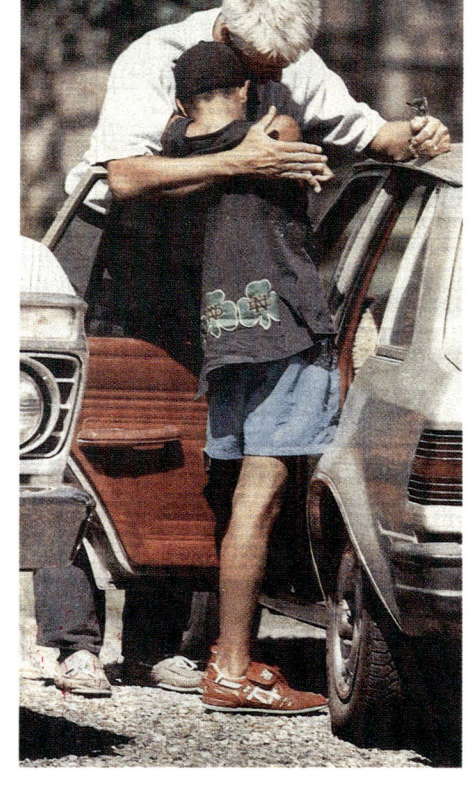

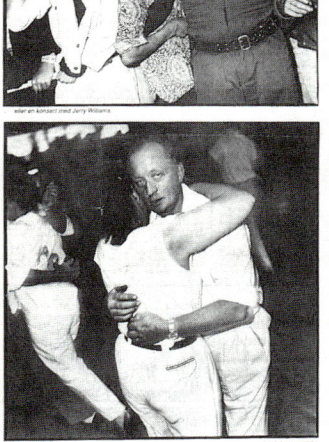

Dagens Nyheter
Stockholm, Sweden

Susanne Walstrom, Photographer

PHOTOJOURNALISM Portfolio • Design

(PORTFOLIO)
BRONZE

The Miami Herald

Patrick Farrell, Photographer

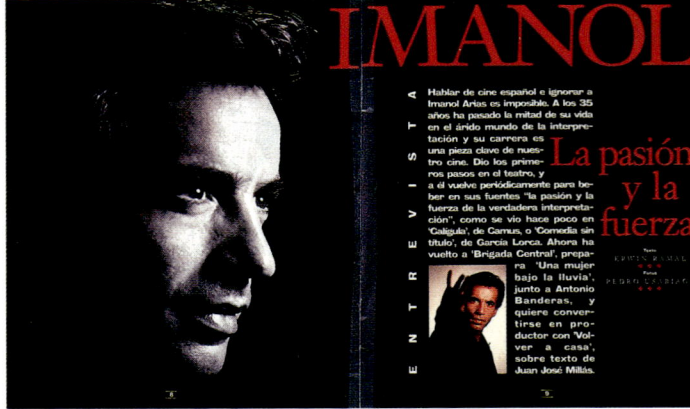

El Sol Magazine
Madrid, Spain

Miguel Gonzalez, Photo Chief; Rodrigo Sanchez, Design Chief; Ricardo Salvador, Illustration Chief; Amparo Redondo, Designer; Cristina Marti, Designer; Pedro Usabiaga, Photographer

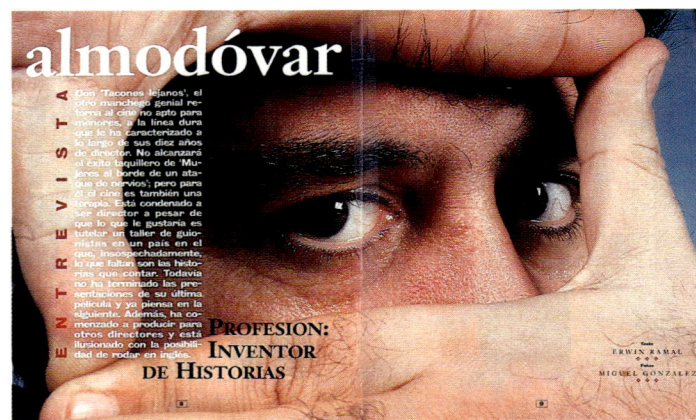

El Sol Magazine

Miguel Gonzalez, Photo Chief & Photographer; Rodrigo Sanchez, Design Chief; Ricardo Salvador, Illustration Chief; Amparo Redondo, Designer; Cristina Marti, Designer

Robert Lockwood Jr.
And The Cleveland Blues Connection

Dollar bills, quarters and cigarette packs form haphazard piles on the tables at Brothers Lounge, where the Swiss chalet interior of the listening room clashes with the simple steel-door entrance to this bar on the Cleveland-Lakewood border. At least one night a month, this is a room with a view of the blues.

Familiar guitar riffs begin as a couple in their late 40s makes their way to the small clearing that serves as a dance floor. Four songs into the second set of the evening, the guy who's been howling as if he were in the bleachers at a Browns game seems to have disappeared. Couples and foursomes, some wearing black Harley-Davidson T-shirts with tattered jeans, others in sharply pressed, button-down-collared sports shirts, are polite in their applause but seem just as intent on maintaining their private conversations.

"Sweet Home, Chicago" is the song. For blues fans who may never have been to Chicago's Maxwell Street Market or Jazz Record Mart, the song conjures up images of a rumble-tumble lifestyle they may know only from John Belushi and Dan Aykroyd in "The Blues Brothers." But for band leader Robert Lockwood Jr., 76, the song is more than a fond remembrance of the city he left behind 30 years ago: It's the first song he learned to play on the guitar, and he learned it more than 60 years ago from the man

By Bill Lammers — Photographs By Dale Omori

SILVER

The Plain Dealer Sunday Magazine

David Pickel, Design Director; Dale Omori, Photographer

PHOTOJOURNALISM Design

The Philadelphia Inquirer Magazine

Bert Fox, Art Director and Designer; Jessica Helfand, Design Director; Jonathan Wilson, Photographer; Tom Gralish, Photo Editor; T.A. Frail, Writer

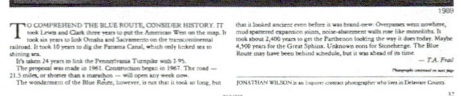

Lexington Herald-Leader

Jim Jennings, AME Graphics; Malcolm Stallons, Design Desk Chief; Ron Garrison, Photographer

BRONZE

The Spokesman-Review & Spokane Chronicle

Scott Sines, Photo Editor & Designer; Neal Pattison, Editor & Designer; Kit King, Chief Photographer; Fred King, Editor; John Kafentzis, Editor

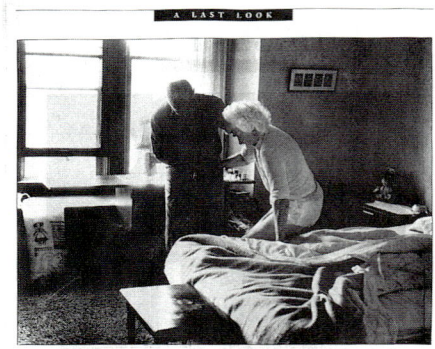
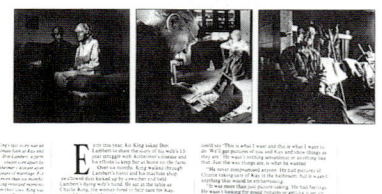

The Spokesman-Review & Spokane Chronicle

Neal Pattison, AME; Scott Sines, Photo Editor; Vince Grippi, Graphics Editor; Chuck Carter, Chief Artist; Jim Allen, News Editor; Staff Photographers

The Spokesman-Review & Spokane Chronicle

Scott Sines, Photo Editor; Kit King, Chief Photographer; Jim Allen, News Editor

Design Portfolio

SILVER

The Spokesman-Review & Spokane Chronicle

Scott Sines, Photo Editor

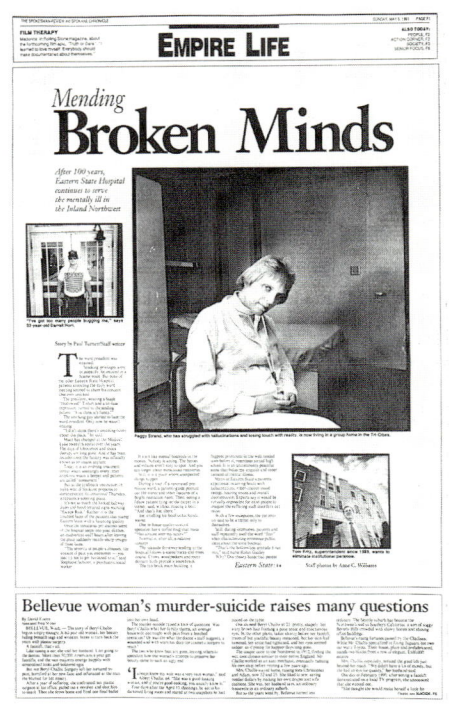

PHOTOJOURNALISM Design Portfolio

BRONZE

The Philadelphia Inquirer Magazine

Bert Fox, Art Director & Designer; Jessica Helfand, Design Director; Tom Gralish, Photo Editor; T.A. Frail, Editor & Writer

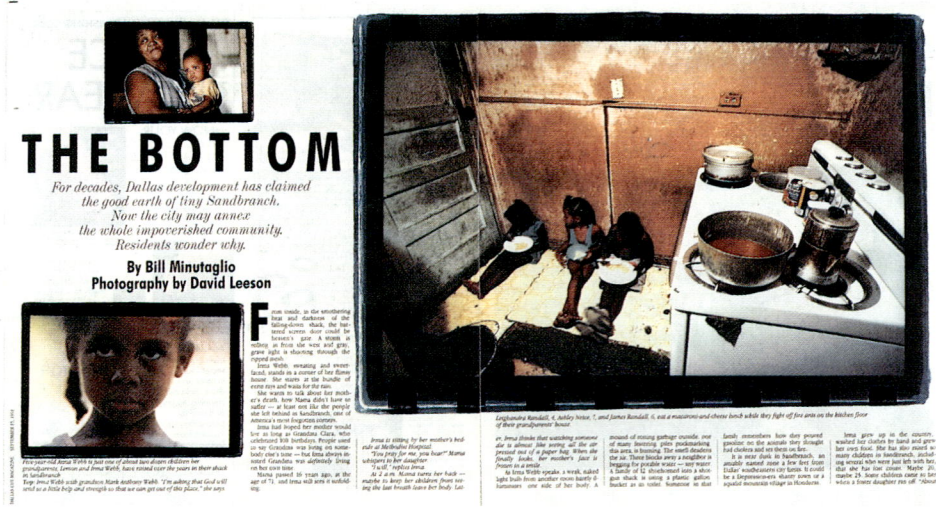

The Dallas Morning News / Dallas Life Magazine

Lesley Becker, Art Director and Designer; David Leeson, Photographer & Illustrator; Erich Schlegel, Photographer & Illustrator; William Snyder, Photographer & Illustrator; Alison Victoria, Photographer & Illustrator

CHAPTER NINE

Illustration

ILLUSTRATION Black & White

BRONZE
El Mundo
Ricardo Martinez, Illustration Editor

SILVER
El Mundo
Madrid, Spain
Ricardo Martinez, Illustration Editor

El Mundo
Ulises Culebro, Illustrator; Carmelo Caderot, Art Director & Designer

BRONZE
El Mundo
Ricardo Martinez, Illustration Editor

El Mundo
Ricardo Martinez, Illustration Editor

El Mundo
Ricardo Martinez, Illustration Editor

El Mundo
Ricardo Martinez, Illustration Editor

El Mundo
Samuel Velasco, Graphics Artist

ILLUSTRATION Black & White

El Mundo
Madrid, Spain
Ricardo Martinez, Illustration Editor

The Richmond News Leader
David Lewis, Graphics Artist

Dallas Observer
Peter Kuper, Illustrator

The Detroit News
Patrick Sedlar, Illustrator

The Philadelphia Inquirer Magazine
Scott Menchin, Illustrator; Bert Fox, Art Director;
Jessica Helfand, Design Director; Ruth M. McNulty,
Writer; Jessica Helfand, Designer

El Nuevo Dia
San Juan, PR

Jose L. Diaz de Villegas, Sr., Art Director, Designer & Illustrator

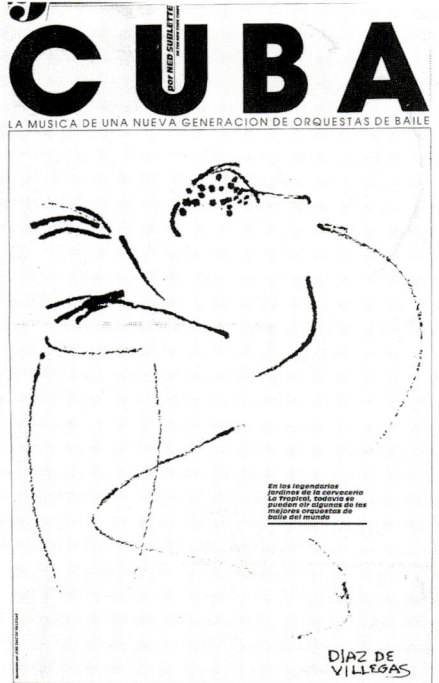

El Nuevo Herald
Miami, FL

Raul Fernandez, Illustrator & Designer; Nuri Ducassi, Art Director; Ivonne Gomez, Writer

Detroit Free Press Magazine

Thomas Thewes/Der Larm, Illustrator; Andrew Hartley, Art Director; Deborah Withey, Design Director

The Anchorage Times

Susan Berry, Designer & Illustrator; Lee Waigand, AME Graphics/Design

The Village Voice

Scott Menchin, Illustrator; Florian Bachleda, Associate Art Director; Wes Anderson, Design Director

San Jose Mercury News

Sam Hundley, Illustrator

ILLUSTRATION Color

The New York Times Magazine

Janet Woolley, Illustrator; Janet Froelich, Art Director; Nancy Harris, Designer; Tom Bodkin, Design Director

The New York Times Magazine

Lane Smith, Illustrator; Janet Froelich, Art Director; Kathi Rota, Designer; Tom Bodkin, Design Director

The New York Times Magazine

Amy Guip, Illustrator; Janet Froelich, Art Director; Kathi Rota, Designer; Tom Brodkin, Design Director

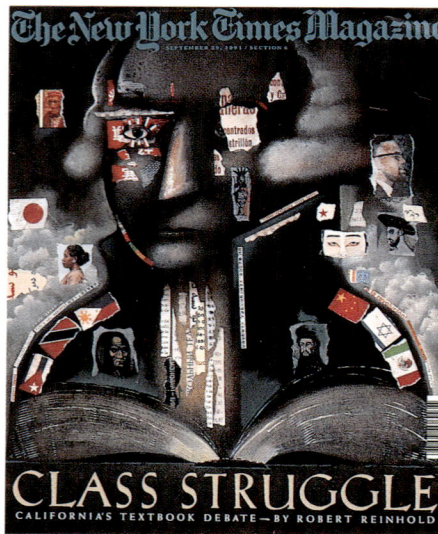

The New York Times Magazine

Henrik Drescher, Illustrator; Janet Froelich, Art Director; Tom Bodkin, Design Director; Kandy Littrell, Designer

American Medical News
Chicago, IL

David Shannon, Illustrator; Barbara Dow, Art Director & Designer

American Medical News

David Shannon, Illustrator; Barbara Dow, Art Director & Designer

SILVER

The New York Times Magazine

Henrik Drescher, Illustrator; Blair Drawson, Illustrator; Michael Bartalos, Illustrator; Amy Guip, Illustrator; Janet Woolley, Illustrator; Marshall Arisman, Illustrator; Brian Cronin, Illustrator; Janet Froelich, Art Director & Designer; Tom Bodkin, Design Director

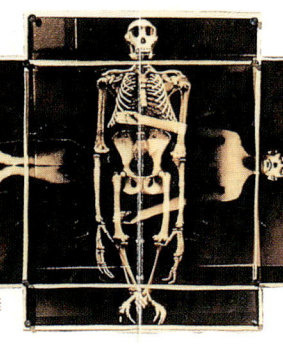

ILLUSTRATION Color

Anchorage Daily News
Dee Boyles, Illustrator & Designer

Anchorage Daily News
Pete Spino, Illustrator & Designer; Galie Jean-Louis, Art Director

Anchorage Daily News
Pete Spino, Art Director, Designer & Illustrator

El Nuevo Dia
San Juan, PR
Jose L Diaz de Villegas, Jr., Art Director, Designer & Illustrator

Anchorage Daily News
Dee Boyles, Illustrator & Designer

The Anchorage Times
James Havens, Illustrator & Designer; Lee Waigand, AME Graphics/Design

Bangor Daily News
Eric Zelz, Art Director & Illustrator

Dayton Daily News
Ted Pitts, Illustrator

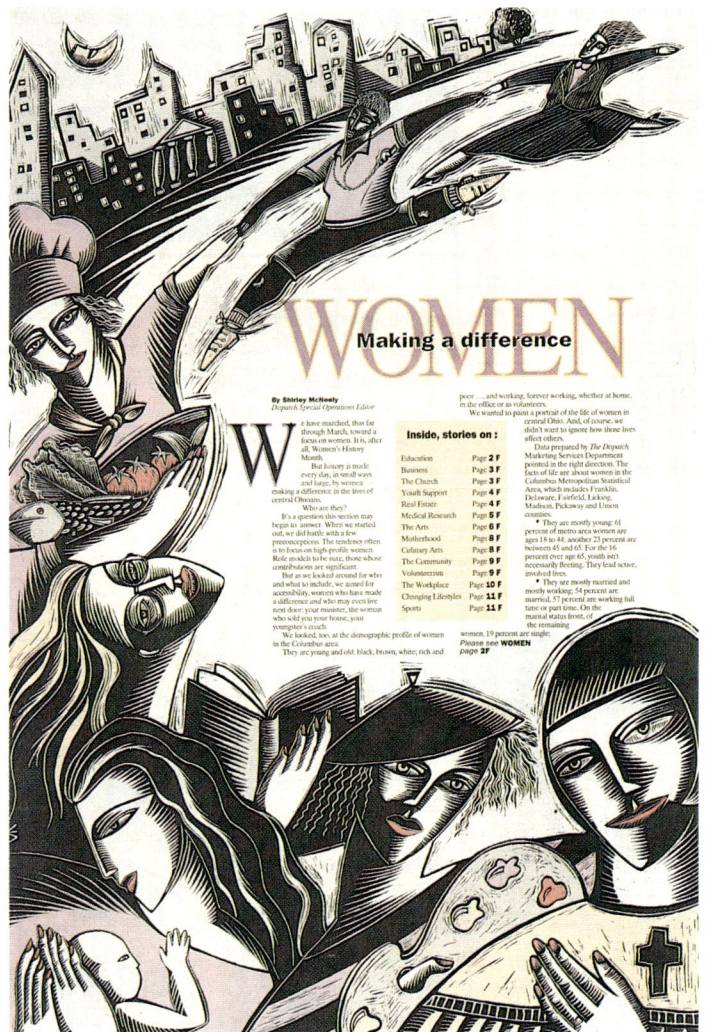

St. Louis Post-Dispatch
John Shew, Artist

The Columbus Dispatch
Evangelia Philippidis, Artist; Scott Minister, Art Director; Becky Kover, Special Section Coordinator

ILLUSTRATION Color

Detroit Free Press
John Labbe, Illustrator; Steve Anderson, Art Director & Designer; Deborah Withey, Design Director

Detroit Free Press Magazine
John Labbe, Illustrator; Andrew Hartley, Art Director; Deborah Withey, Design Director

Detroit Free Press
Andrea Wisnewski, Illustrator; Claire Innes, Art Director & Designer; Deborah Withey, Design Director

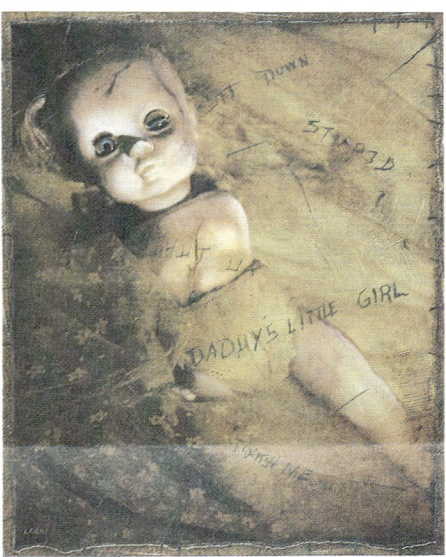

Detroit Free Press
Warren Gebert, Illustrator; Deborah Withey, Art Director & Design Director; Steve Anderson, Designer

Detroit Free Press Magazine
John Labbe, Illustrator; Andrew Hartley, Art Director; Deborah Withey, Design Director

The Detroit News

Glynnis Sweeny, Illustrator & Designer; Wes Bausmith, Art Director

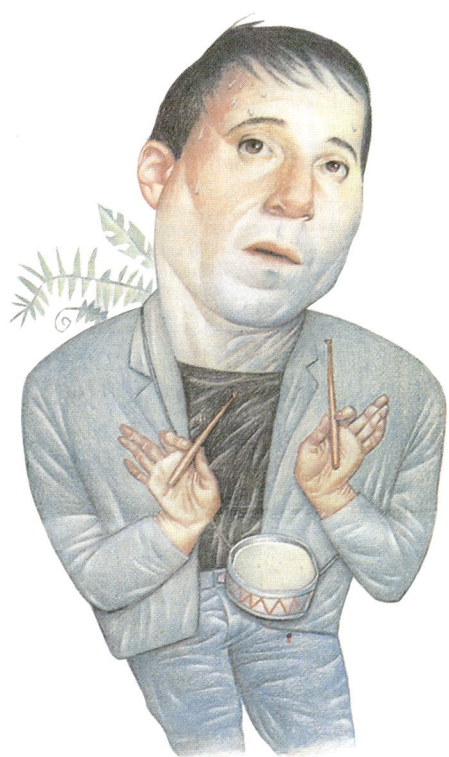

St. Petersburg Times

Don Morris, Illustrator; Trich Redman, Art Director

Financial Times
London, England

James Ferguson, Illustrator; Phillip Thompson, Art Director & Designer

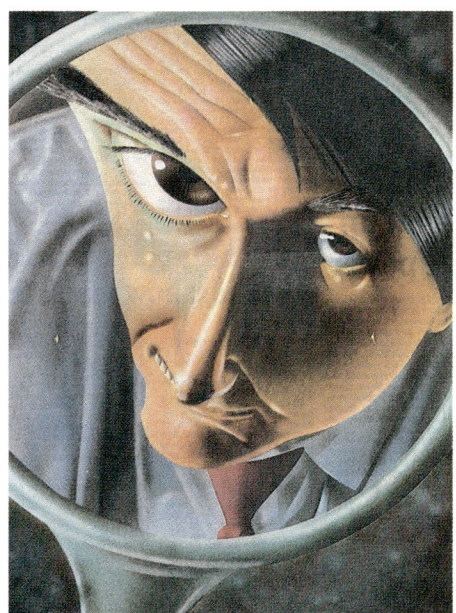

Dayton Daily News

Randy Palmer, Illustrator; Pat Rini, Page Designer

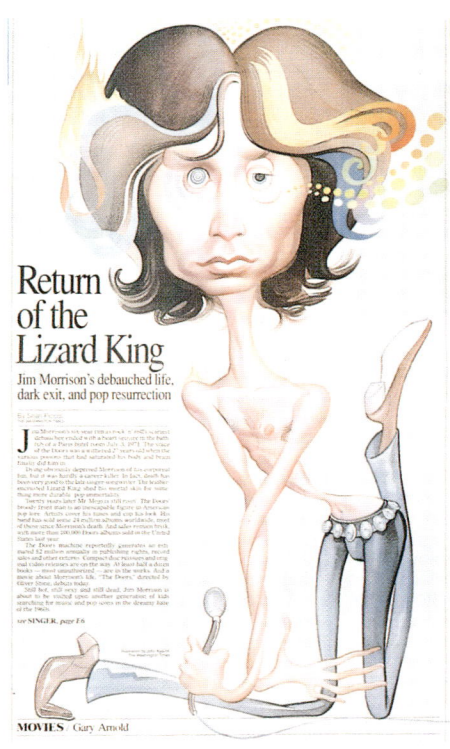

The Washington Times

John Kascht, Illustrator & Designer; Dolores Motichka, Art Director

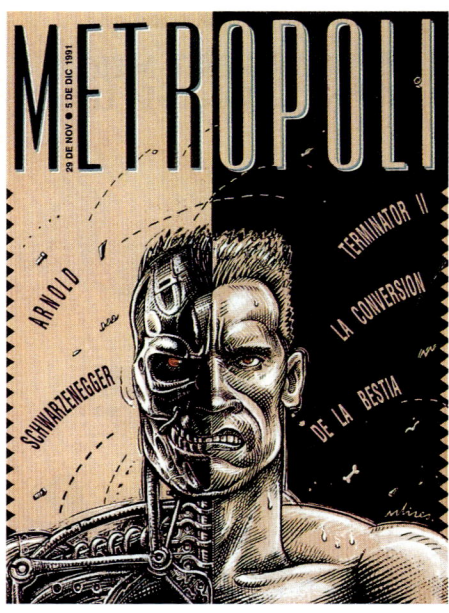

El Mundo / Metropoli
Madrid, Spain

Ulises Culebro, Illustrator & Designer; Carmelo Caderot, Art Director & Designer

ILLUSTRATION Color

El Nuevo Herald
Miami, FL

Nuri Ducassi, Illustrator & Designer; Olga Connor, Editor

The Kansas City Star

Ving Ha, Illustrator; Tom Dolphens, Design Director

El Nuevo Herald

Nuri Ducassi, Illustrator & Designer; Olga Connor, Editor

El Nuevo Herald

Nuri Ducassi, Illustrator & Designer; Olga Connor, Editor

El Nuevo Herald

Nuri Ducassi, Illustrator & Designer; Olga Connor, Editor

The Miami Herald

Phill Flanders, Illustrator; Reggie Myers, Illustrator; Nuri Ducassi, Illustrator; Woody Vondracek, Illustrator; Herman Vega, Illustrator; Hiram Henriquez, Illustrator; Ana Lense Larrauri, Illustrator; Raul Fernandez, Illustrator; Patterson Clark, Illustrator; Rhonda Prast, Designer; Randy Stano, Director of Editorial Art & Design

The Miami Herald

Herman Vega, Illustrator; Woody Vondracek, Illustrator; Reggie Myers, Illustrator; Nuri Ducassi, Illustrator; Bert Garcia, Illustrator; Raul Fernandez, Illustrator; Phill Flanders, Illustrator; Ana Lense Larrauri, Illustrator; Patterson Clark, Illustrator; Rhonda Prast, Designer; Randy Stano, Director of Editorial Art & Design

The Miami Herald

Nuri Ducassi, Illustrator; Rhonda Prast, Designer; Randy Stano, Director of Editorial Art & Design

Lexington Herald-Leader

Molly Swisher, Illustrator; Susan Brubaker, Designer; Paula Anderson, Lifestyle Editor; Jim Jennings, AME Graphics

Vendsyssel Tidende
Hjorring, Denmark

Lars Andersen, Illustrator; Kjeld Torbjern, Designer; Birthe Lauritsen, Researcher

ILLUSTRATION Color

The Pittsburgh Press
Stacy Innerst, Illustrator; J. Bruce Baumann, AME Graphics

San Jose Mercury News
Sam Hundley, Illustrator

The Press Democrat
Santa Rosa, CA
Sharon Henry, Graphics Artist

The Philadelphia Inquirer Magazine
Tim Gabor, Illustrator; Bert Fox, Art Director; Jessica Helfand, Design Director & Designer; K. R. Law, Writer

The Philadelphia Inquirer Magazine
Joel Peter Johnson, Illustrator; Bert Fox, Art Director; Jessica Helfand, Design Director & Designer; Jack Smith, Writer

La Presse
Montreal, PQ, Canada
Genevieve Cote, Illustrator; Julien Chung, Art Director; Jocelyne Potelle, Designer

Detroit Free Press Magazine

Dick Rochon, Graphics Artist; Andrew Hartley, Art Director & Designer; Deborah Withey, Design Director

The Washington Post Magazine

Vivian Flesher, Illustrator; Kelly Doe, Deputy Art Director & Designer; Richard Baker, Art Director

The Washington Post Magazine

Brian Cronin, Illustrator; Richard Baker, Art Director & Designer

The Washington Post Magazine

Anthony Russo, Illustrator; Kelly Doe, Deputy Art Director & Designer; Richard Baker, Art Director

The Washington Post Magazine

Peter Kuper, Illustrator; Kelly Doe, Deputy Art Director & Designer; Richard Baker, Art Director

ILLUSTRATION Color

BRONZE

The Washington Post Magazine

Anita Kunz, Illustrator; Richard Baker, Art Director & Designer

BRONZE

The Washington Post Magazine

Anita Kunz, Illustrator; Richard Baker, Art Director & Designer

The Washington Post Magazine

Janet Woolley, Illustrator; Kelly Doe, Deputy Art Director & Designer; Richard Baker, Art Director

BRONZE

The Washington Post Magazine

James Yang, Illustrator; Kelly Doe, Deputy Art Director & Designer; Richard Baker, Art Director

Portfolio

SILVER

Anchorage Daily News

Pete Spino, Art Director, Designer & Illustrator

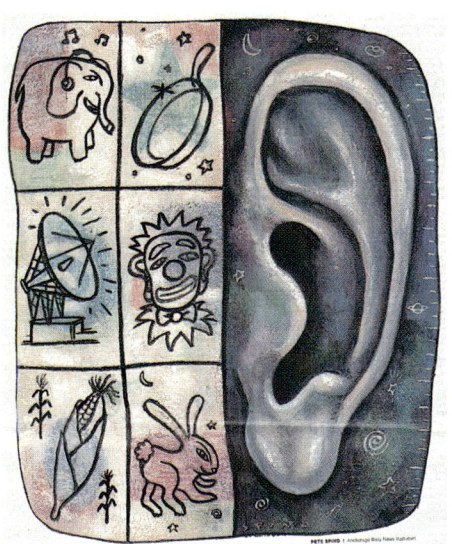

THIRTEENTH EDITION 203

ILLUSTRATION Portfolio

SILVER
The Columbus Dispatch
Evangelia Philippidis, Artist; Scott Minister, Art Director

SILVER
El Mundo
Madrid, Spain

Ricardo Martinez, Illustration Editor

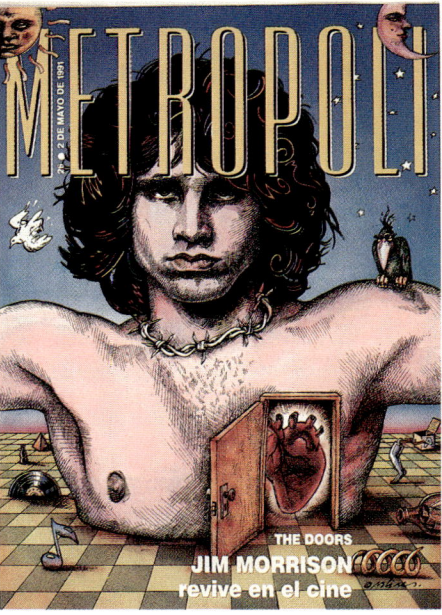

El Mundo

Ulises Culebro, Illustrator & Designer; Carmelo Caderot, Art Director & Designer

ILLUSTRATION Portfolio

Computer Reseller News
Manhasset, NY

Adam Niklewicz, Illustrator; Gene Fedele, Sr. Art Director; Bob DeMarzo, Editor

The Seattle Times

Fred Birchman, Illustrator & Designer; David Miller, Art Director

BRONZE

The Philadelphia Inquirer Magazine

Joel Peter Johnson, Illustrator; Bert Fox, Art Director; Jessica Helfand, Design Director

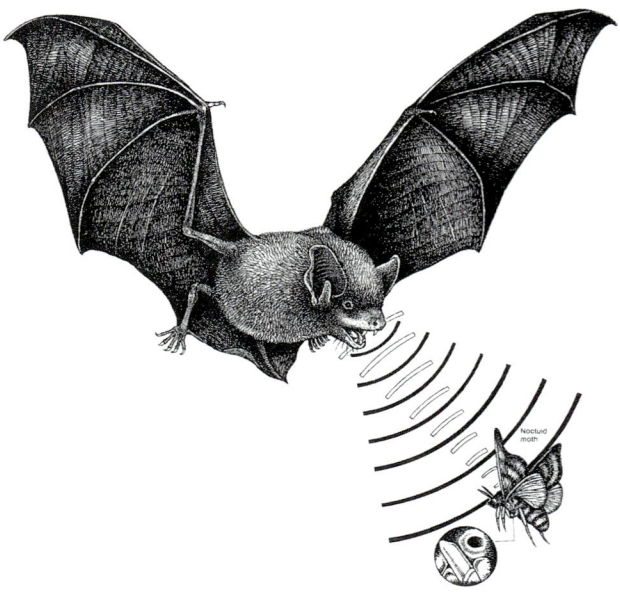

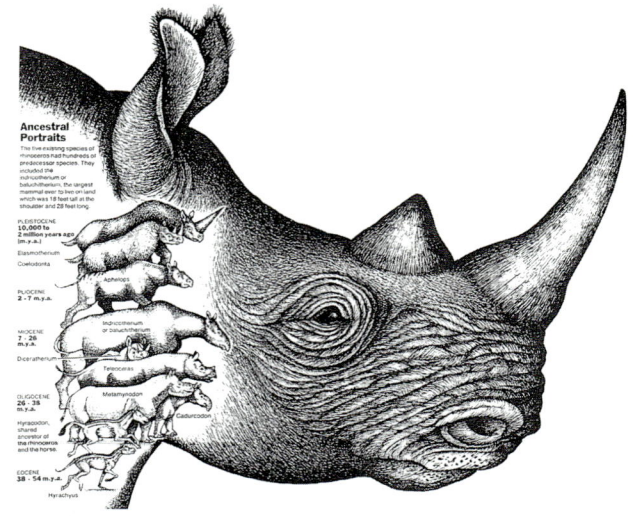

The New York Times

Patricia J. Wynne, Illustrator; Nancy Sterngold, Art Director & Designer; Tom Bodkin, Design Director

El Nuevo Herald & The Miami Herald

Nuri Ducassi, Illustrator, Designer & Art Director; Bill Grant, Sports Design Editor; Tim Burke, Sunday Sports Editor; Rhonda Prast, Features Design Editor; Randy Stano, Director of Editorial Art & Design

The Times-Picayune

Tony O. Champagne, Illustrator

The Detroit News

Glynnis Sweeny, Illustrator & Designer; Wes Bausmith, Art Director

ILLUSTRATION Portfolio

The Albuquerque Tribune
Jeff Neumann, Illustrator

Akron Beacon Journal
Dennis Balogh, Illustrator & Designer

San Jose Mercury News
Sam Hundley, Illustrator

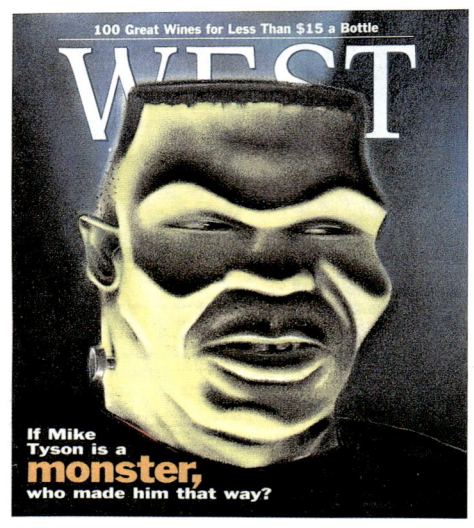

208   THE BEST OF NEWSPAPER DESIGN

CHAPTER TEN

Informational Graphics

INFORMATIONAL GRAPHICS Breaking News, B&W

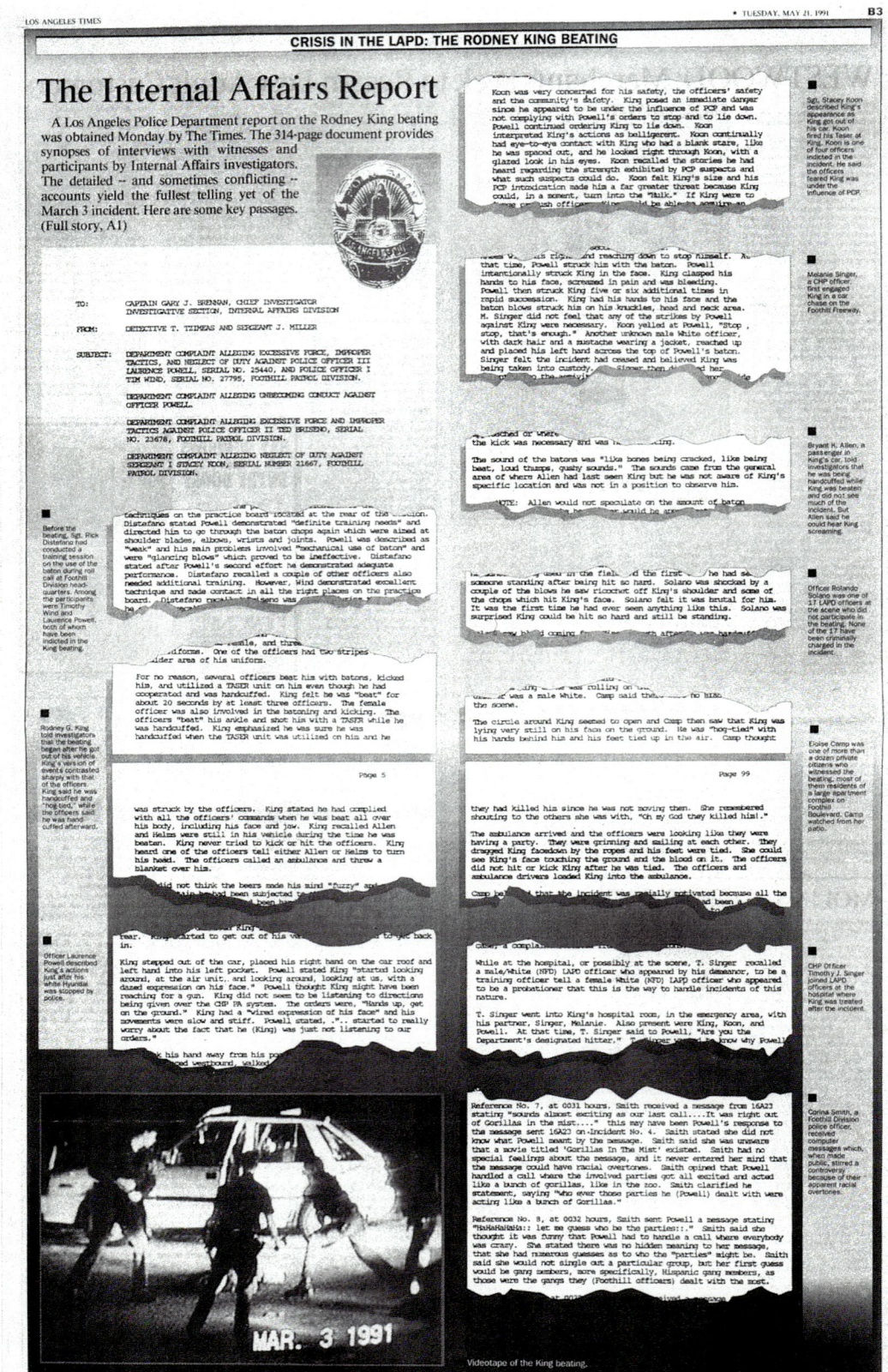

SILVER

Los Angeles Times

Michael Hall, Designer; Sara Lessley, News Editor

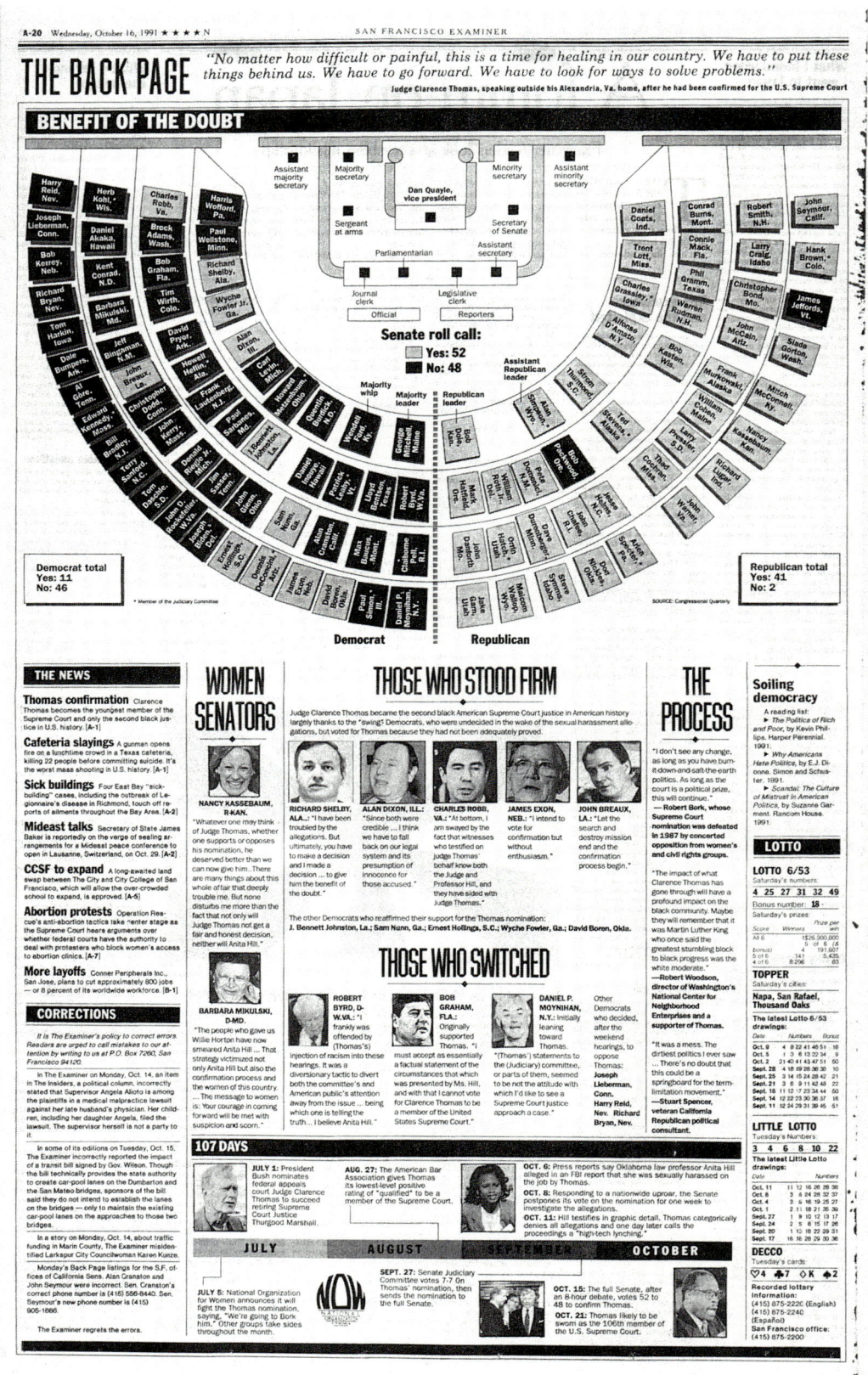

INFORMATIONAL GRAPHICS Breaking News, B&W

The Sunday Times

Phil Green, Graphics Editor/Designer; Cary Cook, Illustrator; Ian Moores, Illustrator; Ian Bott, Illustrator

The Sunday Times
London, England

Phil Green, Graphics Editor/Designer; Chris Sargent, Illustrator; Gary Cook, Illustrator

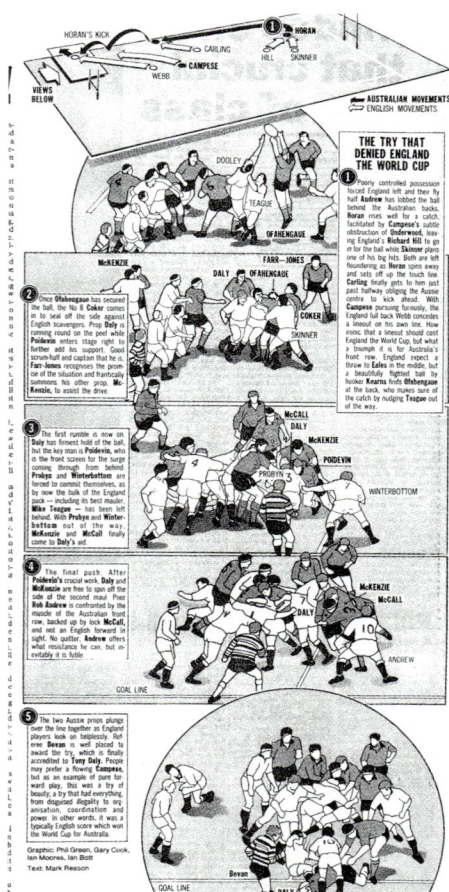

SILVER
The Sunday Times

Phil Green, Graphics Editor, Designer, Illustrator & Researcher; Chris Sargent, Illustrator

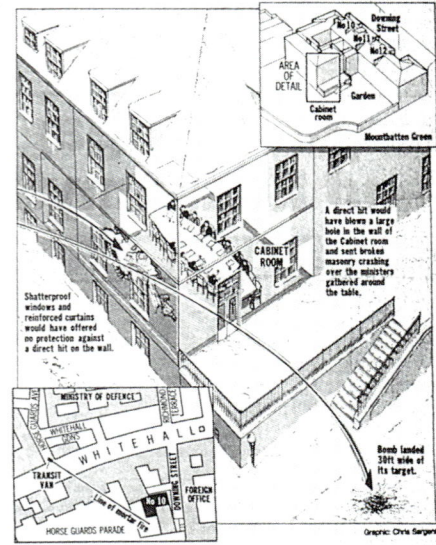

Breaking News, B&W • Color

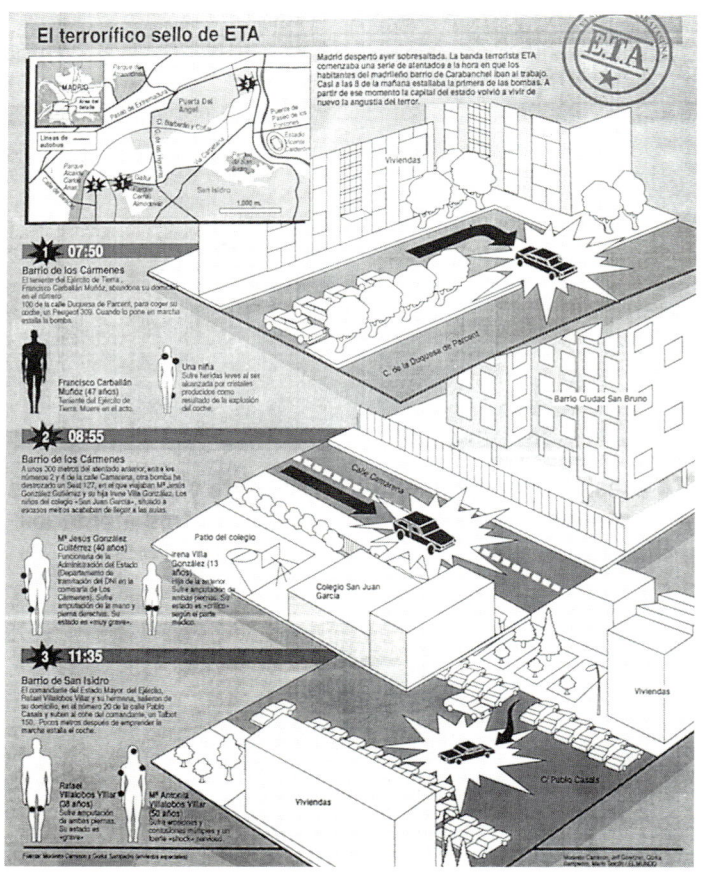

BRONZE

El Mundo
Madrid, Spain

Mario Tascon, Infographics Director; Jeff Goertzen, Art Consultant & Illustrator; Modesto Carrasco, Illustrator; Gorka Sampedro, Illustrator; Juan Velasco, Illustrator; Samuel Velasco, Illustrator; Ulises Culebro, Illustrator

The New York Times

Joe Ward, Designer, Graphics Editor; Tom Bodkin, Design Director

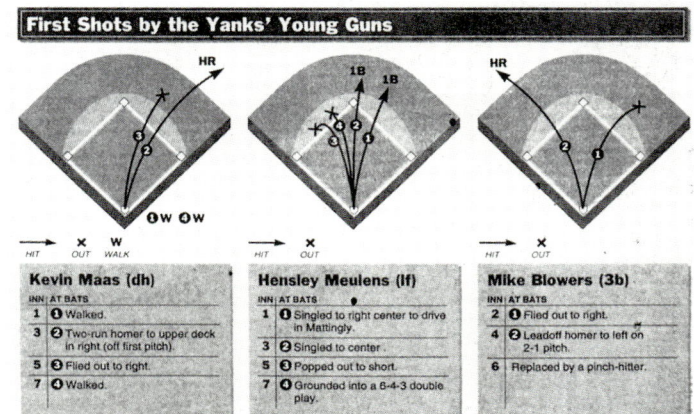

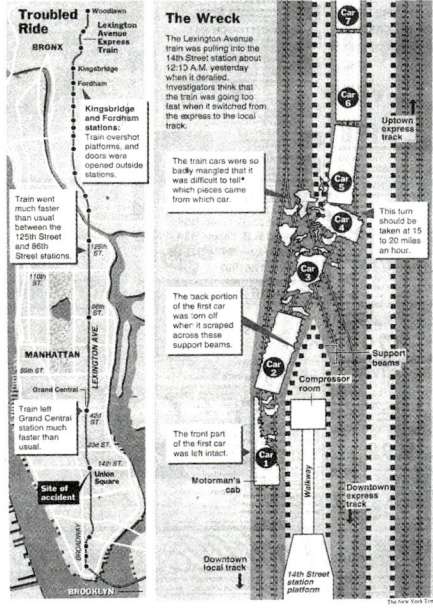

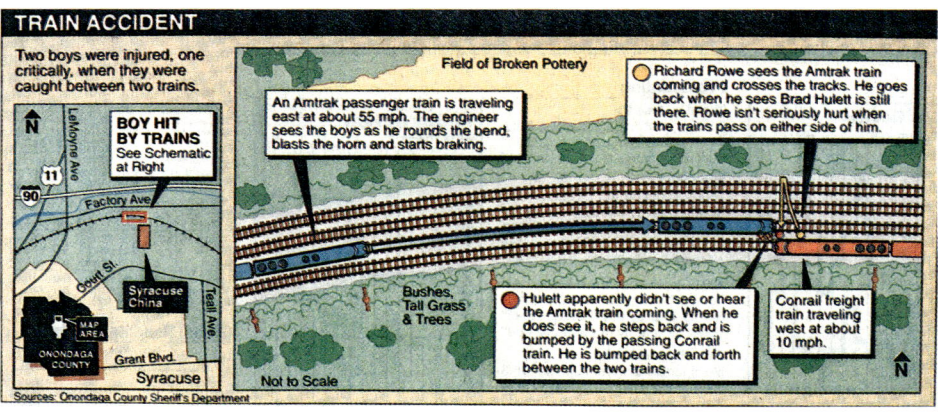

(BREAKING NEWS, COLOR)

The Post-Standard
Syracuse, NY

Peter Allen, Illustrator & Designer

BRONZE

The New York Times

Margaret O'Connor, Art Director; John Papasian, Illustrator; Megan Jaegerman, Illustrator; Anne Cronin, Graphics Editor; Tom Bodkin, Design Director

INFORMATIONAL GRAPHICS Breaking News, Color

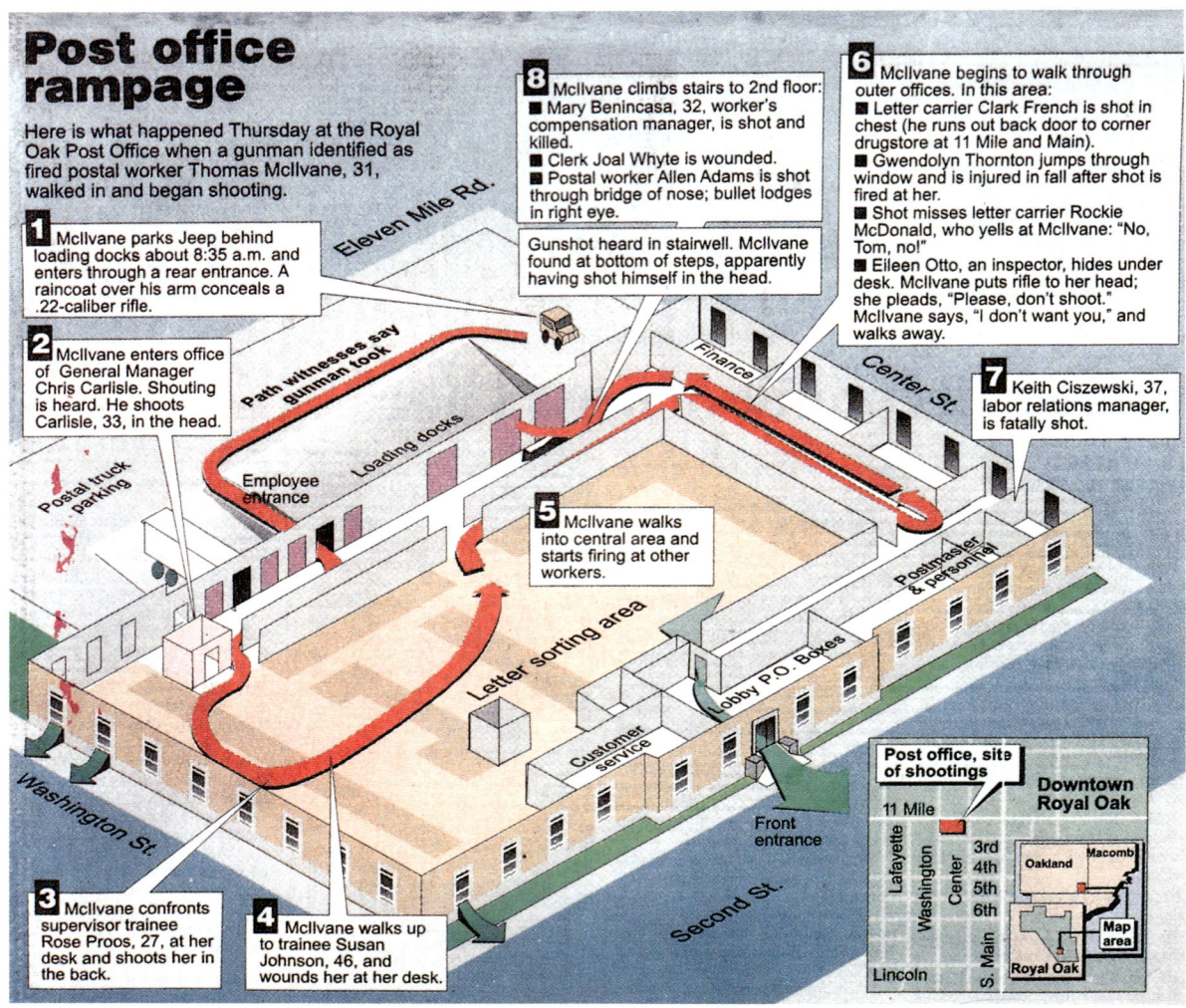

SILVER

The Detroit News

David Pierce, Artist; Kenneth Knight, Artist; Robert Richards, Artist; Patrick Sedlar, Artist; Robert Graham, Graphics Art Director; Dierck Casselman, AME Graphics/Design; Felix Grabowski, Graphics Director; Michele Fecht, Assistant Graphics Editor; Patricia Vegella, Researcher

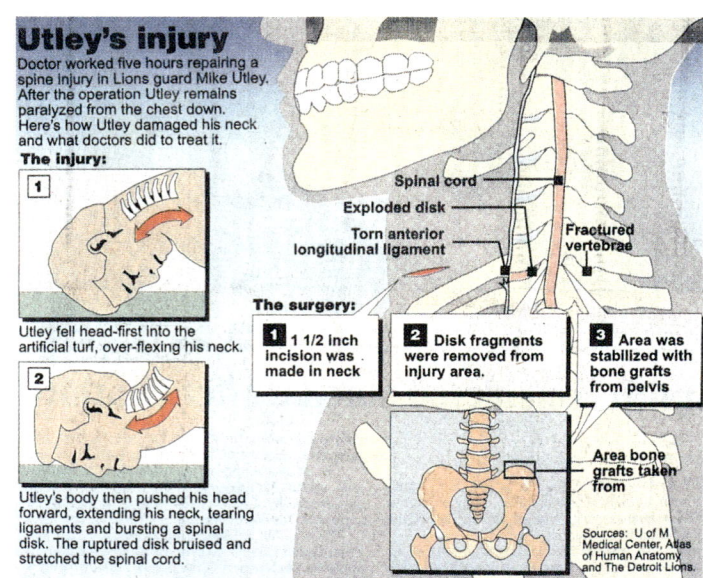

BRONZE

The Detroit News

Sidney Jablonski, Artist; Felix Grabowski, Graphics Director; Aaron Hightower, Artist; David Pierce, Asst. Graphics Editor

The Detroit News

Aaron Hightower, Artist; Robert Richards, Artist; David Pierce, Assistant Graphics Editor

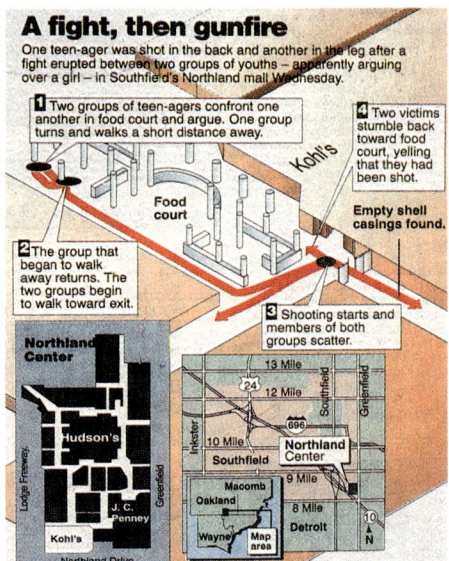

The Virginian-Pilot / Ledger-Star
Norfolk, VA

Bill Pitzer, Illustrator

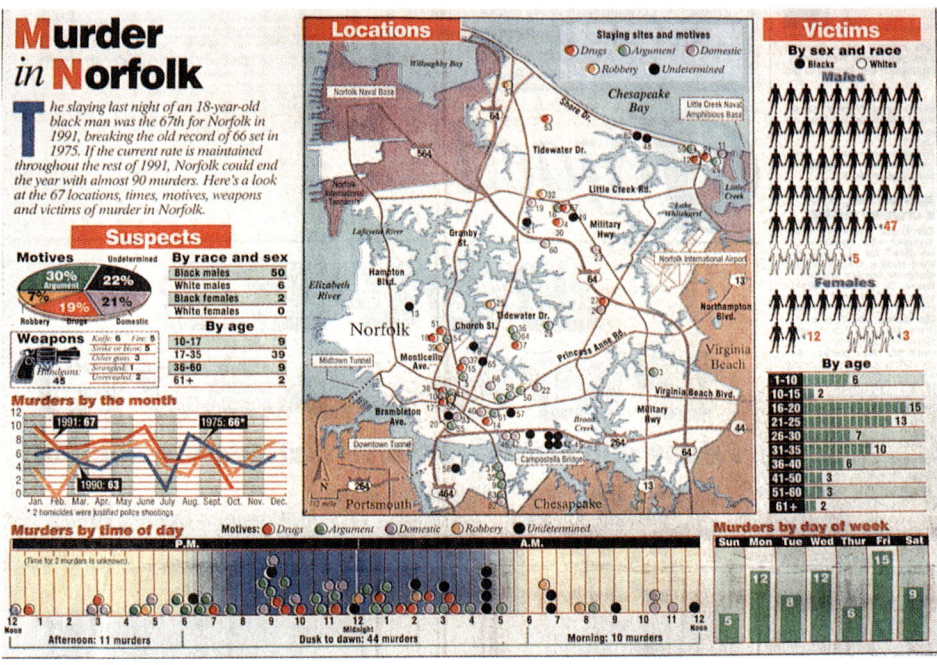

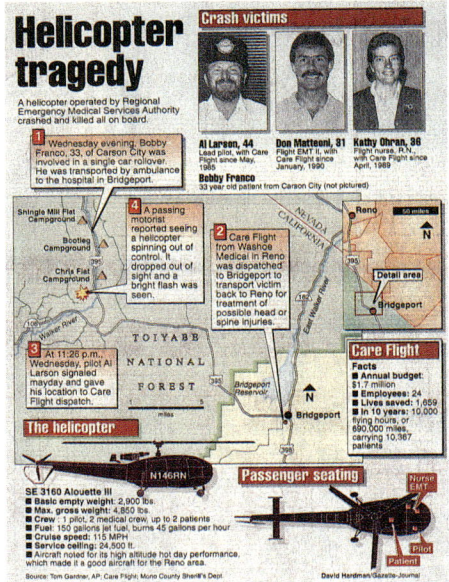

Reno Gazette-Journal

Dave Hardman, Graphics Director

BRONZE
The Houston Chronicle

B.C. Oren, Graphics Reporter

THIRTEENTH EDITION 215

INFORMATIONAL GRAPHICS   Breaking News, Color

BRONZE

The Times-Picayune
Michael Jantze, Infographic Artist

San Francisco Examiner
Chris Morris, Artist; Kelly Frankeny, Graphics Editor; Stewart Huntington, Graphics Coordinator

The Times-Picayune
James Zisk, Infographic Artist

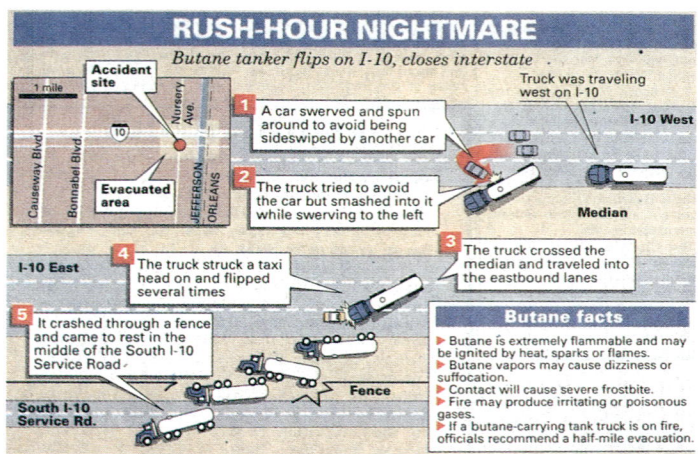

Breaking News Portfolio

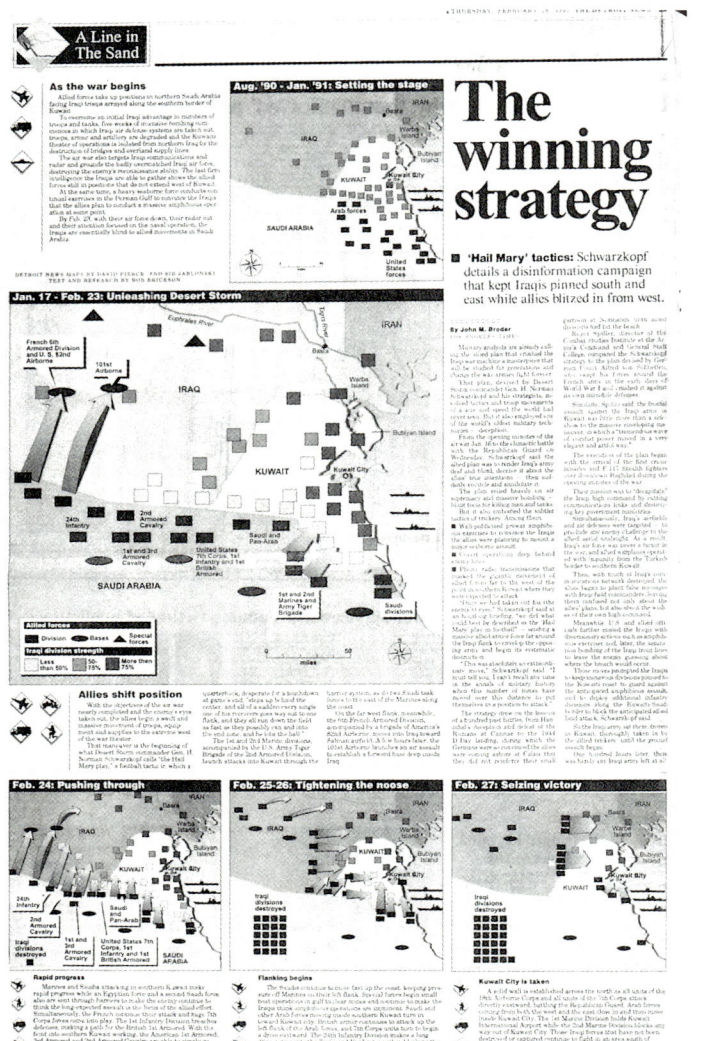

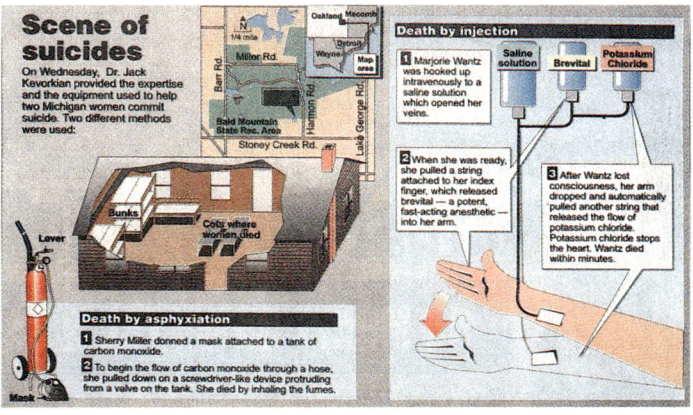

The Detroit News
Informational Graphics Staff

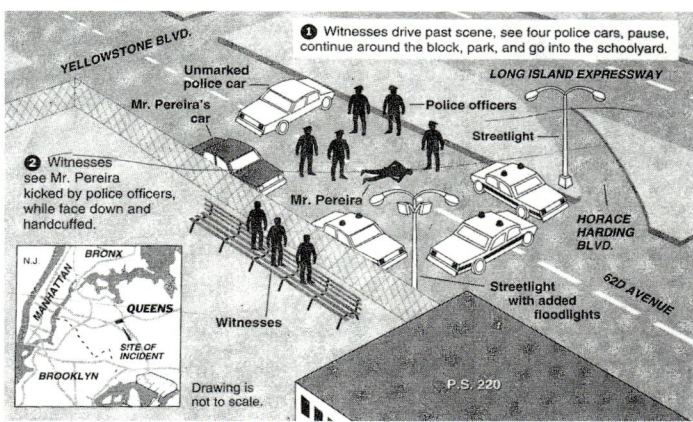

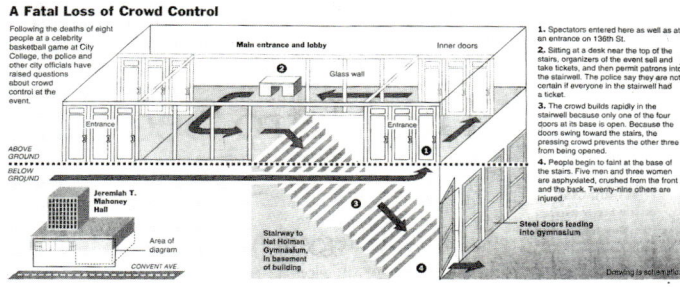

The New York Times
Staff

INFORMATIONAL GRAPHICS Breaking News Portfolio

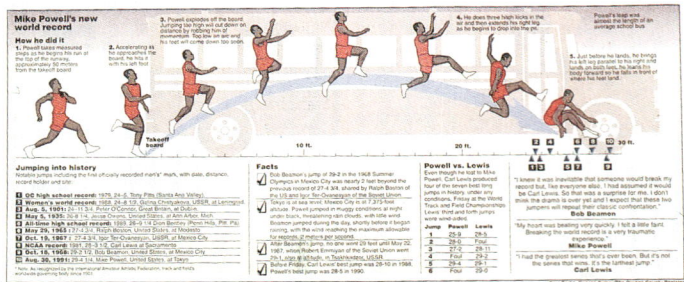

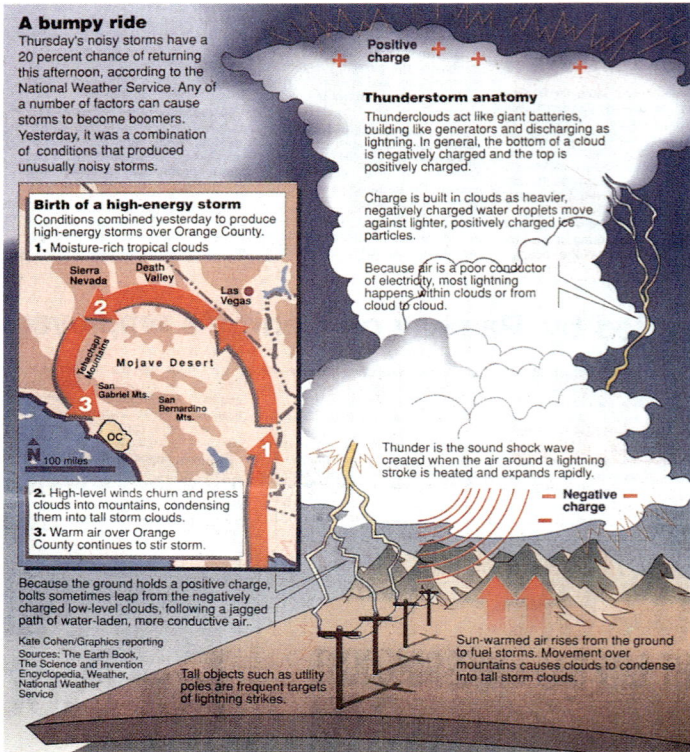

The Orange County Register
Santa Ana, CA

George Turney, Artist

The Sunday Times
London, England

Phil Green, Graphics Editor

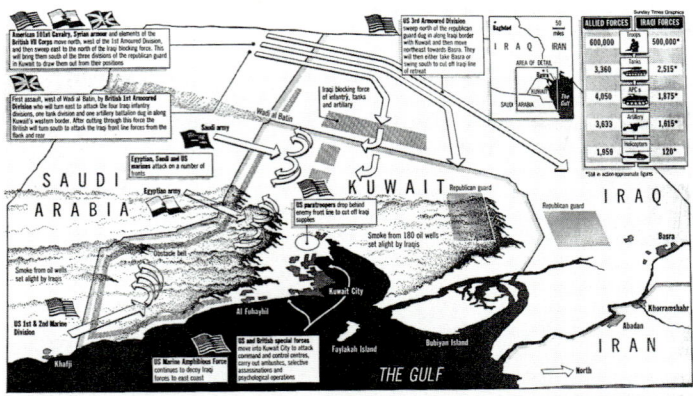

'It will be swift, sudden and devastating'

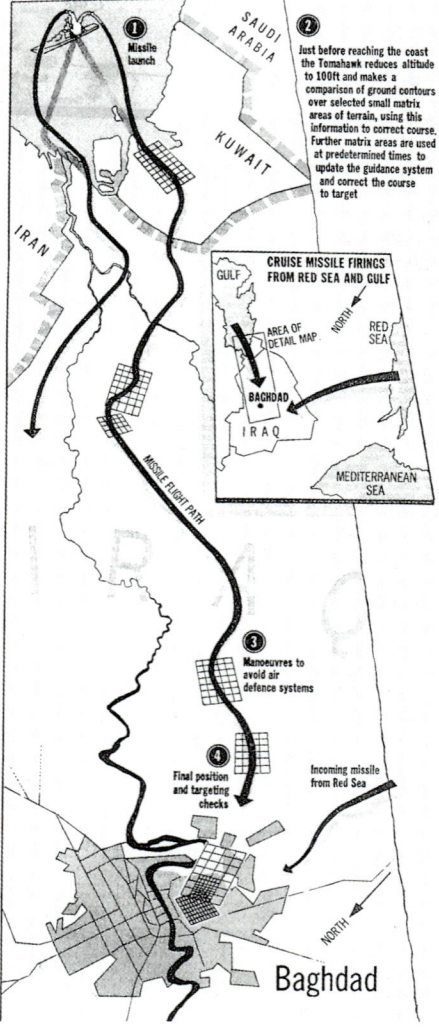

218 THE BEST OF NEWSPAPER DESIGN

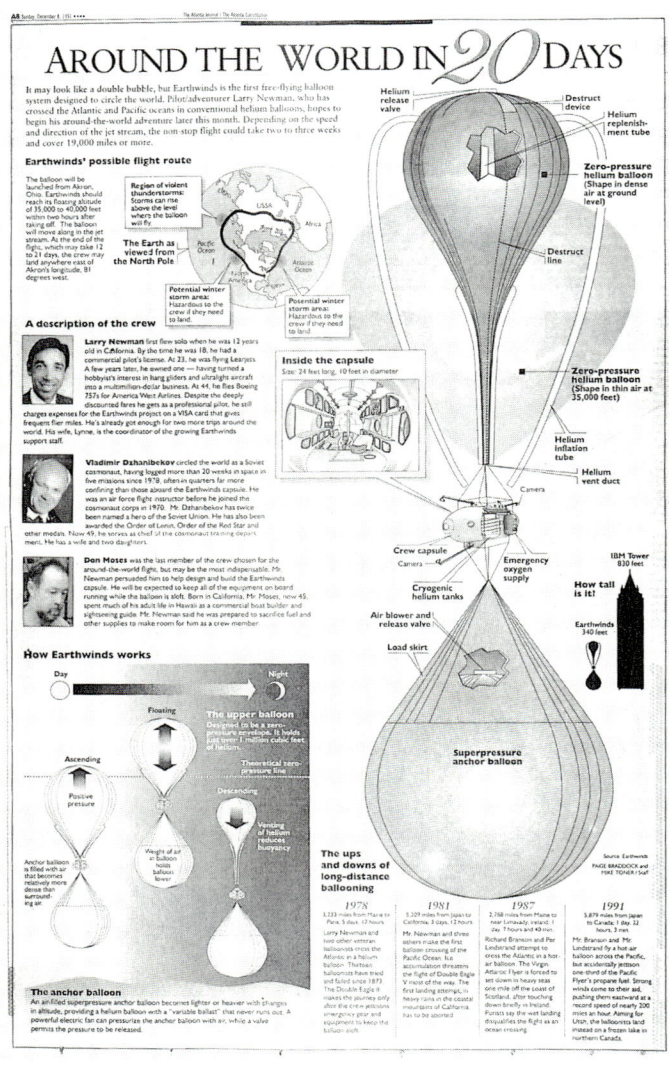

BRONZE

The Atlanta Journal & Constitution

Paige Braddock, Illustrator & Researcher; Mike King, Editor; Mike Toner, Researcher; Tony De Feria, Art Director; Mike Gordon, Design Director

Chicago Tribune

Paige Braddock, Illustrator, Researcher; Dennis Odom, Art Director; Nancy I.Z. Reese, Graphics Editor; Stephen Cvengros, Illustration Editor

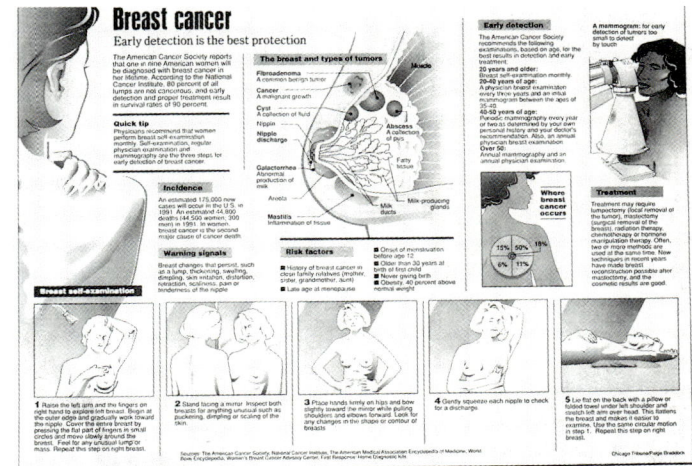

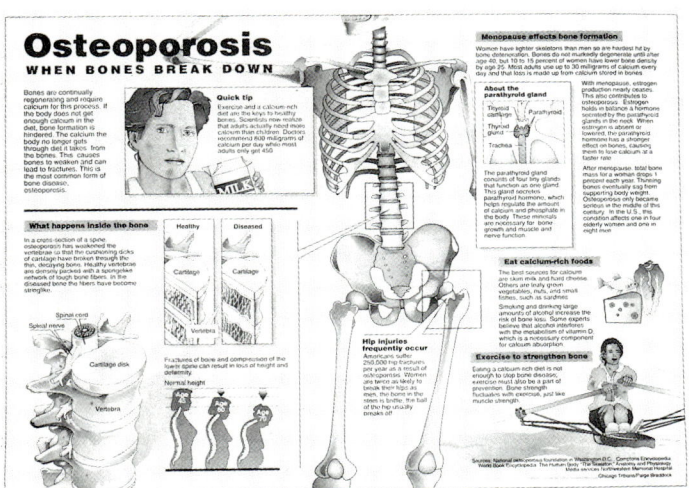

Chicago Tribune

Paige Braddock, Illustrator & Researcher; Dennis Odom, Art Director; Nancy I.Z. Reese, Graphics Editor; Stephen Cvengros, Illustration Editor

Chicago Tribune

Stephen Ravenscraft, Illustrator & Researcher; Vasin Douglas, Illustrator & Researcher; Rick Tuma, Illustrator; Dennis Odom, Art Director; Nancy I.Z. Reese, Graphics Editor; Stephen Cvengros, Illustration Editor

INFORMATIONAL GRAPHICS Black & White

Detroit Free Press

Moses Harris, Chief Artist; Laura Varon Brown, Graphics Director; Ted Williamson, Assistant Graphics Editor; Ron Dzwonkowski, Deputy City Editor; John Goecke, Design Director; City Desk Reporters

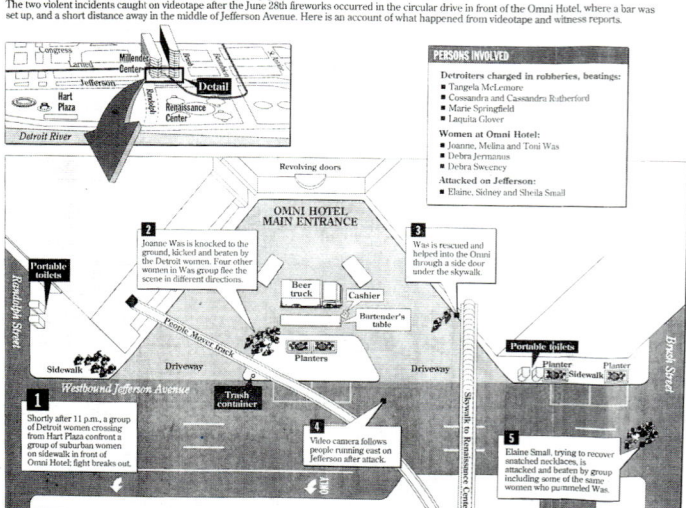

Detroit Free Press

Martha Thierry, Artist; Laura Varon Brown, Graphics Director; Ted Williamson, Assistant Graphics Editor

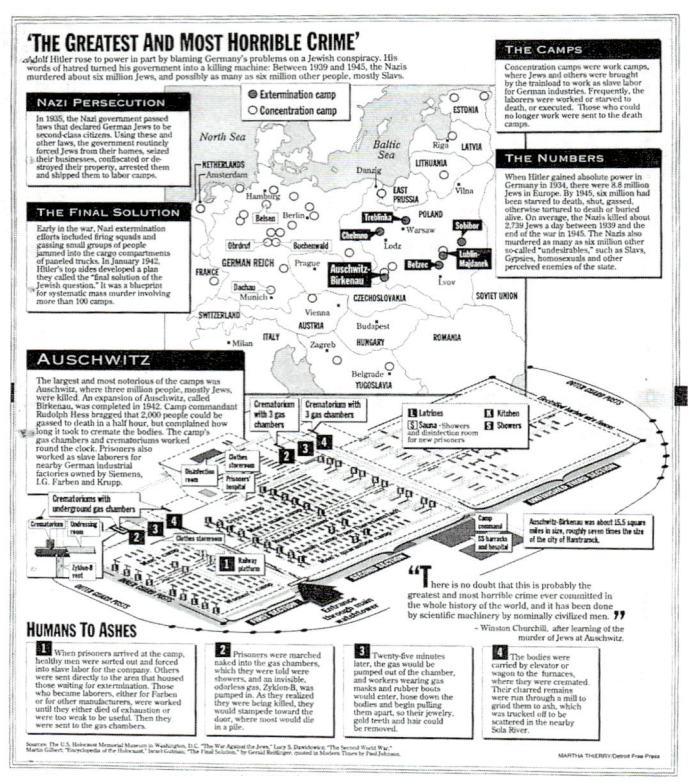

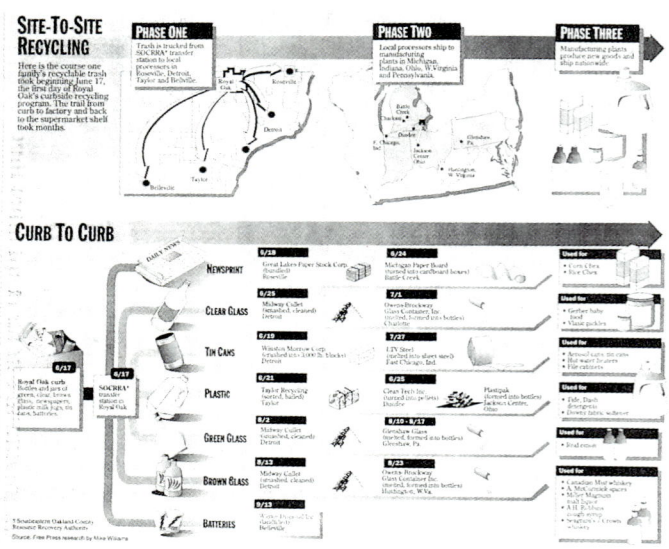

Detroit Free Press

Hank Szerlag, Artist; Laura Varon Brown, Graphics Director; Ted Williamson, Assistant Graphics Editor; Mike Williams, Reporter; Kathy O'Gorman, Assistant City Editor

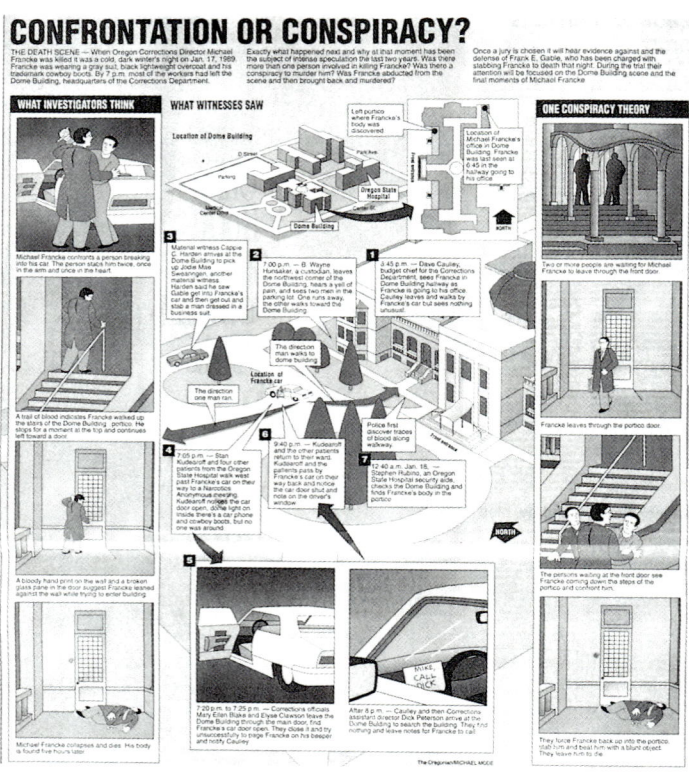

The Oregonian

Michael Mode, Staff Artist; Mark Wigginton, Art Director

The Detroit News

David Pierce, Artist; Michele Fecht, Assistant Graphics Editor; Marla Camp, Graphics Editor

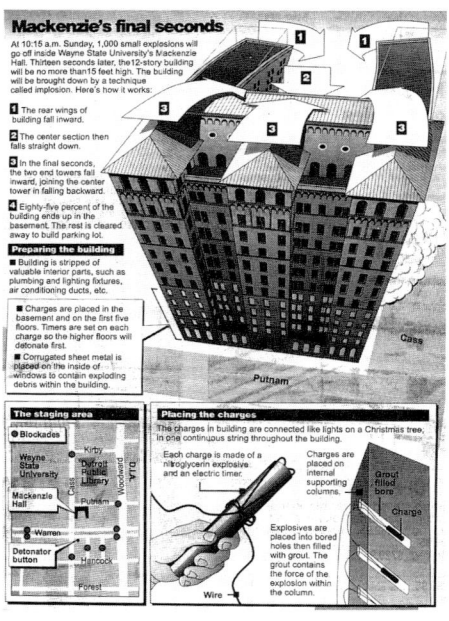

The Detroit News

David Pierce, Artist; Patricia Vegella, Researcher; Sidney Jablonski, Artist; Michele Fecht, Asst. Graphics Editor

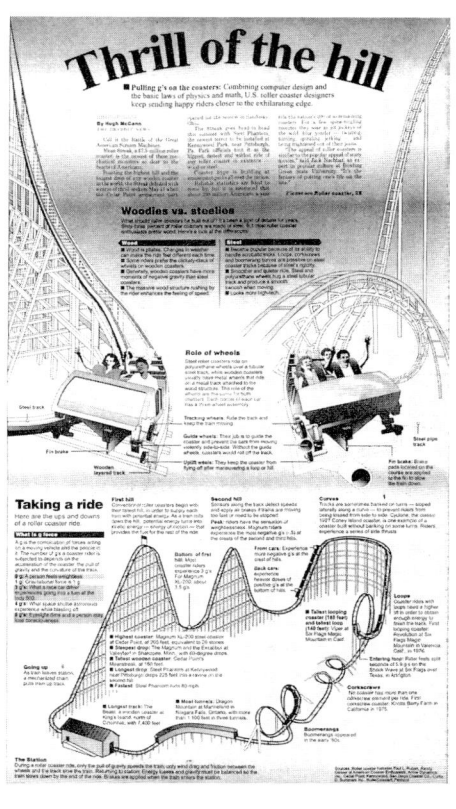

The Detroit News

David Pierce, Artist; Michele Fecht, Assistant Graphics Editor; Alan Stamm, Deputy National Editor

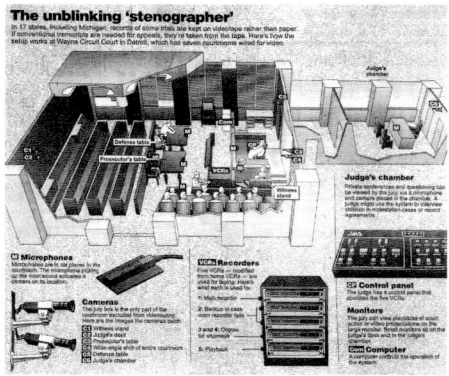

The National Sports Daily

Frank O'Connell, Illustrator & Designer; Karl Gude, Art Director

Los Angeles Times / Orange County Edition

Dennis Lowe, Artist

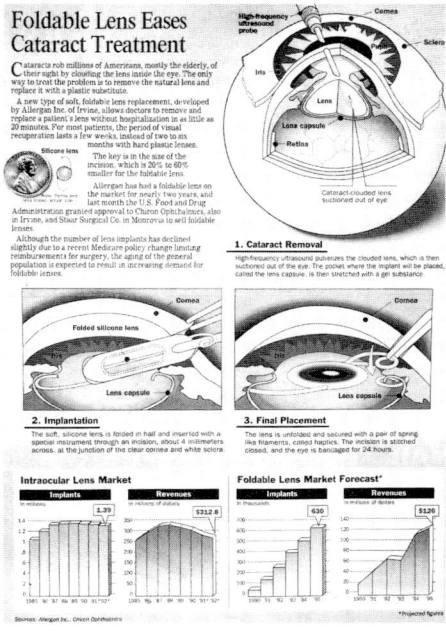

Los Angeles Times / Orange County Edition

Dennis Lowe, Artist; Dallas Jackson, Researcher

THIRTEENTH EDITION 221

INFORMATIONAL GRAPHICS Black & White

Gannett News Service
Arlington, VA

Frank Pompa, Art Coordinator

Honolulu Star-Bulletin

Kevin Hand, Graphics Artist

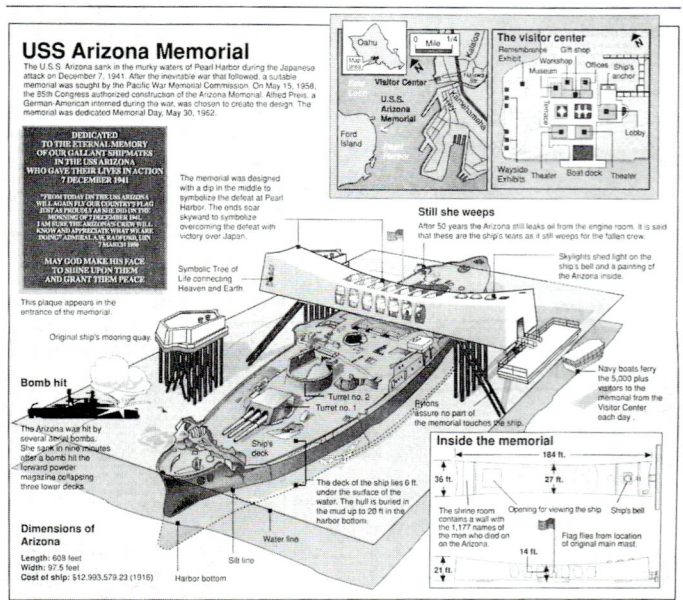

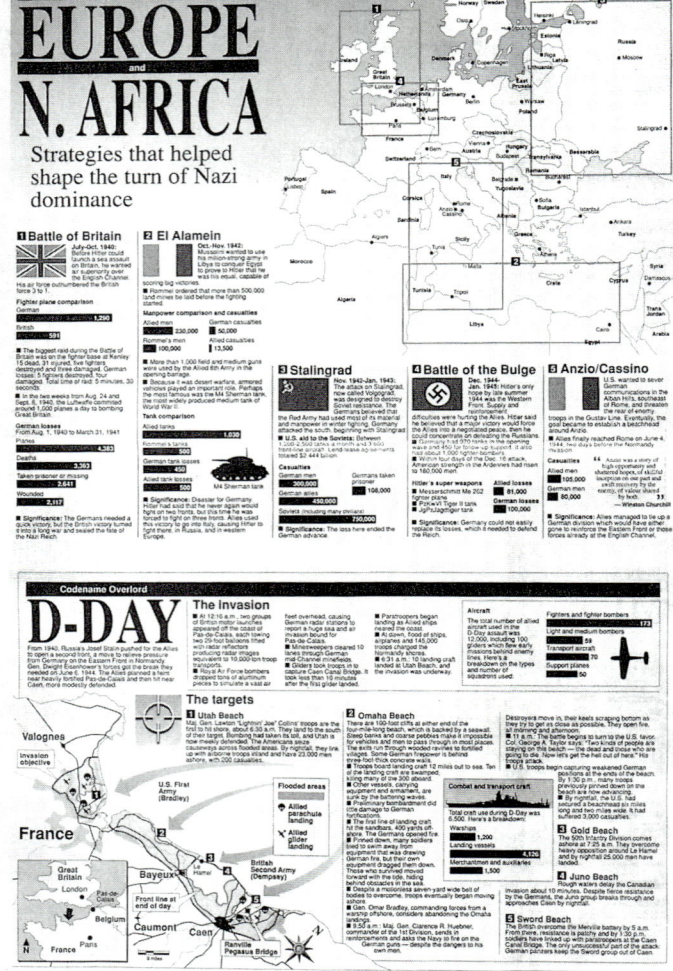

El Mundo
Madrid, Spain

Mario Tascon, Infographics Director; Jeff Goertzen, Art Consultant; Samuel Velasco, Illustrator

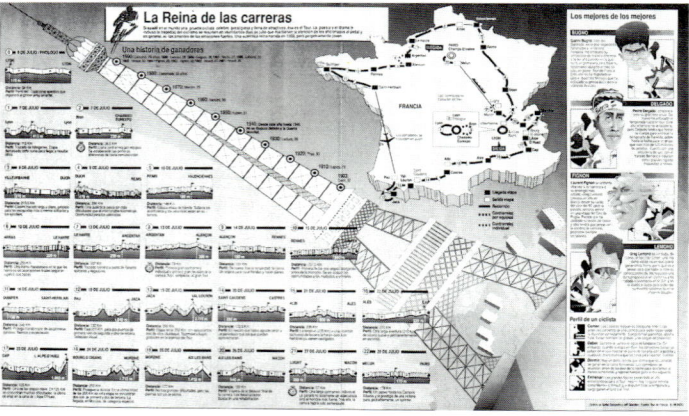

El Mundo

Gorka Sampedro, Illustrator; Mario Tascon, Infographics Director; Jeff Goertzen, Art Consultant & Illustrator

The New York Times

Joe Ward, Graphics Editor; Stephen Kroninger, Illustrator; Paul Winfield, Writer; Tom Bodkin, Design Director

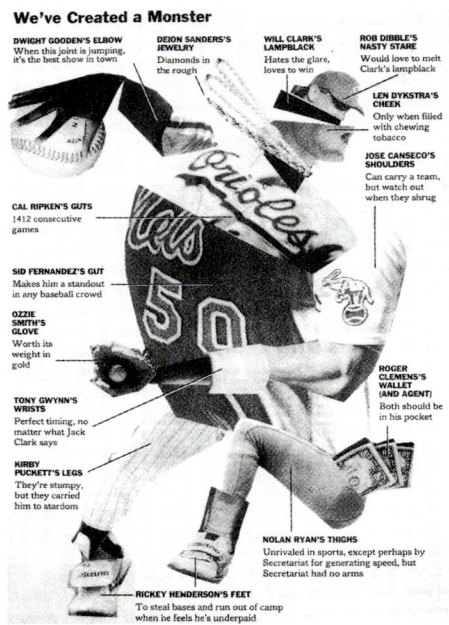

The New York Times

Nancy Stemgold, Art Director; Tom Bodkin, Design Director; Dimitry G. Schidlovsky, Illustrator

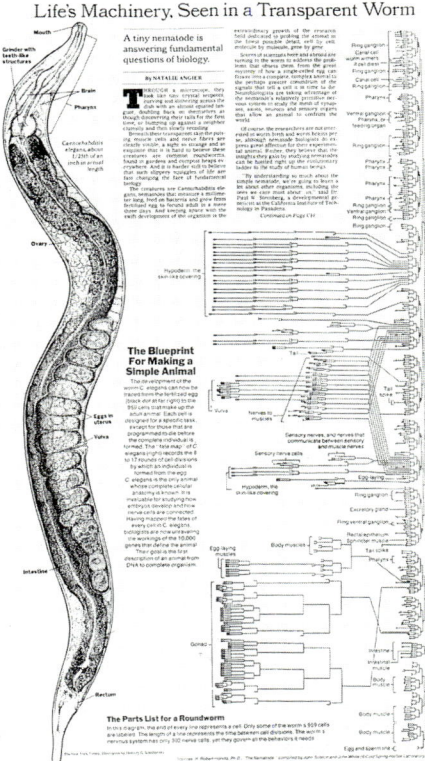

The New York Times

Peter C.T. Elsworth, Graphics Editor; Greg Ryan, Art Director; Tom Bodkin, Design Director

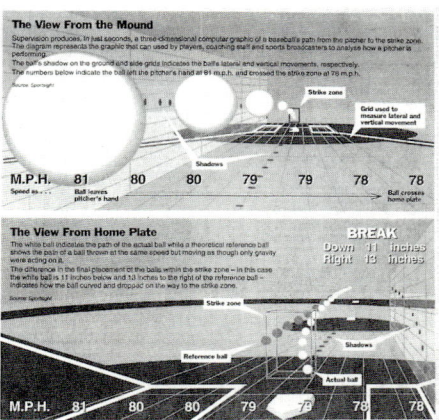

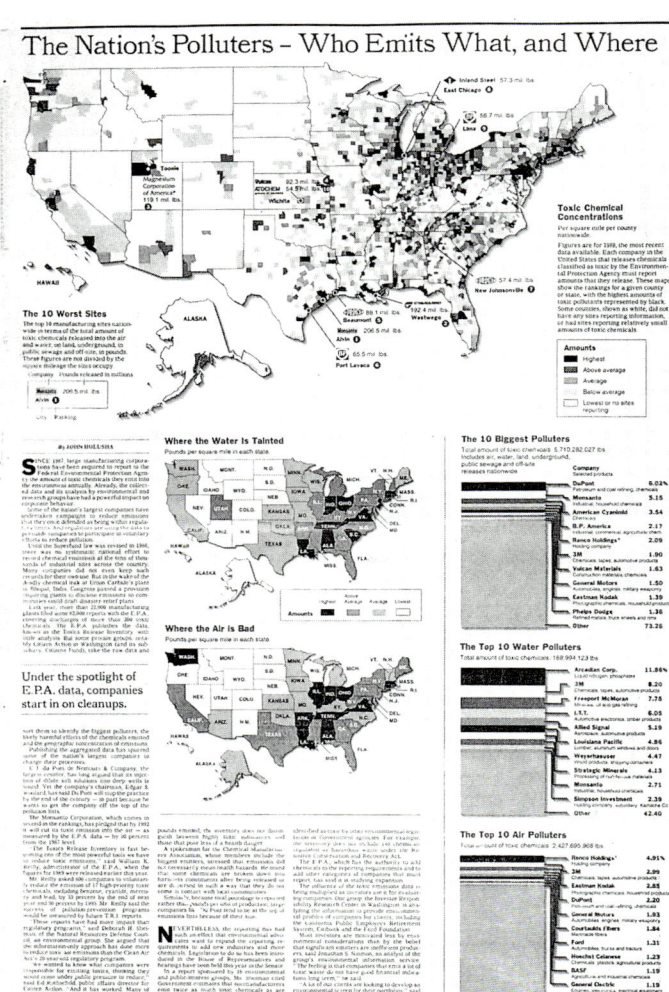

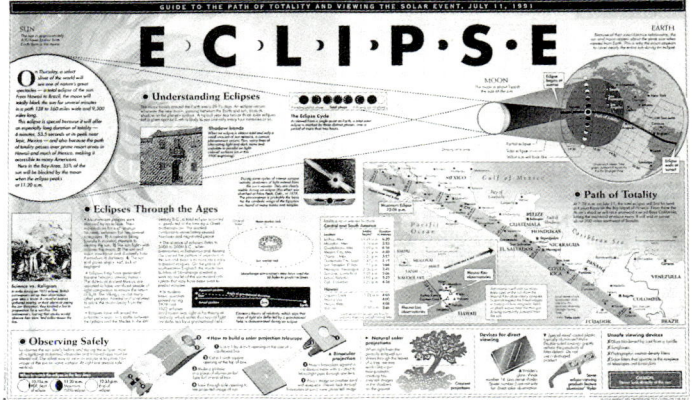

San Francisco Chronicle

Steve Outing, Graphics Editor; Steve Kearsley, Illustrator; Kristine Strawser, Illustrator

BRONZE

The New York Times

Ty Ahmad-Taylor, Graphics Editor; Greg Ryan, Art Director; Tom Bodkin, Design Director

INFORMATIONAL GRAPHICS Black & White • Color

(BLACK & WHITE)
The Plain Dealer
Steve Little, Staff Artist

Akron Beacon Journal
Art Krummel, Artist

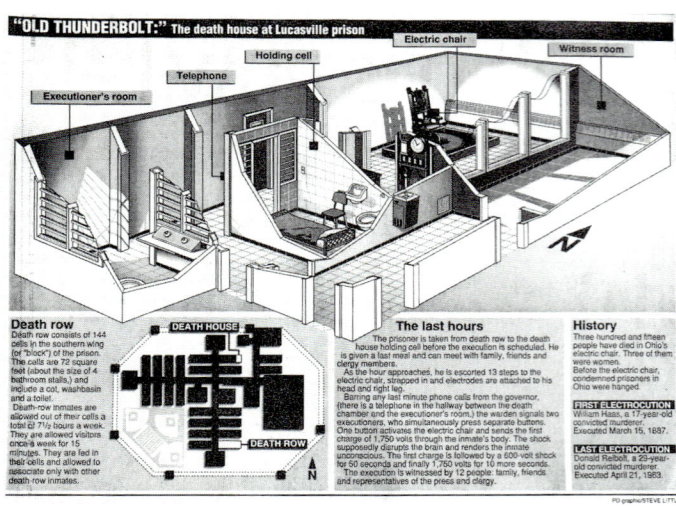

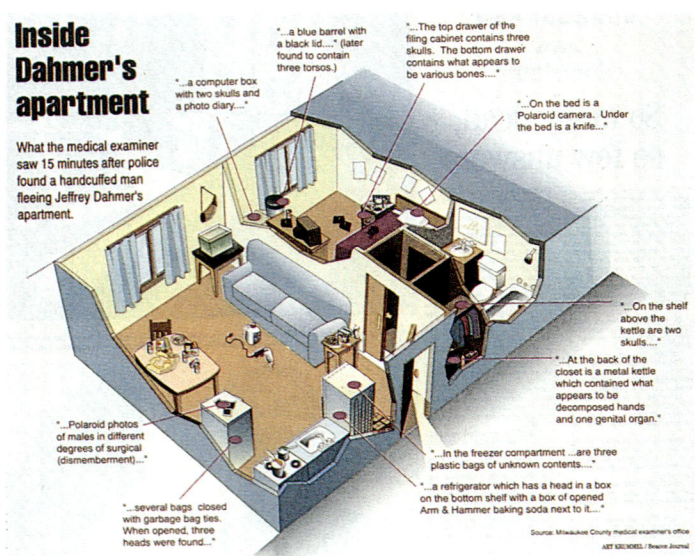

The Arizona Daily Star
Tucson, AZ

Bill Pitzer, Illustrator & Designer; Chuck Kramer, Research/Editing; Charlie Leight, Art Director

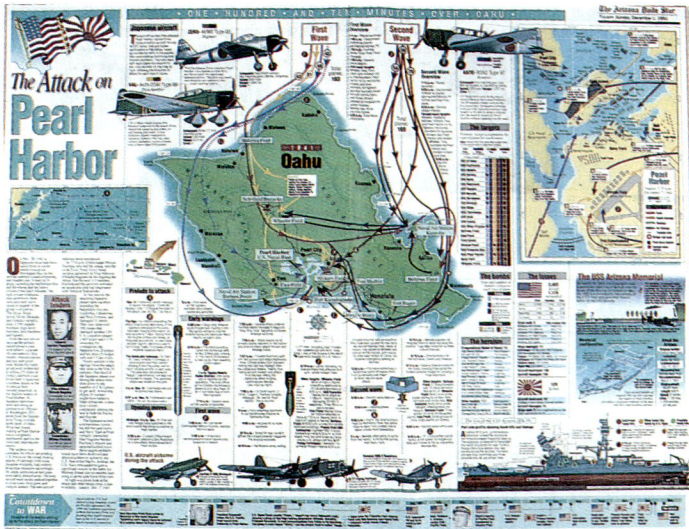

The Arizona Republic
Phoenix, AZ

Don Foley, Artist; Pete Watters, Graphic Coordinator

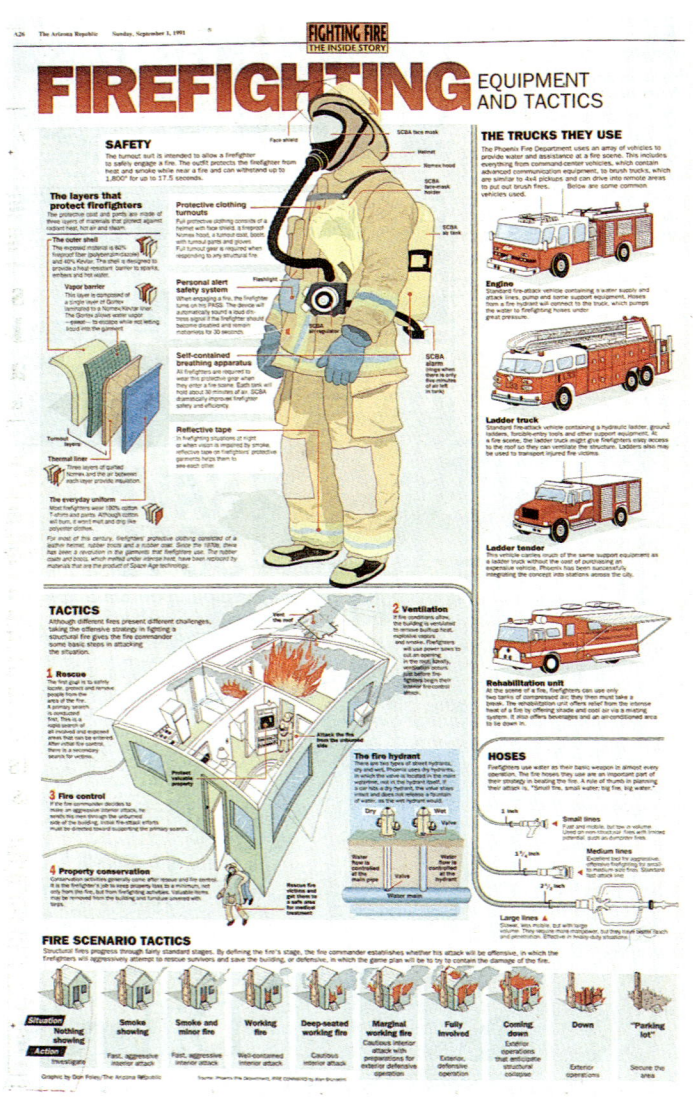

Color

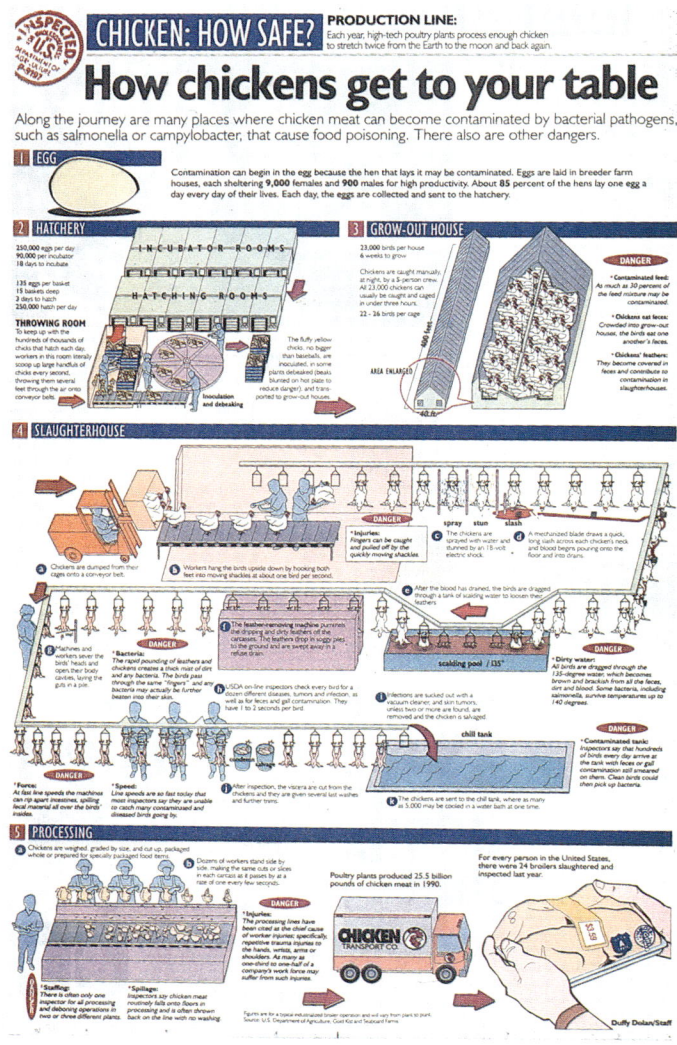

BRONZE
The Atlanta Journal & Constitution
Duffy Dolan, Illustrator & Researcher; Lee Hotz, Editor; Tony De Feria, Art Director; Mike Gordon, Design Director

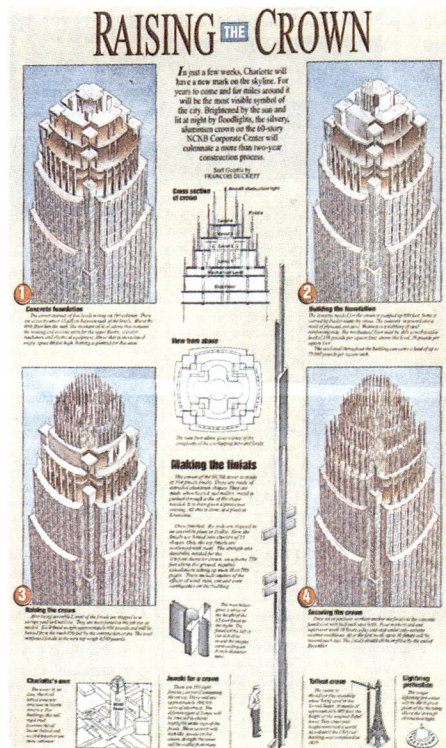

The Charlotte Observer
Francois Duckett, Illustrator & Researcher; Mike Homan, Art Director & Designer

BRONZE
The Boston Globe
Neil C. Pinchin, InfoGraphics Designer; Cynthia Daniels, Art Director

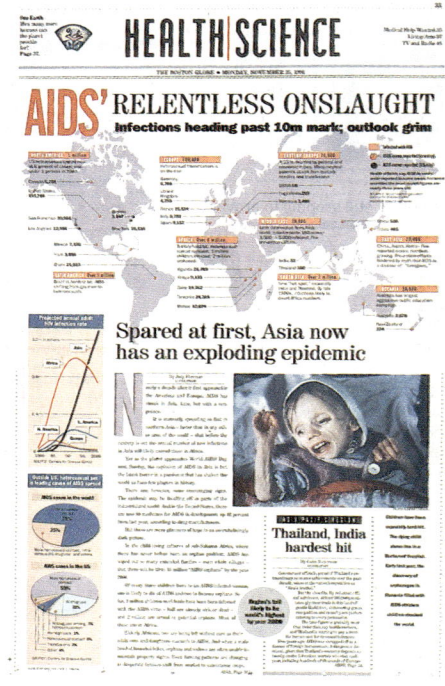

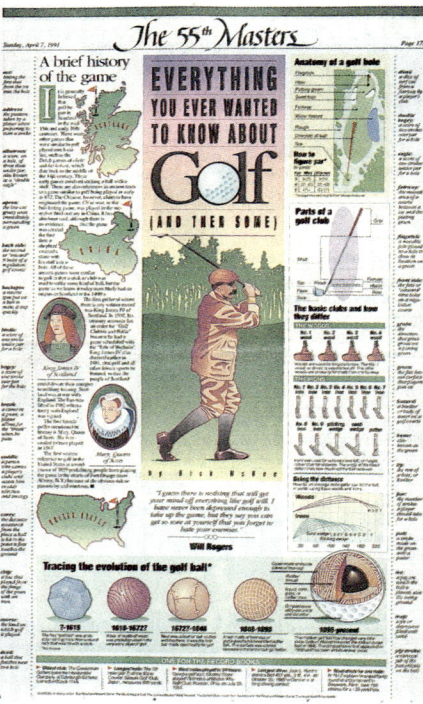

The Augusta Chronicle
Rick McKee, Chief Artist

THIRTEENTH EDITION 225

INFORMATIONAL GRAPHICS Color

Chicago Tribune

Paige Braddock, Illustrator & Researcher; Rick Tuma, Illustrator; Don Sena, Researcher; Stephen Ravenscraft, Illustrator; Julie Sheer, Researcher; Dennis Odom, Art Director & Illustrator; Nancy I.Z. Reese, Graphics Editor; Stephen Cvengros, Illustration Editor; Terry Volpp, Art Director; Enrique Rodriguez, Illustrator

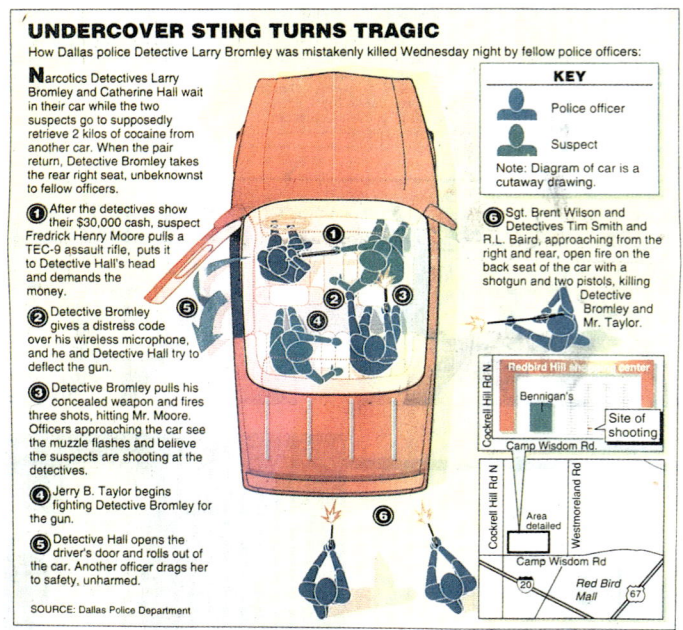

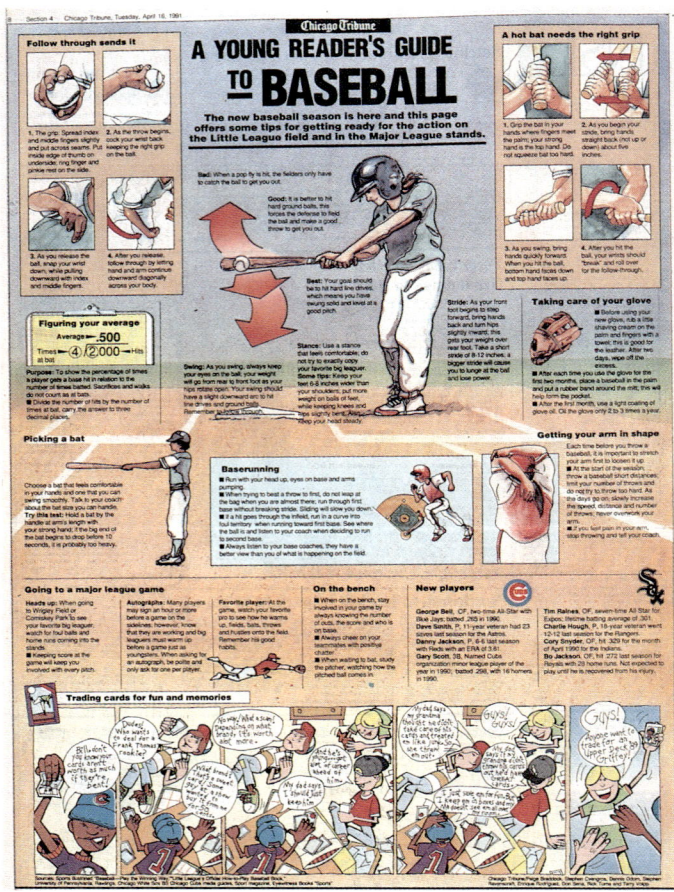

BRONZE

The Dallas Morning News

Ed Kohorst, Art Director; Laura Stanton, Illustrator & Designer; Ed Owens, Graphic Reporter

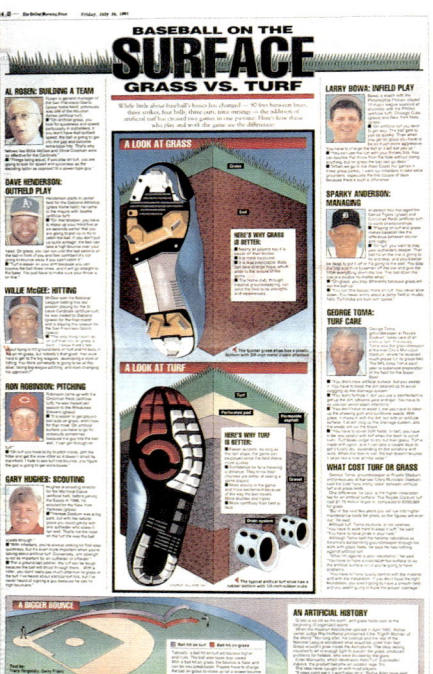

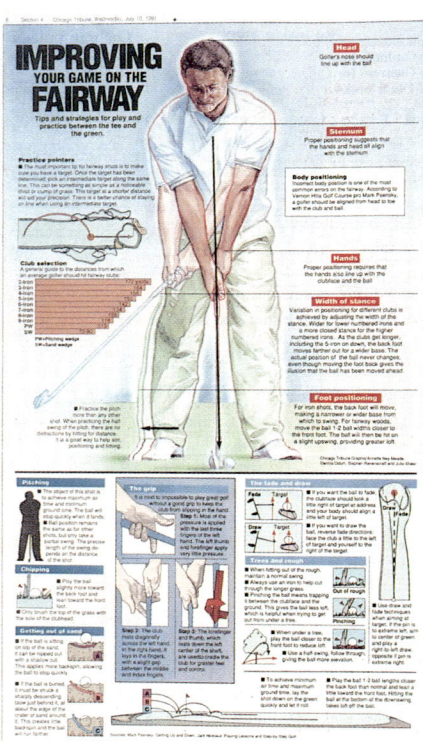

The Dallas Morning News

Clif Bosler, Designer; Ed Kohorst, Art Director

Chicago Tribune

Stephen Ravenscraft, Illustrator & Researcher; Dennis Odom, Art Director, Designer & Illustrator; Julie Sheer, Researcher; Stephen Cvengros, Illustration Editor; Annette Ney Meade, Researcher

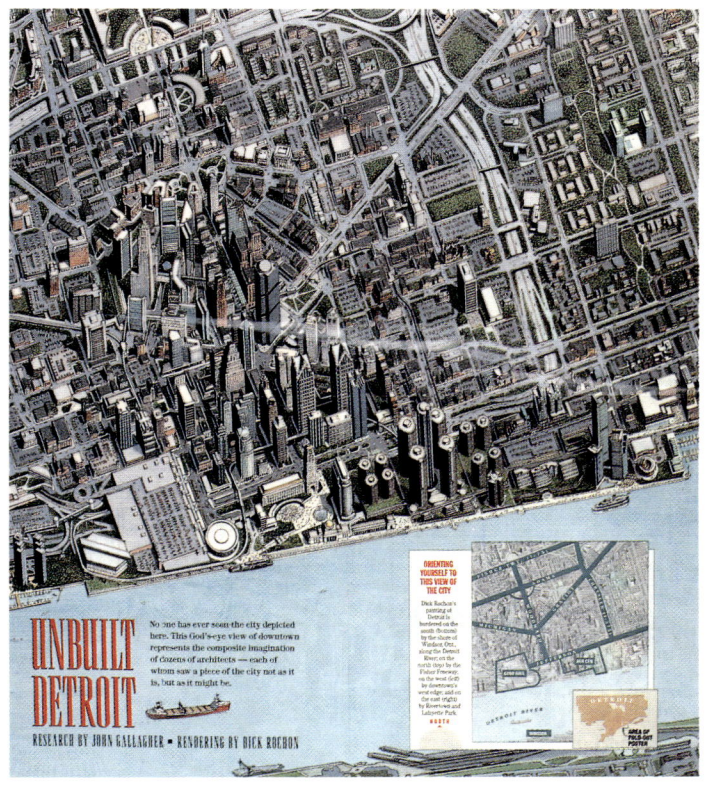

Detroit Free Press

Andrew Hartley, Art Director & Designer; Dick Rochon, Artist; John Gallagher, Researcher; Brian Dickerson, Editor; Geri Lama, Copy Editor; Mary Henry, Quebecor; Deborah Withey, Design Director

Detroit Free Press Magazine

Andrew Hartley, Art Director & Designer; Dick Rochon, Artist; John Gallagher, Researcher; Brian Dickerson, Editor; Geri Lama, Copy Editor; Mary Henry, Quebecor; Deborah Withey, Design Director

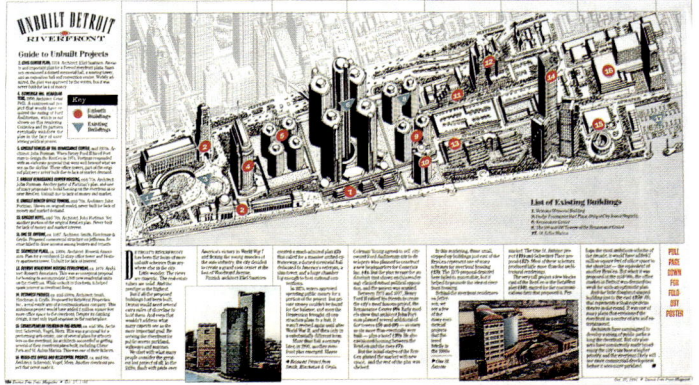

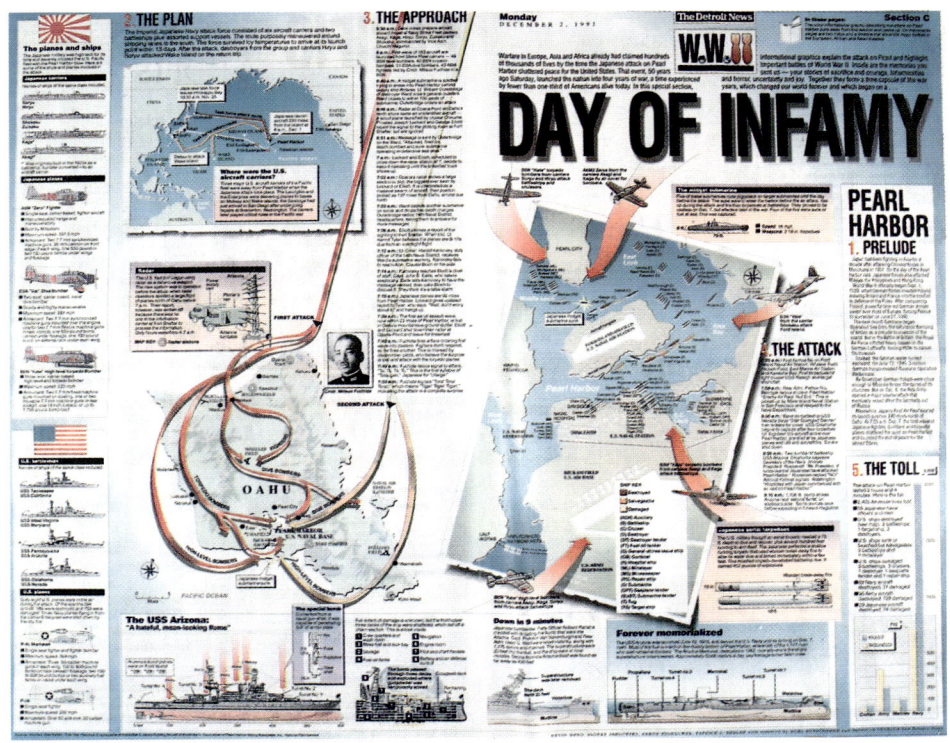

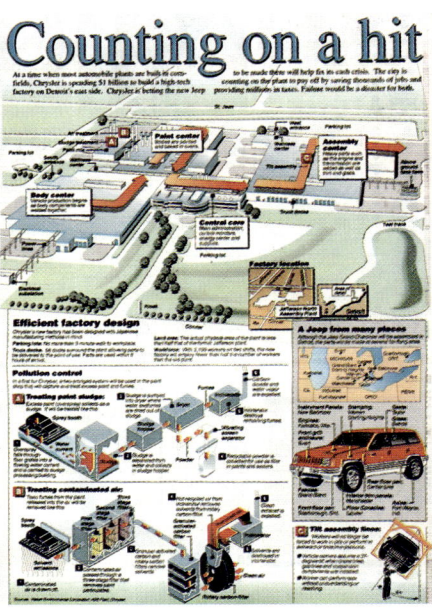

The Detroit News

Sidney Jablonski, Artist; David Pierce, Artist; Michele Fecht, Assistant Graphics Editor

The Detroit News

Sidney Jablonski, Artist; Aaron Hightower, Artist; Patrick Sedlar, Artist; Kevin Hand, Artist; Patricia Vegella, Researcher; Burl Burlingame, Researcher; Michele Fecht, Assistant Graphics Editor; Dierck Casselman, AME Graphics/Design

THIRTEENTH EDITION 227

INFORMATIONAL GRAPHICS Color

BRONZE
The Detroit News

David Pierce, Artist & Designer; Michele Fecht, Assistant Graphics Editor; Patricia Vegella, Researcher

The Miami Herald

Wes Albers, Assistant News Editor; Rick Brownlee, Info Graphic Artist; Herman Vega, Designer; Randy Stano, Director of Editorial Art & Design

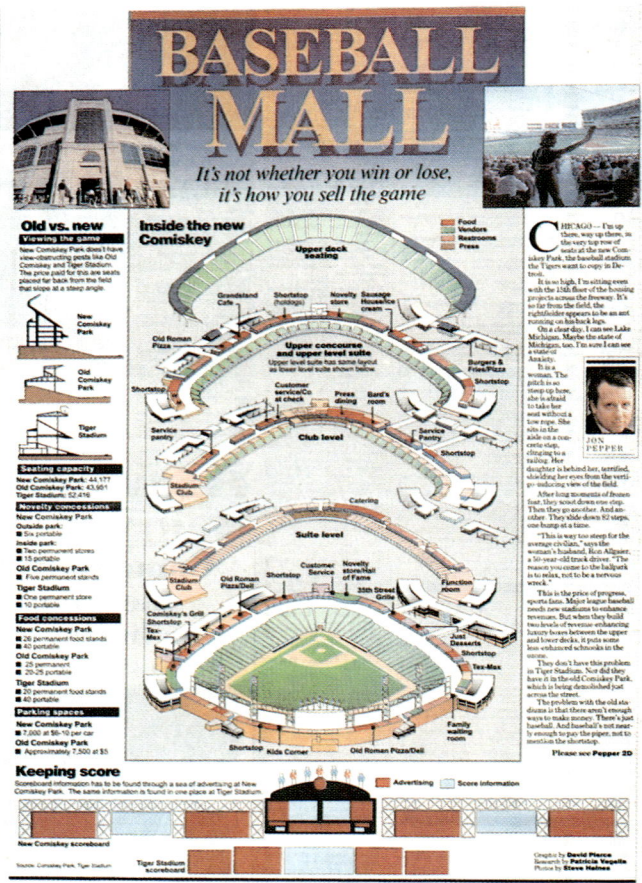

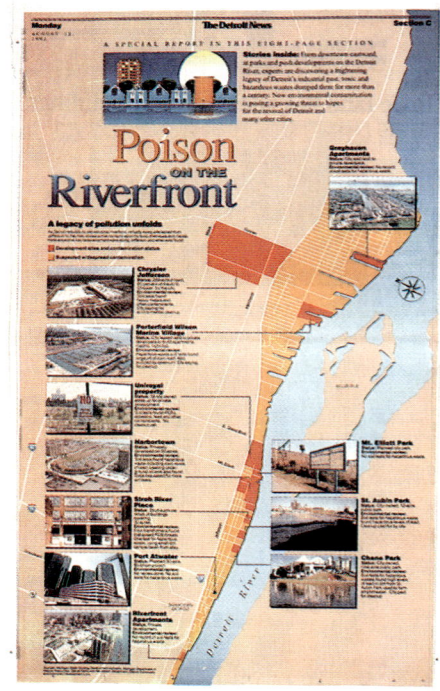

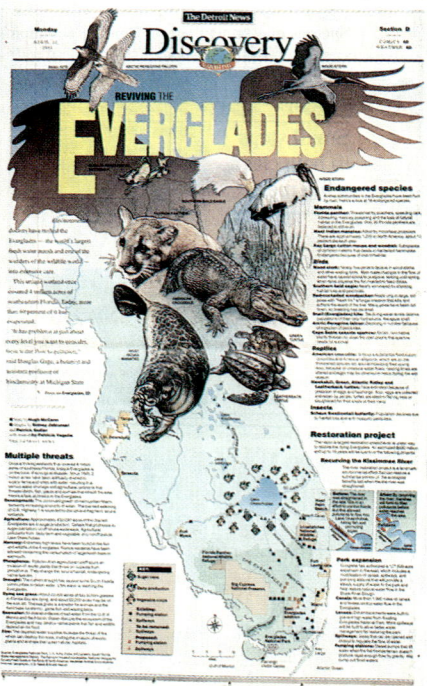

The Detroit News

Sidney Jablonski, Artist; Aaron Hightower, Artist; Robert Graham, Graphics Art Director; Dierck Casselman, AME Graphics/Design; Michele Fecht, Assistant Graphics Editor

The Detroit News

Sidney Jablonski, Artist; Patrick Sedlar, Artist; Robert Graham, Art Director; Michele Fecht, Assistant Graphics Editor; Patricia Vegella, Researcher

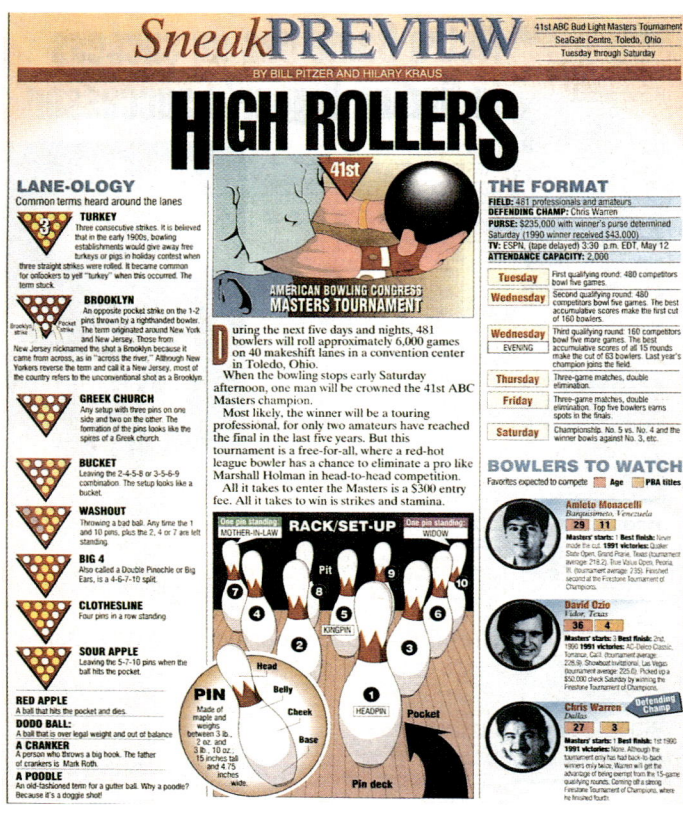

BRONZE

The National Sports Daily

Bill Pitzer, Illustrator & Designer; Karl Gude, Art Director; Don DeMaio, AME Graphics

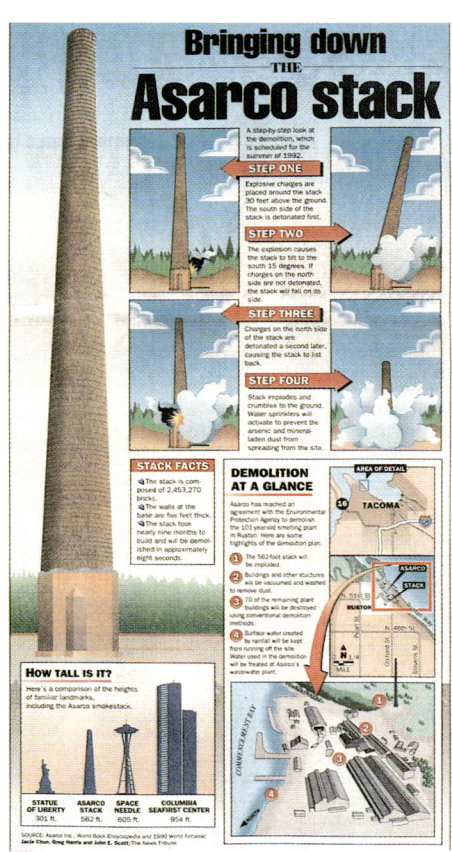

The Morning News Tribune
Tacoma, WA

John E. Scott, News Artist/Designer; Greg Harris, News Artist/Designer; Jacie Chun, News Artist; Greg Anderson, Director of Art & Photography

The Oregonian

Steve Cowden, Artist; Mark Wigginton, Art Director

The Oregonian

Steve Cowden, Artist; Mark Wigginton, Art Director

THIRTEENTH EDITION 229

INFORMATIONAL GRAPHICS Color

The Post-Standard
Syracuse, NY

Michael A. Braia, Illustrator, Designer & Researcher

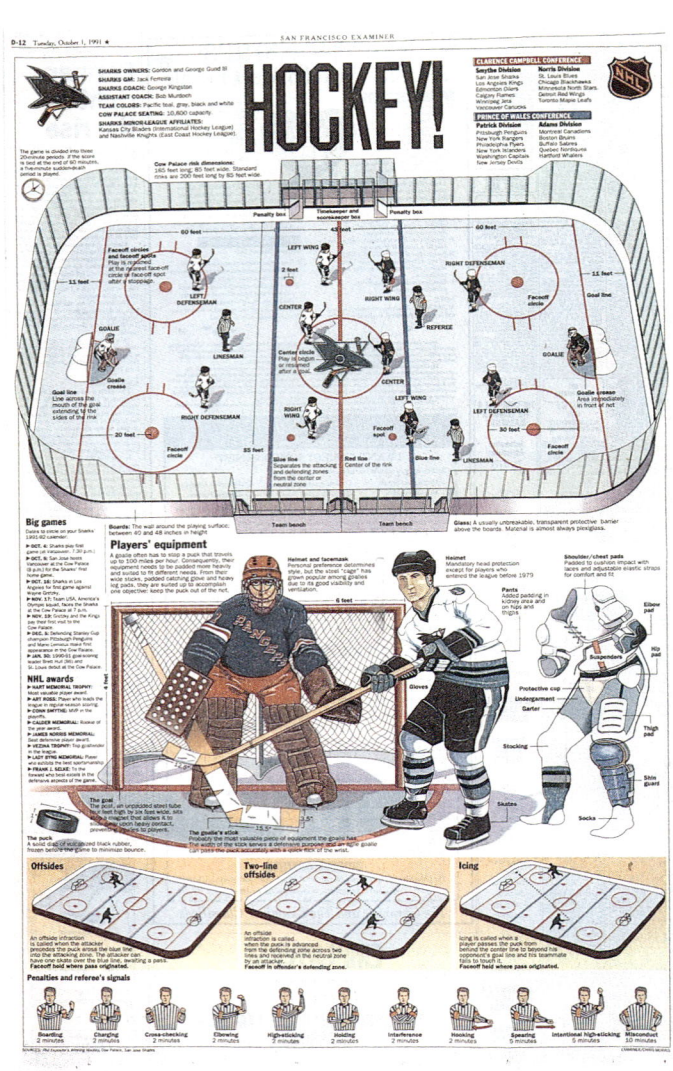

San Francisco Examiner

Chris Morris, Artist; Kelly Frankeny, Graphics Editor; Ross McKeon, Researcher

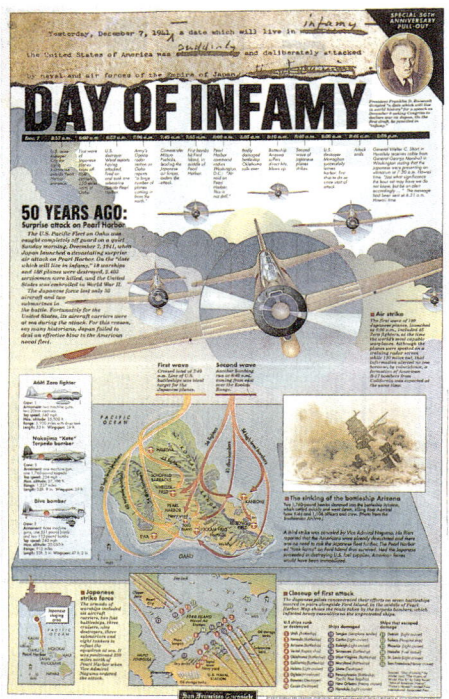

San Francisco Chronicle

Steve Outing, Graphics Editor; Steve Kearsley, Illustrator; Kristine Strawser, Illustrator; Bruce Krefting, Illustrator; Ed Rachles, Illustrator; Scott Wilson, Researcher

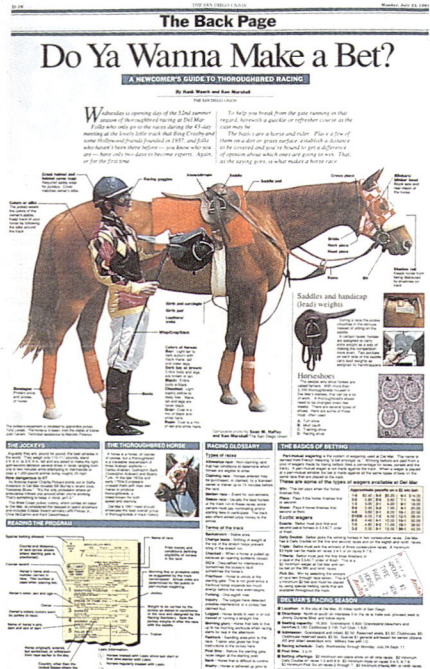

The San Diego Union

Ken Marshall, Designer & Writer; Hank Wesch, Writer; Sean M. Haffey, Photographer

230 THE BEST OF NEWSPAPER DESIGN

BRONZE
Seattle Post-Intelligencer
Duane Hoffmann, Art

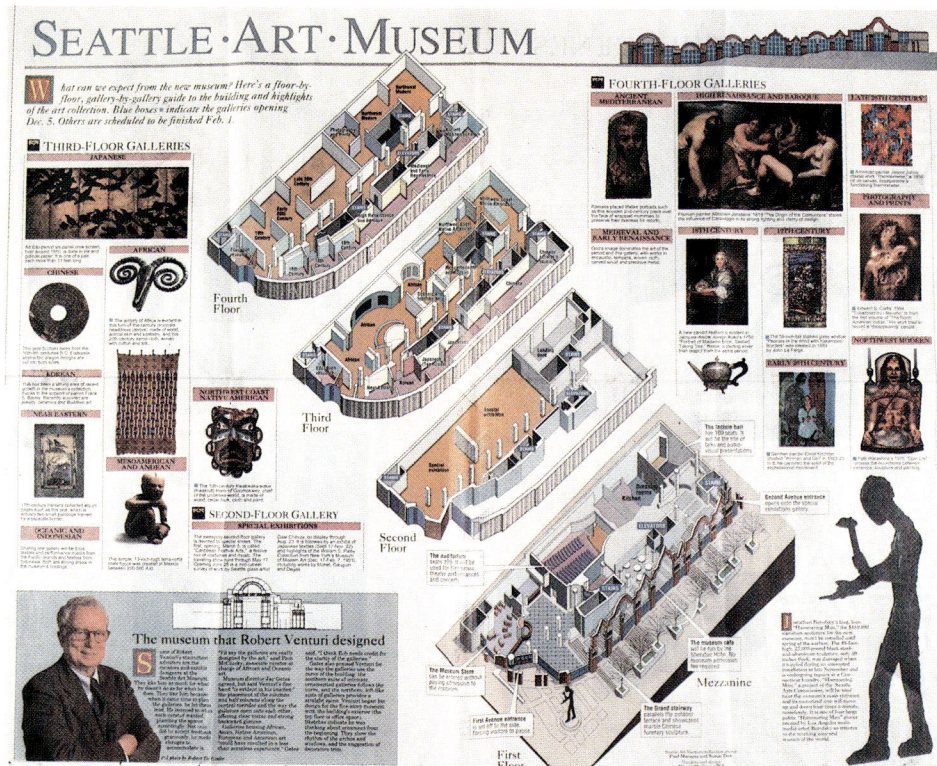

The Seattle Times
Rob Kemp, Designer & Artist; Fred Case, Reporter

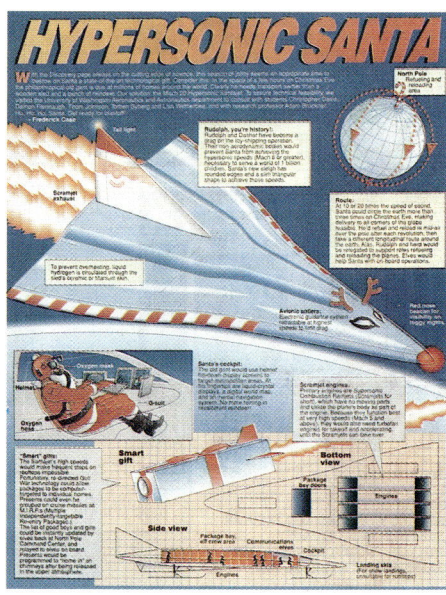

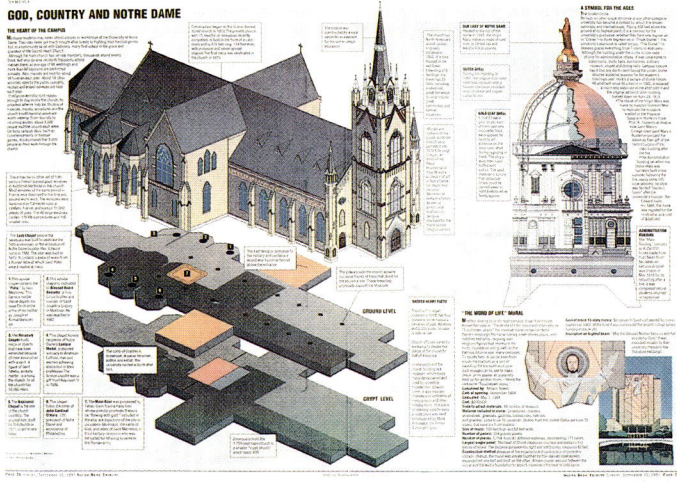

South Bend Tribune
Michael Brugh, Illustrator & Researcher; Diane Stephen, Researcher; David Kordalski, Art Director

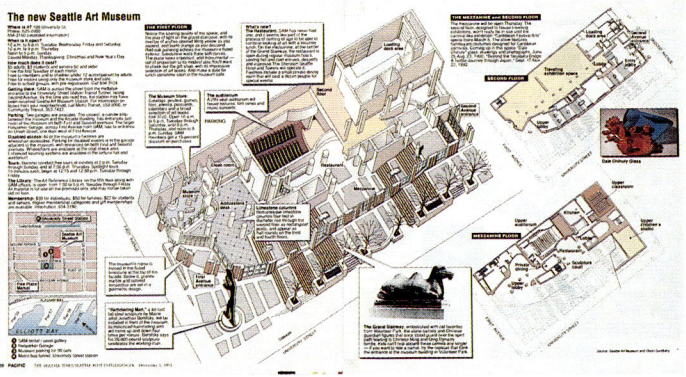

The Seattle Times
James McFarlane, Illustrator; David Miller, Art Director; Robin Fogel, Designer

INFORMATIONAL GRAPHICS Color

Syracuse Herald American
Tom Schmitt, Illustrator & Designer

The Virginian-Pilot / Ledger-Star
Norfolk, VA

Bill Pitzer, Illustrator & Designer

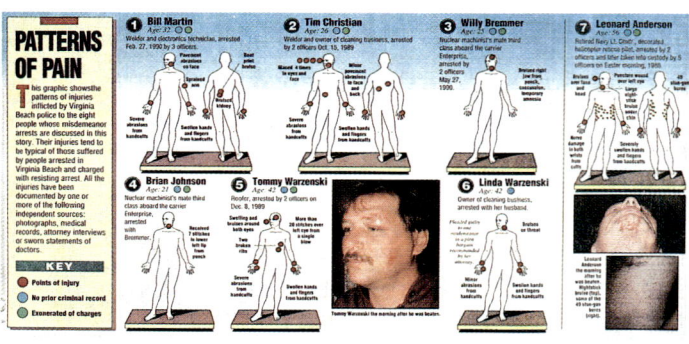

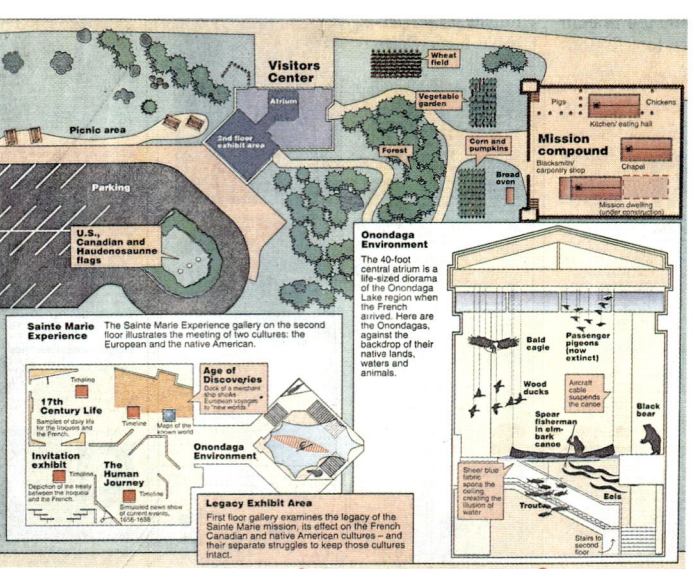

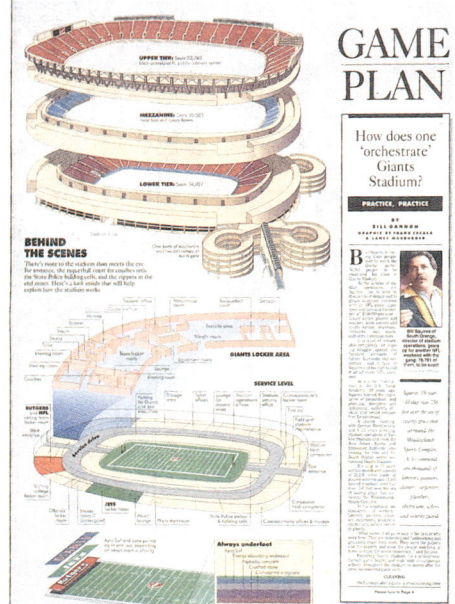

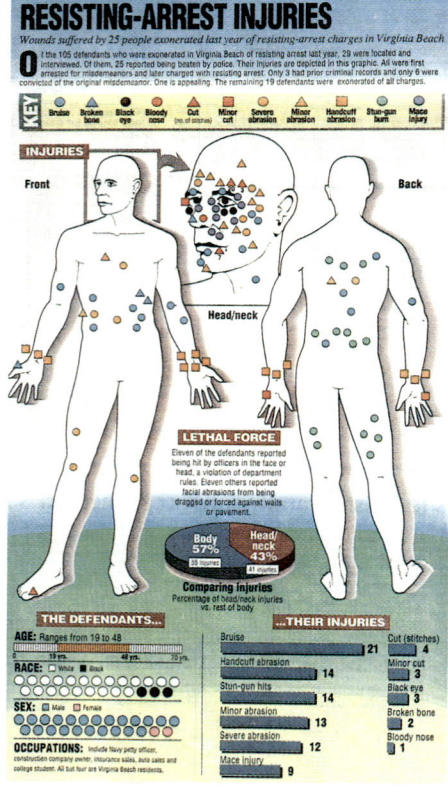

The Star-Ledger
Newark, NJ

Frank Cecala, Computer Artist; Lance Marburger, Computer Artist; Lisa Zollinger, Art Director & Designer

The Virginian-Pilot / Ledger-Star
Bill Pitzer, Illustrator & Designer

Syracuse Herald American
Tom Schmitt, Illustrator, Designer & Researcher

Portfolio

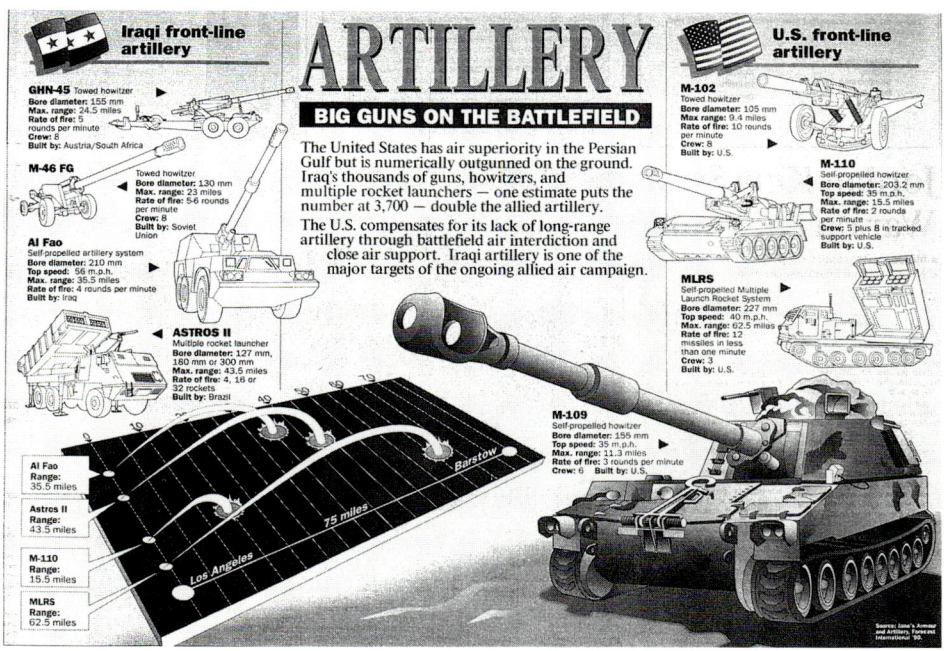

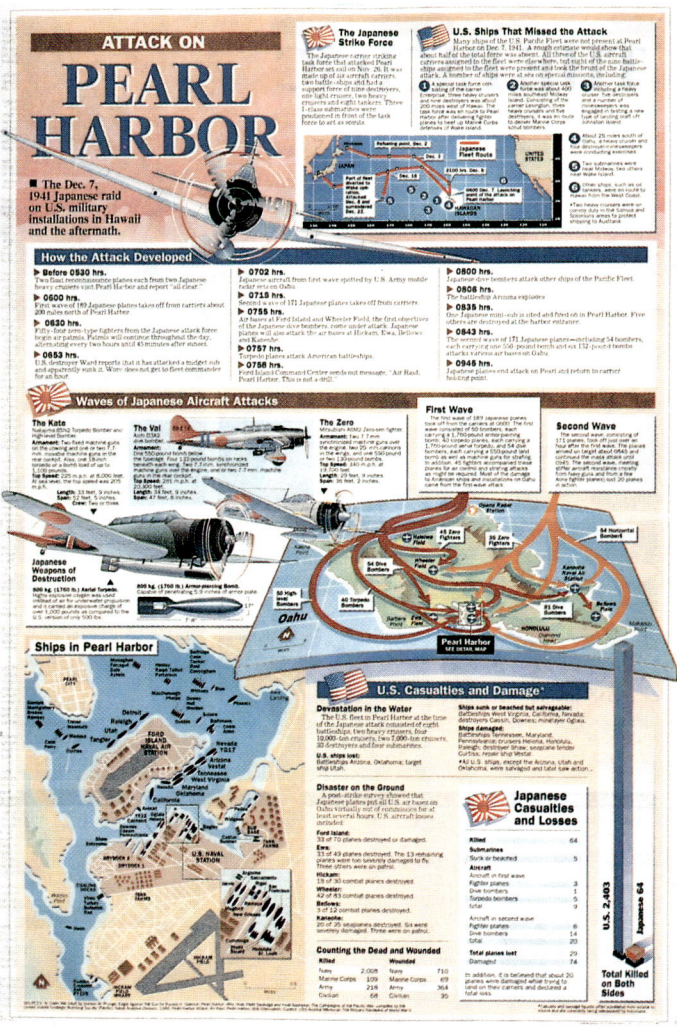

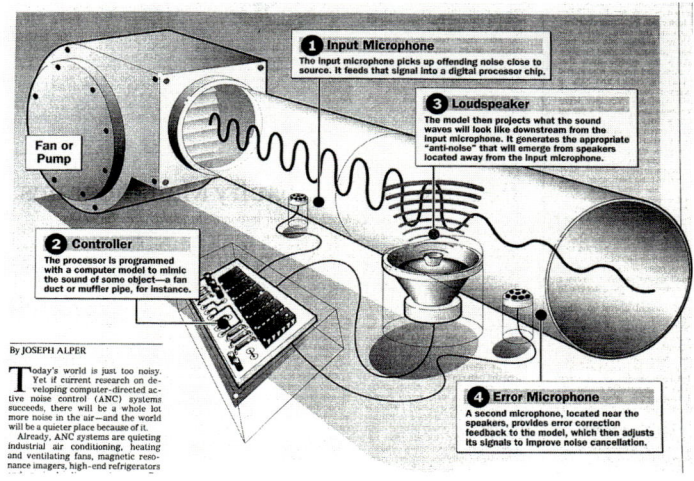

SILVER

Los Angeles Times

Bill Dunn, Art Director; Anders Ramberg, Designer and Illustrator

INFORMATIONAL GRAPHICS Portfolio

SILVER
The Oregonian
Steve Cowden, Artist; Mark Wigginton, Art Director

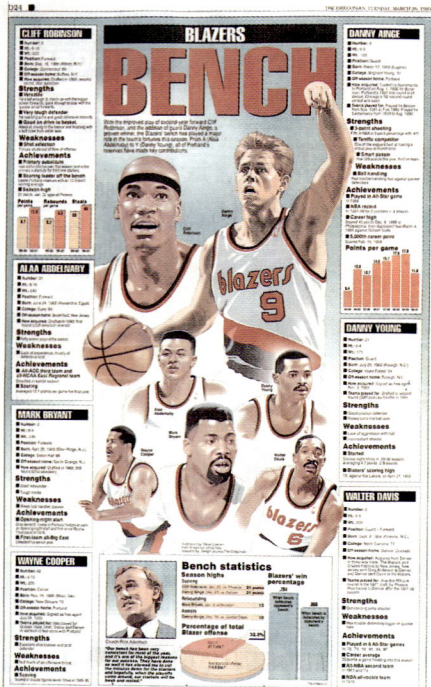

BRONZE
The Dallas Morning News
Clif Bosler, Designer; Ed Kohorst, Art Director

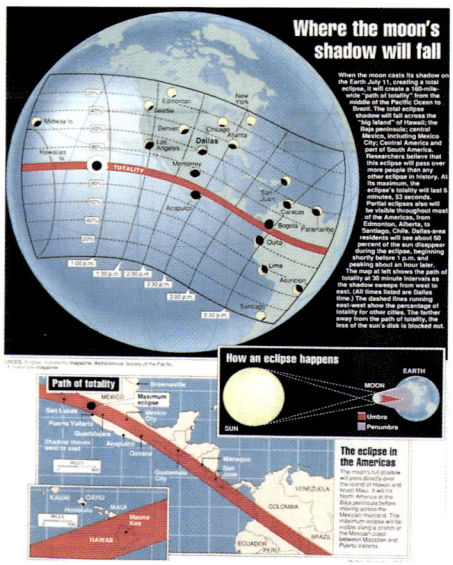

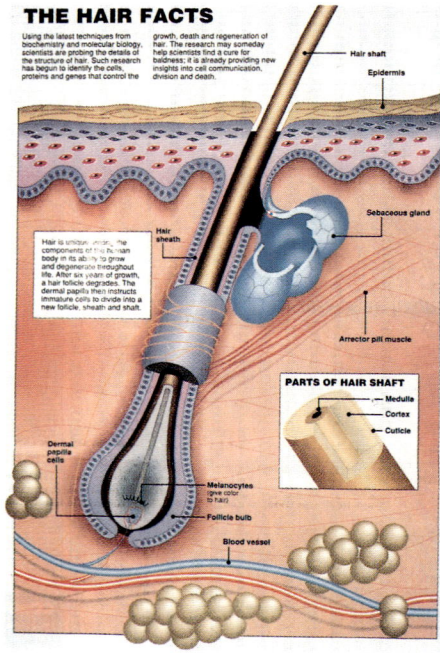

234 THE BEST OF NEWSPAPER DESIGN

The Boston Globe Magazine

Neil C. Pinchin, Info Graphics Designer; Cynthia Daniels, Art Director

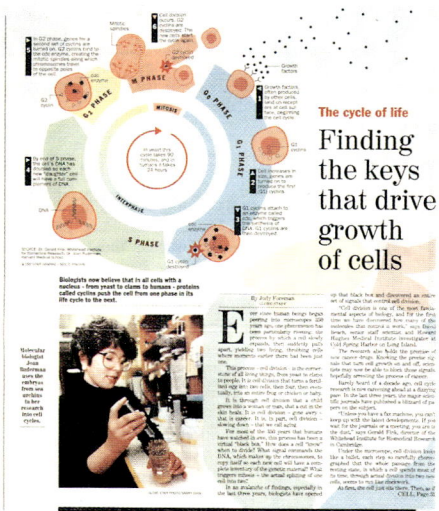

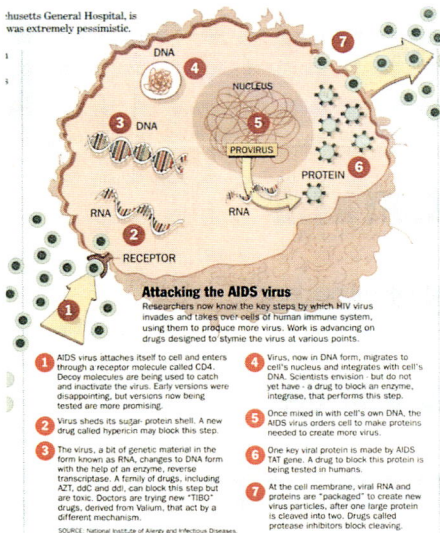

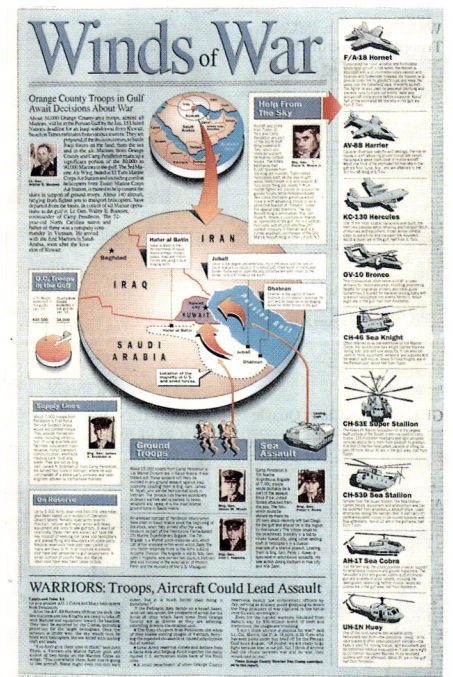

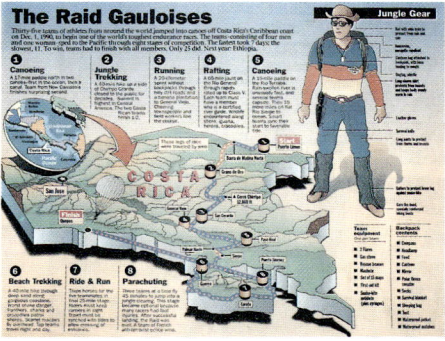

Los Angeles Times / Orange County Edition

David Puckett, Illustrator & Researcher

Los Angeles Times / Orange County Edition

Dennis Lowe, Graphics Artist; Scott Brown, Writer

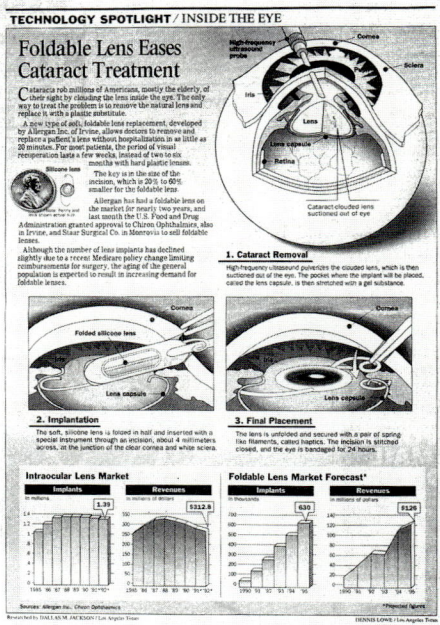

THIRTEENTH EDITION 235

INFORMATIONAL GRAPHICS Portfolio

The Atlanta Journal & Constitution / Chicago Tribune

Paige Braddock, Illustrator & Researcher; Julie Sheer, Researcher; Stephen Cvengros, Art Director, Chicago Tribune; Nancy I.Z. Reese, Graphics Editor; Tony Deferia, Art The Director Atlanta Journal-Constitution

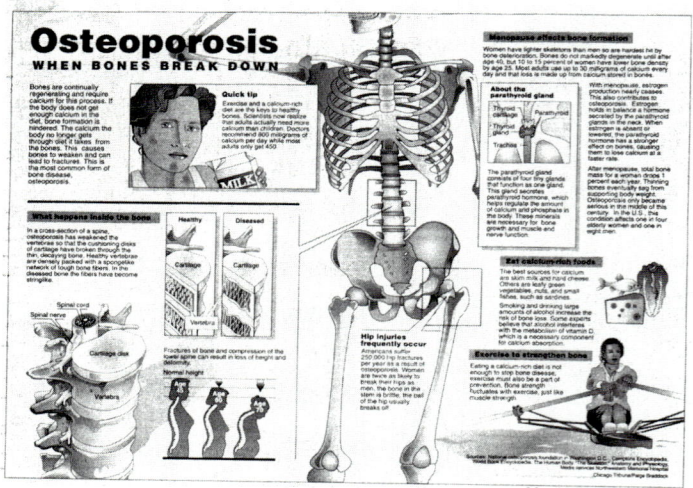

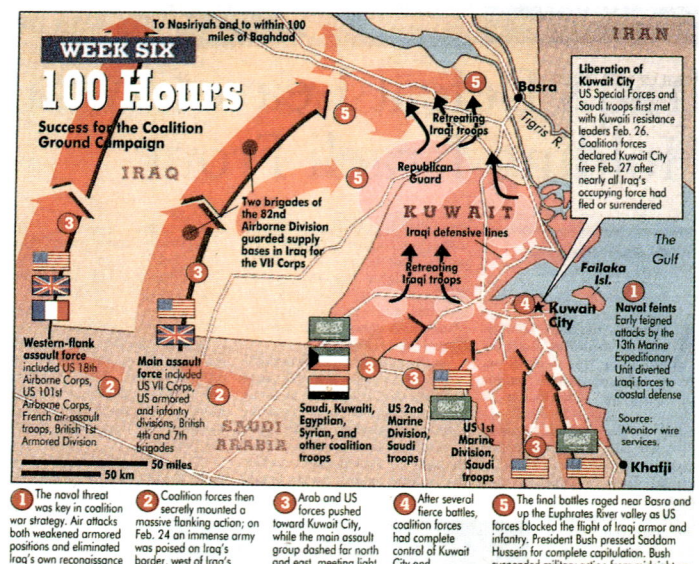

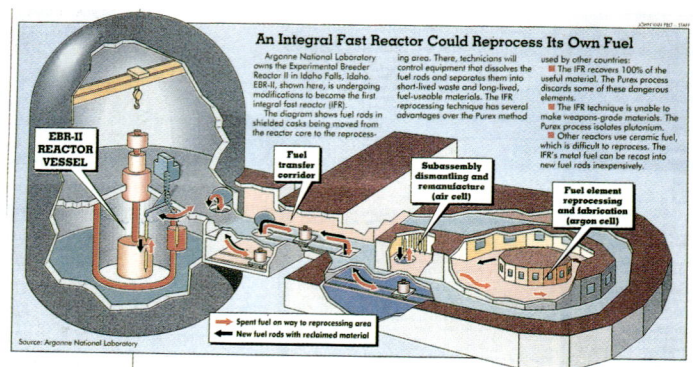

The Christian Science Monitor
Boston, MA

John Van Pelt, Graphics Artist

Star Tribune
Minneapolis, MN

Raymond J. Grumney, Illustrator; Constance Nelson, Reporter; Tim Campbell, News Graphics Editor

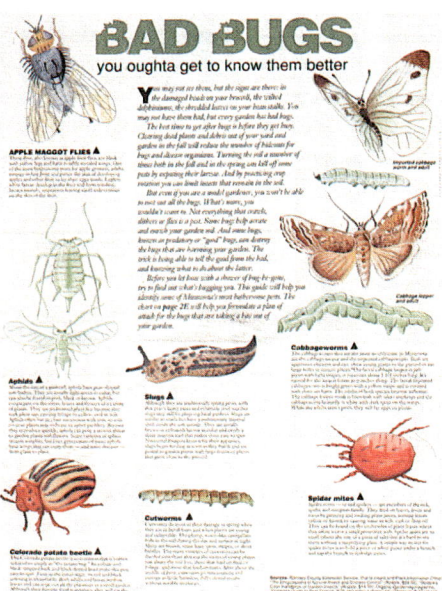

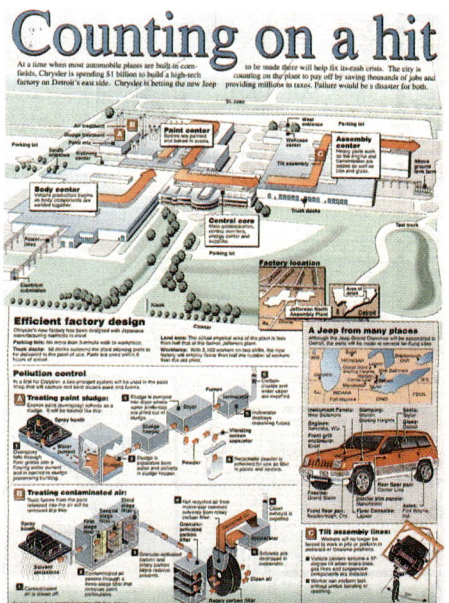

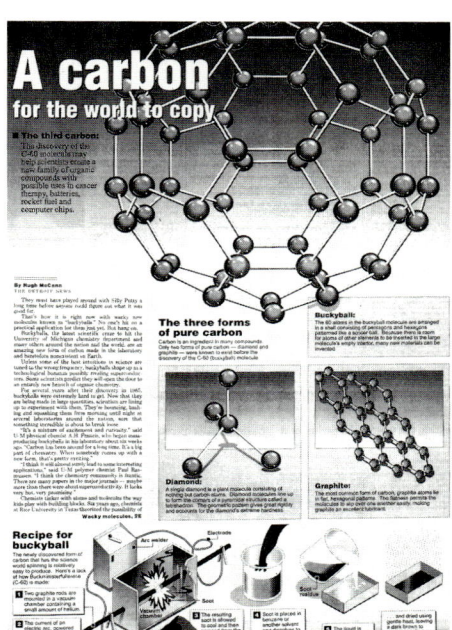

The Detroit News

Sidney Jablonski, Artist

The Orange County Register
Santa Ana, CA

Paul Carbo, Artist

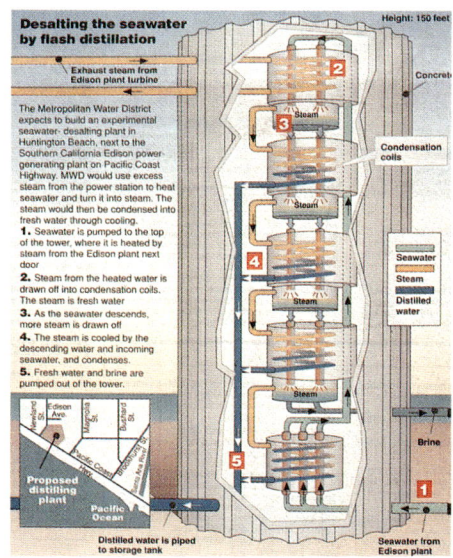

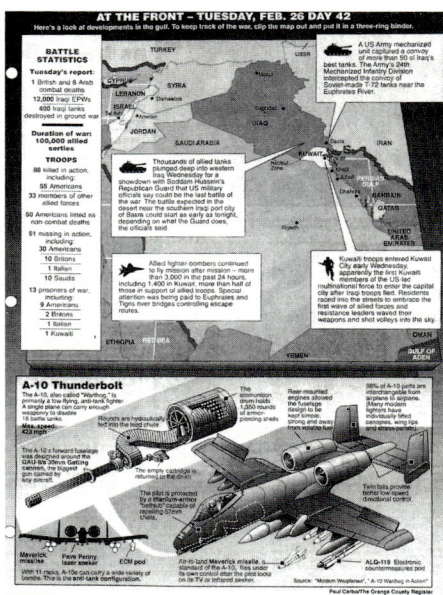

INFORMATIONAL GRAPHICS Portfolio

El Mundo
Madrid, Spain

Mario Tascon, Infographics Director; Jeff Goertzen, Art Consultant; Ulises Culebro, Illustrator; Samuel Velasco, Illustrator; Gorka Sampedro, Illustrator; Modesto Carrasco, Illustrator; Rodrigo Martinez, Researcher

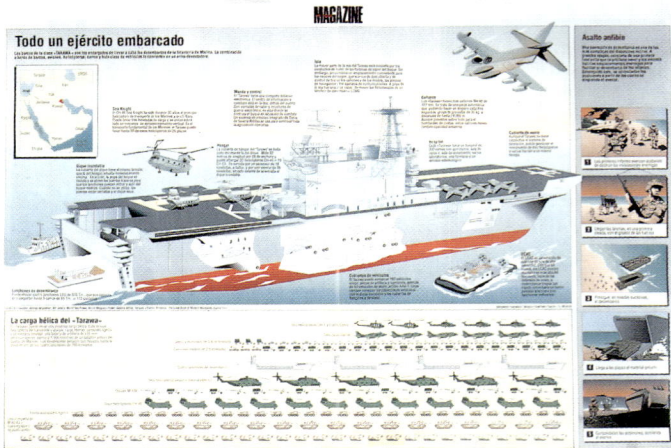

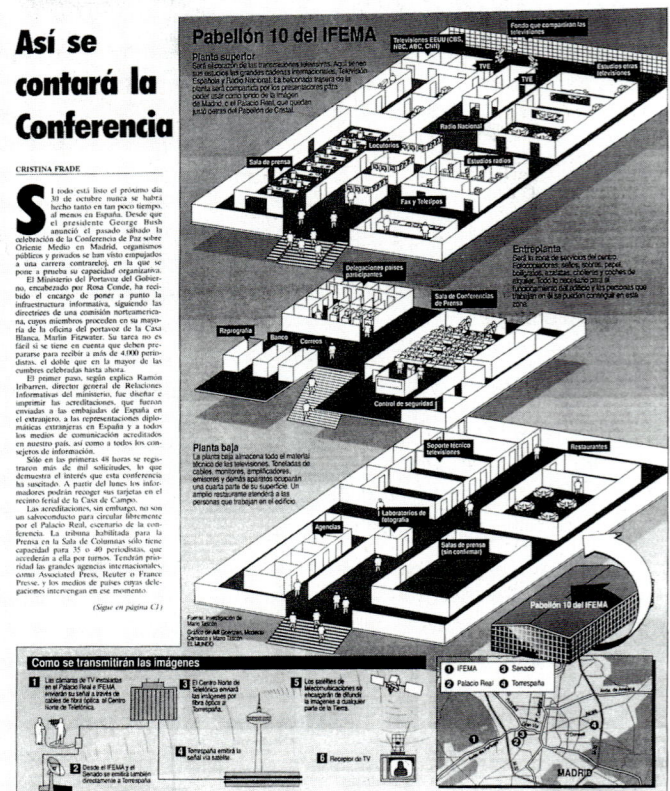

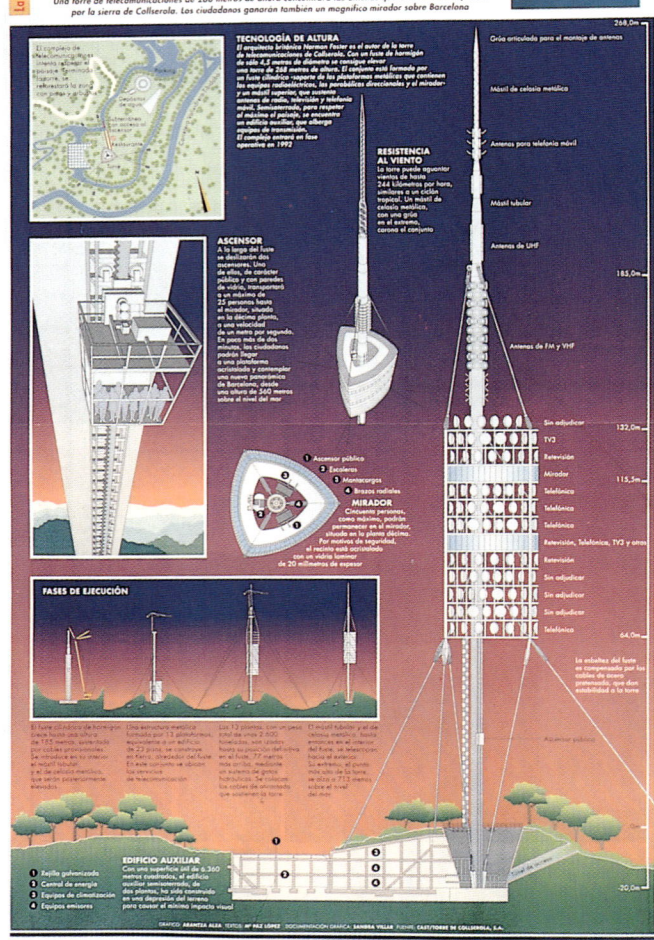

La Vanguardia
Barcelona, Spain

Carlos Perez de Rozas, Art Director; Rosa Mundet, Assistant Art Director; Angels Soler, Infographics Designer; Jordi Bague, Infographics Designer; Rafael Salas, Infographics Designer; Josep Ramos, Infographics Designer; Sandra Villar, Infographics Designer; Rosa Maria Anechina, Infographics Designer; Jordi Paris, Senior Infographics Designer; Enric Guell, Infographics Designer

San Francisco Examiner

Chris Morris, Artist; Kelly Frankeny, Graphics Editor

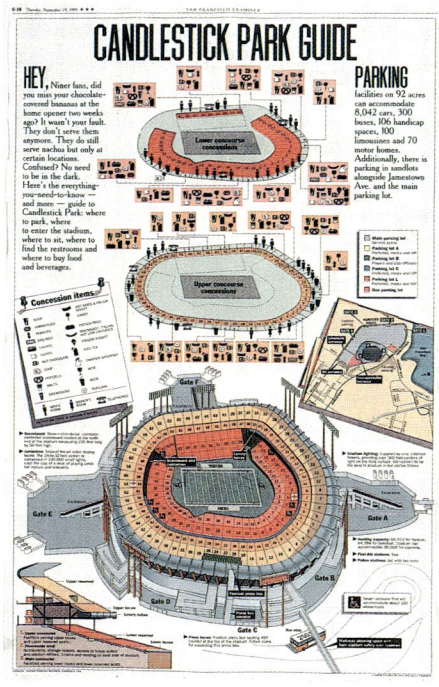

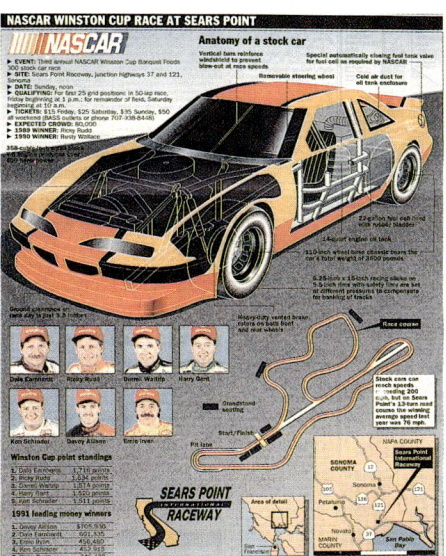

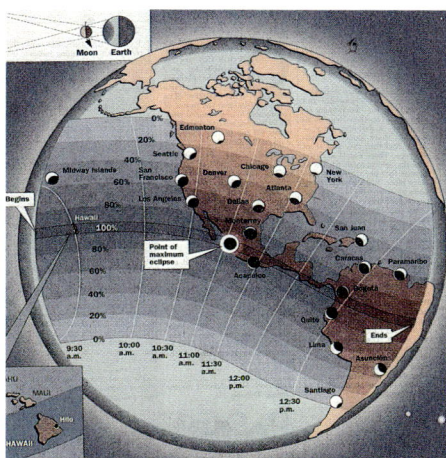

San Francisco Examiner

Joe Shoulak, Artist; Kelly Frankeny, Graphics Editor

The Seattle Times

Rob Kemp, Graphics Artist

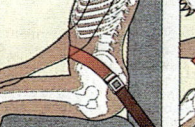
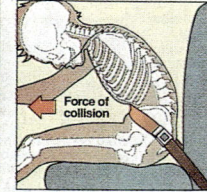
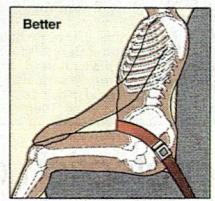
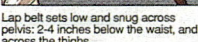
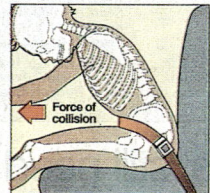
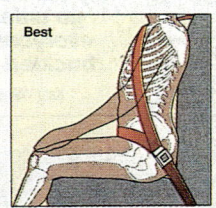
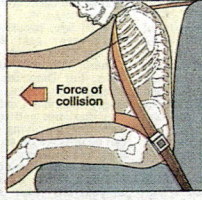

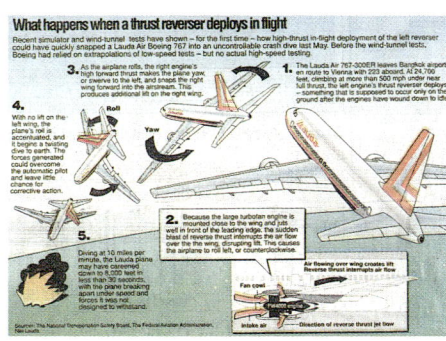

THIRTEENTH EDITION 239

INFORMATIONAL GRAPHICS Portfolio

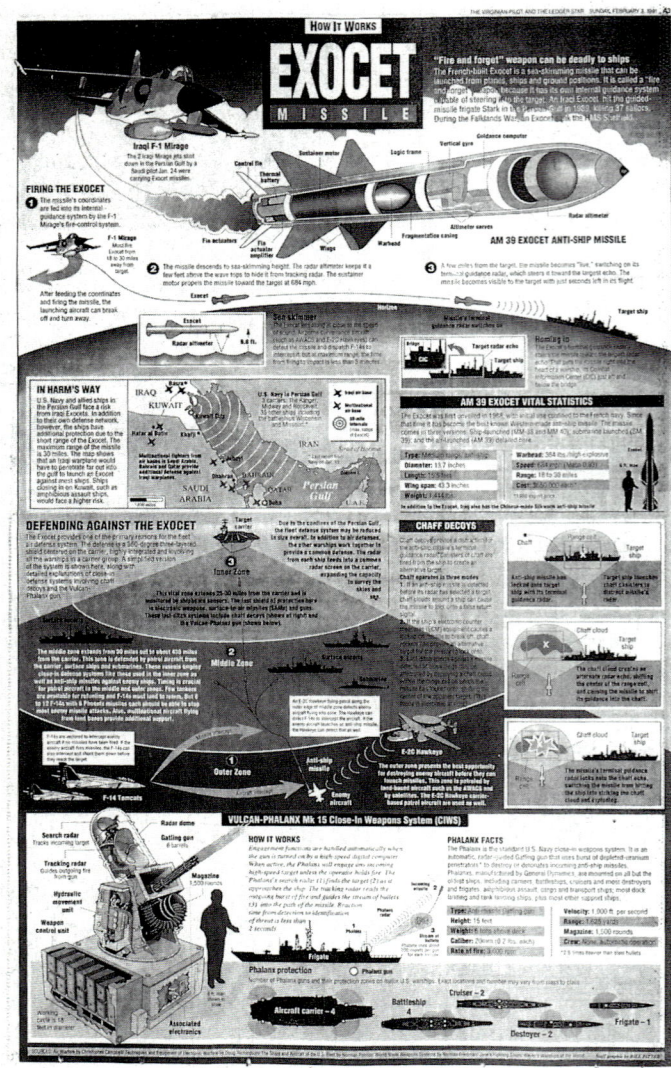

The Virginian-Pilot / Ledger-Star
Norfolk, VA

Bill Pitzer, Illustrator & Designer

The Virginian-Pilot / Ledger-Star

Janet Shaughnessy, Staff Artist

240   THE BEST OF NEWSPAPER DESIGN

CHAPTER ELEVEN

Miscellaneous

MISCELLANEOUS Overall • Decorative Typography

The Wall Street Journal Reports

Greg Leeds, Design Director & Designer; Joe Dizney, Art Director & Designer

The Wall Street Journal Reports

Greg Leeds, Design Director & Designer; Joe Dizney, Art Director & Designer

SILVER

The Wall Street Journal Reports

Greg Leeds, Design Director and Designer; Joe Dizney, Art Director & Designer

The Wall Street Journal Reports

Greg Leeds, Art Director & Designer; Dennis Ortiz Lopez, Typographer

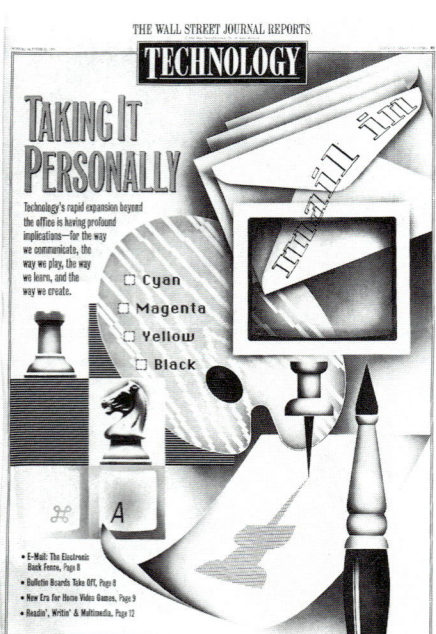

(DECORATIVE TYPOGRAPHY)

The Wall Street Journal Reports

Greg Leeds, Art Director & Designer; Lloyd Miller, Illustrator

The Wall Street Journal Reports

Joe Dizney, Art Director & Designer; Alison Seiffer, Illustrator

242 THE BEST OF NEWSPAPER DESIGN

Decorative Typography

GOLD
The Wall Street Journal Reports
Greg Leeds, Design Director and Designer; Wendy Wray, Illustrator

MISCELLANEOUS Decorative Typography • Overall Redesign

The Anchorage Times
Susan Berry, Illustrator & Designer; Lee Waigand, AME Graphics/Design

The Dallas Morning News
Bob Shema, Designer

BEFORE

AFTER

(OVERALL REDESIGN)

BRONZE

Akron Beacon Journal
Susan Mango Curtis, Art Director & Designer; Randy Miller, Consultant

The Philadelphia Inquirer Magazine
Bert Fox, Art Director & Photo Editor; Jessica Helfand, Design Director & Designer; Greg Gorman, Photographer; Paula Court, Photographer

244 THE BEST OF NEWSPAPER DESIGN

Overall Redesign

The Des Moines Register

Mario Garcia, Designer; Lyle Boone, AME Graphics

Daily Press
Newport News, VA
Staff

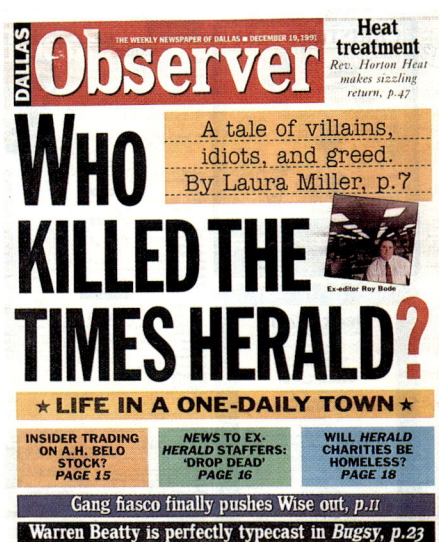

Dallas Observer
Dan Zedek, Art Director

THIRTEENTH EDITION 245

MISCELLANEOUS Overall Redesign

BEFORE

AFTER

Reno Gazette-Journal
Staff

Financial Times of Canada
Toronto, ON

Barbara Hyland, Publisher; Steve Lawrence, Editor; Gary Hall, Art Director; Norman Eyolfson, Illustrator; Tony Sutton, Design Consultant

The Globe and Mail / Montreal Magazine

Susan Casey, Creative Director; Paul Sullivan, Editorial Director; Jim Cormier, Editor

Section Redesign

Akron Beacon Journal
Susan Mango Curtis, Art Director & Designer; Randy Miller, Consultant

Akron Beacon Journal
Susan Mango Curtis, Art Director & Designer; Randy Miller, Consultant

Reno Gazette-Journal
Staff

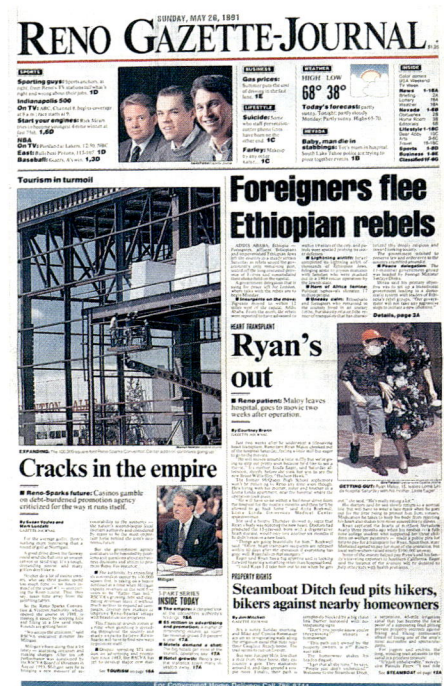

The Des Moines Register
Mario Garcia, Designer; Lyle Boone, AME Graphics

The New York Times
Tom Bodkin, Art Director & Design Director; Fred Norgaard, Designer; Margaret O'Connor, Designer; Sam Reep, Designer; Seth Feaster, Graphics Editor; Rich Meislin, Graphics Editor; Donald Parsons, Graphics Editor; Joe Ward, Graphics Editor

BRONZE

The New York Times
Tom Bodkin, Design Director & Art Director; Sam Reep, Designer; Margaret O'Connor, Designer; Rich Meislin, Graphics Editor; Anne Cronin, Graphics Editor

THIRTEENTH EDITION 247

MISCELLANEOUS Section Redesign

The Detroit News

Dierck Casselman, AME Graphics/Design; Robert Graham, Graphics Art Director; Felix Grabowski, Graphics Director; Mark Lett, AME/National & Business; Ray Jeskey, Deputy Business Editor; Sidney Jablonski, Artist; Mary Harris, Copy Editor

BRONZE
Detroit Free Press

Steve Anderson, Designer; Deborah Withey, Design Director & Designer

BRONZE
The Detroit News

Dierck Casselman, AME Graphics/Design; Felix Grabowski, Graphics Director; Mark Lett, Editor; Steve Kaskovich, Editor; Patrick Sedlar, Artist; Mary Harris, Copy Editor

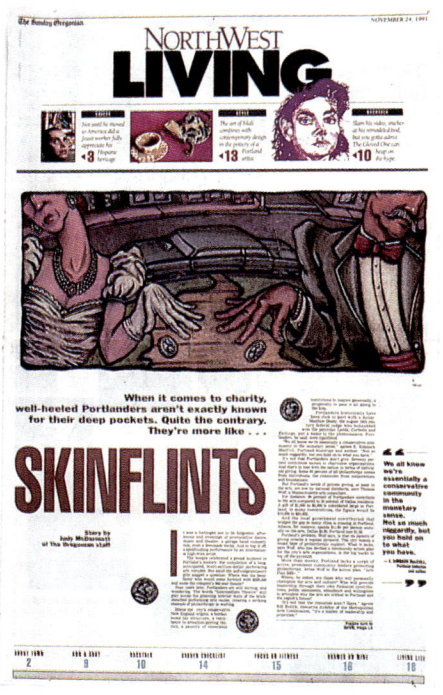

BRONZE
The Oregonian

Tim Harrower, Designer; Michelle Wise, Designer; Mark Wigginton, Art Director

Dayton Daily News

Ted Pitts, Designer; John Thomson, AME Graphics; Randy Palmer, Illustrator; Scott Bateman, Editor

BRONZE
The Eagle-Tribune
Lawrence, MA

Alan Jacobson, Designer; Bill Pitzer, Artist

248 THE BEST OF NEWSPAPER DESIGN

Section • Page Redsigns

The Greensboro News & Record

Alan Jacobson, Designer; Tim Rickard, Designer; Margaret Baxter, Designer

The Post and Courier
Charleston, SC

Staff

San Jose Mercury News

Bryan Monroe, Design Director; Sam Hundley, Designer; Holly Hayes, Section Editor; Robin Doussard, Entertainment Editor

The Post-Standard
Syracuse, NY

Michael A. Braia, Designer

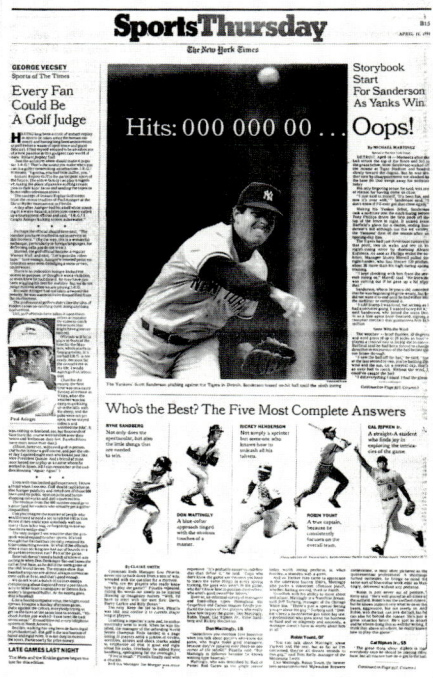

(PAGE REDESIGN)

The New York Times

Tom Bodkin, Design Director & Art Director; Margaret O'Connor, Designer; Sam Reep, Designer

BRONZE

The New York Times

Tom Bodkin, Design Director & Art Director; Margaret O'Connor, Designer; Sam Reep, Designer; Rich Meislin, Graphics Editor; Anne Cronin, Graphics Editor

THIRTEENTH EDITION 249

MISCELLANEOUS Page Redesign

BEFORE

SILVER
Malibu Surfside News
Anne Soble, Redesign Director; Brian D. Fox, Design Consultant; Cindy Luck, Design Consultant

AFTER

Pittsburgh Post-Gazette
Anita Dufalla, Art Director & Designer; Joe Zeff, Designer; Christopher Pett-Ridge, AME

Pittsburgh Post-Gazette
Joe Zeff, Designer; Anita Dufalla, Art Director; Christopher Pett-Ridge, AME

BRONZE
Pittsburgh Post-Gazette
Anita Dufalla, Art Director & Designer; Joe Zeff, Designer; Christopher Pett-Ridge, AME

The Washington Post
Wendy C. Ross, News Editor

BEFORE

SILVER
The Detroit News
Dale Peskin, AME

AFTER

THIRTEENTH EDITION 251

MISCELLANEOUS   Page Redesign • Miscellaneous

BRONZE
The Miami Herald
Ana Lense Larrauri, Designer; Jim Watters, Business Monday Editor; Rex Seline, Business Section Editor; Randy Stano, Director of Editorial Art & Design

Philadelphia Gay News
John Mandes, Editor; Tim Landt, Associate Editor/Graphics; Gary L. Day, Associate Editor/Features

Philadelphia Gay News
John Mandes, Editor; Tim Landt, Associate Editor/Graphics; Gary L. Day, Associate Editor/Features

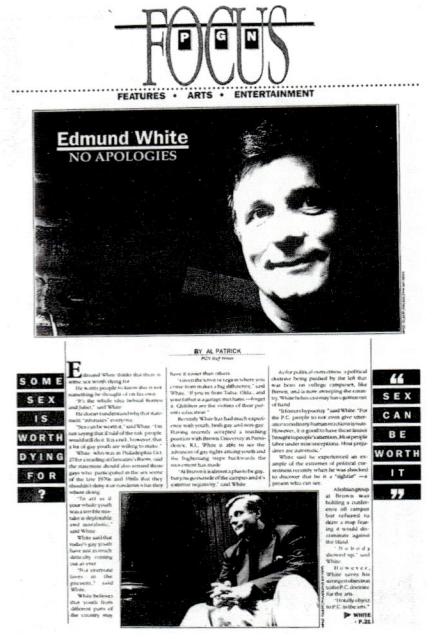

(MISCELLANEOUS)
The Globe and Mail
Toronto, ON, Canada

Tony Sutton, Art Director, Designer & Editor; Brian Gable, Illustrator; Tony Jenkins, Illustrator; Alex Groen, Illustrator

Detroit Free Press
Jef Capaldi, Designer; Deborah Withey, Design Director

Akron Beacon Journal
Susan Mango Curtis, Art Director & Designer; Randy Miller, Consultant; Terence Oliver, Illustrator & Designer

Index of Winners

By Name

A • B

Aguillard, Beth, 98
Ahmad-Taylor, Ty, 223
Albers, Wes, 140, 228
Allen, Jim, 184
Allen, Peter, 213
Allen, Terry, 121, 163
Allsopp, Lucy, 111
Aloisio, Richard, 89
Alstetter, Rob, 44
Alvarez, Lamberto, 103
Andersen, Lars, 199
Anderson, Cathy, 22, 44, 50, 147
Anderson, Greg, 229
Anderson, Jenny, 75
Anderson, Kathy, 98
Anderson, Paula, 199
Anderson, Steve, 35, 91, 140, 157, 196, 248
Anderson, Wes, 191
Anechina, Rosa Maria, 74, 238
Arisman, Marshall, 125, 193
Asmussen, Don, 161
Astor, Josef, 127, 172
Atseff, Tim, 27, 41-42, 64-65, 151

Babb, G.W., 43
Bachleda, Florian, 160, 191
Badovich, Theresa, 151
Bague, Jordi, 74, 238
Baker, Bill, 59
Baker, Richard, 122, 126, 164, 169, 201-202
Bakinowski, Carol, 48
Balogh, Dennis, 208
Bandy, Lee Ann, 81, 96
Barbante, Ben, 173
Barbey, Jacques, 102
Bard, Rich, 86
Barick, Marty, 161
Barrera, Ralph, 43
Barrick, Marty, 159
Bartalos, Michael, 125, 193
Bartholomay, Lucy, 77, 121, 123, 126, 128, 163
Baseman, Gary, 159
Bateman, Scott, 248
Baumann, J. Bruce, 200
Bausmith, Wes, 87, 96, 157, 170, 175, 197, 207
Baxter, Margaret, 249
Becker, Lesley, 177, 186
Belil, Anna, 81
Bell, Julia Barry, 38
Benavidas, Antonio, 112
Benge, George, 33
Bengelsdorf, Peter, 67
Berg/Mira, Micke, 171
Berke, George, 24, 42
Bernardino, Minnie, 96
Berry, Susan, 191, 244
Berthet, Jacqueline, 106
Beyette, Beverly, 135
Bialer, Steven, 144
Bing, Christopher, 143, 166
Biondo, Michael, 94
Birchman, Fred, 206
Bisher, Nanette, 23, 38-39, 66-67, 139
Blackwell, Patrick, 104, 140
Blake, Marty, 123, 163
Blanding, John, 97
Bleck, Cathie, 104, 141
Blitt, Barry, 118
Boake, Kathy, 117
Bock, Betsy, 48
Bodkin, Tom, 6, 29, 34, 37, 48, 74, 78, 82, 84, 89, 92-93, 104, 109, 120, 124-125, 127, 140-141, 158, 169, 172-173, 192-193, 206, 213, 223, 247, 249
Boone, Lyle, 245, 247
Borgert, Tim, 23
Bosler, Clif, 226, 234
Bott, Ian, 212
Boyles, Dee, 94, 96, 194
Braddock, Paige, 219, 226, 236
Bradford, Christy, 54
Bradsher, Keith, 74
Braia, Michael A., 230, 249
Brainerd, Brian, 134
Brandt, Bob, 24, 67
Braulio Martinez, Raul, 99
Breite, Thea, 26, 119, 148, 169-170, 175
Brennan-Hall, Kate, 98
Brewer, Linda, 93
Brodkin, Tom, 192
Brodner, Steve, 160
Brokema, Tim, 144
Brophy, Peter M., 34
Brown, Laura Varon, 46, 58-59, 220
Brown, Mike, 50, 54-55
Brown, Nelson, 26
Brown, Scott, 61-62, 235
Brownlee, Rick, 140, 228
Brubaker, Susan, 199
Bruce, Don, 37
Brugh, Michael, 231
Bryant, Michael, 172
Buchan, Barbara, 111
Buchanan, Todd, 78, 169
Buckley, Chris, 105
Burke, Philip, 91, 93
Burke, Tim, 207
Burlingame, Burl, 227
Burns, Charles, 120
Burrows, Alex, 26, 71, 138
Burzynski, Sue, 22
Byrne, Kevin, 22, 41, 48, 66-67
Bzdek, Vince, 134

C • D

Caderot, Carmelo, 38, 43-44, 112-113, 119, 140, 188, 197, 205
Caglage, Evans, 100-101, 156, 171
Callanan, Brian, 142
Camp, Marla, 56, 221
Campbell, Mike, 25, 135
Campbell, Tim, 237
Canfield, Ken, 69
Capaldi, Jef, 252
Caparros, Monica, 81
Carannante, Greg, 101
Carbo, Paul, 39, 237
Cardon, Michelle, 139
Carey, Art, 177
Carlile, Amy, 102
Carrasco, Modesto, 44, 213, 238
Carroll, Tim, 97
Carter, Chuck, 184
Case, Fred, 231
Casey, Robert, 168
Casey, Susan, 116-118, 126, 128, 165, 246
Casselman, Dierck, 22, 41, 44, 50, 54-56, 133, 214, 227-228, 248
Cataffo, Linda, 71
Cavaretta, Joe, 170
Ceballos, John, 119
Cecala, Frank, 232
Champagne, Tony O., 37, 207
Charlton, Aldona, 97, 104
Chenoweth, Robin, 103
Choplin, Santa, 119
Christopher, Henry, 22, 42, 57
Chun, Jacie, 229
Chung, Julien, 200
Ciardiello, Joe, 148
Cioffi, Ron, 173
Clark, Patterson, 86, 199
Clark, Tim, 98
Cline, Bo Hok, 70
Cochran, Mick, 46, 119
Coddington, Ron, 75
Coleman, Joe, 102
Coleman, Michael, 133
Compton, Paul, 150
Comte, Michel, 127, 172
Condor, Bob, 144
Cone, William, 75
Connor, Olga, 95, 198
Cook, Cary, 212
Copeland, Dennis, 140
Corbera, Joan, 81, 131
Cormier, Jim, 246
Corn, Brian, 46
Corr, John, 176
Cote, Genevieve, 200
Cotter, Dan, 23, 33
Court, Paula, 244
Cousins, Patricia, 108
Cowden, Steve, 73, 132, 229, 234
Cowles, David H., 86, 91
Cox, Christine, 70
Cox, Gerald, 71
Cox, Tracy, 166
Craven, Eric, 33
Cronin, Anne, 29, 213, 247, 249
Cronin, Brian, 114, 125-126, 193, 201
Crowe, Tracy, 93, 96
Culebro, Ulises, 44, 75, 112, 119, 188, 197, 205, 213, 238
Curley, John, 31
Curtis, Susan Mango, 244, 247, 252
Cutler, David, 96, 148
Cvengros, Stephen, 39, 135, 219, 226, 236

Daby, William K., 26
Dalgleish, Pam, 176
Dandy, Steve, 17
Daniels, Cynthia, 108-109, 154, 225, 235
Darti, Cristina, 123
Davidson, John, 48
Davis, Karen, 103, 136
Davis, Mike, 71
Day, Gary L., 252
De Feria, Tony, 43, 219, 225
De Michiell, Robert, 143
de Miguel, Manuel, 38, 43-44, 112-113, 140
Deane, Donna, 96
Decker, John, 71
Deferia, Tony, 236
DeMaio, Don, 229
DeMarzo, Bob, 206
Demi-Smith, David, 150
Dempsey, Laura, 23
Dengler, John L., 33
Denk, James, 32, 35
DeRobertis, Vic, 152
deVinci, Leonardo, 163
Diaz, Al, 140
Diaz, J. Albert, 135
Diaz de Villegas, Jr., Jose L, 87, 194
Diaz de Villegas, Sr., Jose L., 87, 191
Dickerson, Brian, 227
Dixon, Bob, 17
Dizney, Joe, 114, 137-139, 143, 242
Doe, Kelly, 122, 201-202
Dolan, Duffy, 225
Dolan, Mark, 178
Dolphens, Tom, 198
Donovan, Liz, 140
Douglas, Vasin, 219
Doussard, Robin, 249
Dow, Barbara, 192
Downs, Patrick, 135
Drawson, Blair, 125-126, 193
Drescher, Henrik, 121, 125, 192-193
Drummond, Deborah, 166
Drury, Christian Potter, 99
Ducassi, Nuri, 95, 111, 191, 198-199, 207
Duckett, Francois, 225
Dufalla, Anita, 72, 91, 250-251
Duke, William, 89
Dunlap-Shohl, Pamela, 176
Dunn, Bill, 61, 63, 233
Dykes, Steve, 96
Dzwonkowski, Ron, 220

E • F

Ealy, Charles, 48
Eanes, Lori, 166
Edge, Lara, 135
Edwards, Craig, 151
Edwards, Michael, 96
Eidem, Stina, 111
Eisenbart, Rene, 73
Eisert, Sandra, 170
Ekstrom-Frisk, Eleonor, 81
Ellis, Donna, 139
Elsworth, Peter C. T., 223
Enos, Randall, 148, 161
Ericson, Celeste, 70
Ets-Hokin, Joshua, 88
Evans, Mark, 110
Ewing, John, 161
Eyolfson, Norman, 246

Fabris, John, 22-23, 38-39, 41, 48, 66-67, 139
Farnham, Rebecca, 113
Farrell, Patrick, 182
Faust, Scott, 56
Feaster, Seth, 247
Fecht, Michele, 56, 214, 221, 227-228
Fedele, Gene, 206
Feinberg, Ron, 43
Ferguson, James, 197
Fernandez, Raul, 191, 199
Fiedler, James, 16, 22, 42, 57, 150
Fila, Bob, 102
Finberg, Howard I., 102
Finkel Rebach, Nannette, 105, 159
Finley, Bernadette, 41, 67
Fisher, Dan, 41, 147
Flanders, Phill, 199
Flesher, Vivian, 201
Foelich, Janet, 78
Fogel, Robin, 231
Foley, Don, 224
Forst, Don, 30
Fox, Bert, 78, 123, 169, 172, 176-177, 180, 184, 186, 190, 200, 206, 244
Fox, Brian D., 250
Frail, T. A., 78, 177, 184, 186
Frankeny, Kelly, 40, 46-47, 75, 108, 211, 216, 230, 239
Freistedt, Mark, 43
French, Thomas, 133
Froelich, Janet, 6, 120, 124-125, 127, 169, 172-173, 192-193
Fullwiler, Nancy, 82
Furno, Dick, 148

G • H

Gable, Brian, 252
Gabor, Tim, 200
Gajdel, Edward, 36, 128
Gallagher, John, 227
Garcia, Bert, 199
Garcia, Mario, 245, 247
Garrison, Ron, 184
Gavrilovich, Peter, 46
Gay, Jerry, 19, 114
Gay, Stephanie, 34
Gebert, Warren, 196
Gerjevic, Frank, 25
Germain, Bernadette, 105, 113
Ghiglione, Kevin N., 128
Gili, Oberto, 122
Glaser, Marilyn, 103
Goecke, John, 22, 26, 46, 58, 220
Goertzen, Jeff, 44, 75, 213, 222, 238
Goldberg, Nancy Lynn, 86
Goldsmith, Gary, 133
Gomez, Ivonne, 191
Gonzales, Paul, 63
Gonzalez, Miguel, 119, 123, 171, 182
Goode, Jeff, 159
Gordon, Dennis, 35, 38
Gordon, Mike, 43, 219, 225
Gorman, Greg, 244
Gosfield, Josh, 127
Grabowski, Felix, 23, 36, 50, 54-56, 84, 214, 248
Graham, Kevin, 26
Graham, Robert, 41, 54-56, 133, 214, 228, 248
Gralish, Tom, 78, 169, 176-177, 180, 184, 186
Grant, Bill, 207
Grau, Ferran, 81, 131
Gray, Joe, 22, 43-44, 50, 54-55, 147
Greeman, Melanie Stetson, 130
Green, John, 103
Green, Michael, 33
Green, Phil, 212, 218
Green, Rick, 37
Greenfield-Sanders, Timothy, 120
Gregory, Tom, 24, 42
Gressette, Felicia, 99
Grimes, Laura, 73
Grin, Gayle, 101
Grippi, Vince, 26, 168, 184
Griswold, Doug, 75
Gritz, Ligaya, 41, 147
Groecke, John, 58
Groen, Alex, 252
Groesch, Greg, 22, 42, 57
Grossfeld, Stan, 77
Grossman, Ron, 88, 144
Grumney, Raymond J., 237
Gude, Karl, 221, 229
Guell, Enric, 238
Guip, Amy, 125, 192-193
Gulait, Bert, 105
Gurman, David, 142
Gustafson, Mats, 101
Guzy, Carol, 161

Ha, Ving, 198
Habib, Dan, 170, 178
Haffey, Sean M., 40, 230
Hales, Linda, 106
Halfand, Jessica, 177
Hall, Gary, 36, 246
Hall, Michael, 62, 210
Hallinen, Bob, 25
Hamill, Blair, 134
Hand, Kevin, 222, 227
Hanley, Brian, 44
Hanus, Nancy, 22, 41, 50, 54-55, 133, 147
Harbison, Robert, 14, 134
Hardman, Dave, 215
Harris, Greg, 229
Harris, Mary, 23, 248
Harris, Moses, 46, 220
Harris, Nancy, 192

THIRTEENTH EDITION 253

Harrower, Tim, 248
Hartig, Karl, 20
Hartley, Andrew, 121, 164, 173, 191, 196, 201, 227
Hathaway, Emily, 80, 158
Havens, James, 194
Hax, Carolyn, 72
Hayes, Holly, 249
Hayes, Mitchell J., 93, 166
Haynes, David, 166
Helfand, Jessica, 78, 123, 169, 172, 176-177, 180, 184, 186, 190, 200, 206, 244
Heller, Steven, 82
Henderson, Felecia, 43
Henderson, Greg, 32
Hennessy, Phil, 102
Henriquez, Hiram, 140, 199
Henry, Mary, 227
Henry, Mike S., 42
Henry, Sharon, 200
Hernandez, Roberto, 38
Herold, June, 23
Herzberg, Tom, 148
Herzog, Kristin, 23, 35
Hiestand, Scott, 43
Hightower, Aaron, 23, 54, 56, 214-215, 227-228
Hill, Erik, 135
Hinckley, Jeff, 103
Hindley, Richard, 71
Hirsch, Maggie, 75
Hockstein, Steve, 71
Hoey, Peter, 86
Hoffman, Cynthia, 86, 91, 156
Hoffmann, Duane, 231
Hogan, Bill, 88, 102, 144
Holder, Dan, 48
Holt, Dean, 71
Holter, Rick, 104, 113, 133
Homan, Mike, 225
Hoover, Sandra, 19
Horn, Shirley, 134
Hotz, Lee, 225
Houde, Christine, 165
Huff, Don, 48
Humenik, John, 151
Hundley, Sam, 40, 191, 200, 208, 249
Huntemann, Susan, 119, 169, 174-175
Hunter, Alexander, 105
Huntington, Stewart, 46-47, 216
Hyland, Barbara, 36, 246
Hyland, John, 48

I · J

Iken, Hank, 74
Innerst, Stacy, 200
Innes, Claire, 81, 96, 103, 139, 196
Irby, Ken, 24
Ivleva, Victoria, 173

Jablonski, Sidney, 54-55, 214, 221, 227-228, 237, 248
Jackson, Dallas, 221
Jacobson, Alan, 18, 26, 248-249
Jaegerman, Megan, 74, 109, 213
Jantze, Michael, 42, 74, 216

Jareaux, Robin, 89
Jean-Louis, Galie, 84, 89, 94-95, 162, 194
Jenkins, Tony, 252
Jennings, Jim, 71, 184, 199
Jensen, Gregers, 84
Jeskey, Ray, 248
Johanson, Ulf, 81
Johansson, Karin, 81
Johnson, Joel Peter, 200, 206
Johnson, Kim, 46
Johnson, Lynette, 62
Julian, Sheryl, 97

K · L

Kafentzis, John, 26, 168, 184
Kamajian, Alfred T., 84
Kamidoi, Wayne, 22, 58, 84
Kaplan, John, 91, 178
Karabotsos, George, 117-118, 126, 128, 165
Kascht, John, 4, 57, 80, 90-91, 114, 161, 197
Kashi, Ed, 176
Kaskovich, Steve, 23, 36, 248
Kasper, Robert, 106
Kay, Sandy, 63
Kearsley, Steve, 75, 223, 230
Keating, Michael, 16, 22, 25, 27, 42, 57, 149
Keegan, Micheal, 98
Kelly, Colleen, 81
Kemp, Rob, 70, 231, 239
Kendrick, David, 121
Kent, Nancy, 93
Kerr, Thomas, 123
Kesler, W. D., 90
Kessler, Meda, 99, 105
Kim, Yunghi, 97, 123
King, Bill, 32
King, Fred, 140, 184
King, Kit, 26, 140, 167-168, 181, 184
King, Mike, 219
Kingston, Anne, 36
Kitagaki, Paul, 134
Klein, David G., 113
Knight, Kenneth, 43, 56, 214
Kohl, Joseph, 110
Kohorst, Ed, 103, 136, 144, 226, 234
Kolb, George, 149
Kopecky, Robert, 118
Kordalski, David, 231
Koslo, Patrick, 118
Kover, Becky, 195
Kozlowski, Christopher J., 151
Kramer, Chuck, 224
Kraus, James, 166
Kraus, Orlie, 20
Krefting, Bruce, 230
Kreiter, Suzanne, 170
Kroninger, Stephen, 223
Krummel, Art, 224
Krzczuk, Tony, 80, 158
Kuehn, Karen, 127
Kunz, Anita, 122, 202
Kuper, Peter, 190, 201

Labbe, John, 121, 196
Laciura, Phil, 44
Lafuse, Claudia, 139
Lai, Tia, 41
Lama, Geri, 227
Lanchester, Colleen, 133
Landers, Jim, 48
Landt, Tim, 252
Larrauri, Ana Lense, 36, 147, 199, 252
Lauer, Ralph, 99
Lauritsen, Birthe, 199
Law, K. R., 200
Lawrence, Steve, 36, 246
Lawson, John, 73
Lechner, Tammy, 135
Lee, Sheri G., 97, 106-107, 139, 156
Lee, Tim, 82
Leeds, Greg, 114, 137-139, 142-143, 155, 242-243
Leeson, David, 76, 186
Legg, Kathy, 106
Leibovitz, Annie, 126
Leiby, Rich, 96
Leigh, Anne, 37
Leight, Charlie, 224
Lense Larrauri, Ana, 36, 147, 199, 252
Lessley, Sara, 210
Lett, Mark, 23, 248
Levine, Ned, 37
Levy-Liberman, Joni, 166
Lewis, David, 190
Lewis, Tim, 93, 141, 166
Liberman, Joni Levy, 96
Licha, Silvia, 111
Lindsay, John, 93
Little, Steve, 224
Littrell, Kandy, 120, 127, 169, 172-173, 192
Ljung, Hakan, 111
Lopez, Dennis Ortiz, 142, 242
Lopez, Juan, 80
Lovink, Marianne, 118
Lowe, Dennis, 61-62, 221, 235
Lubens, Pauline, 173
Luck, Cindy, 250
Lynn, Bob, 71

M · N

MacBride, Jim, 159
Macedo, Edmundo, 40
Magerl, Chris, 173
Mainguy, Mark, 118
Majeri, Tony, 144
Mallison, Carol Zuber, 48
Mancini, John, 30
Mandes, John, 252
Marburger, Lance, 232
Mark, Mary Ellen, 120, 169
Marshall, Ken, 40, 230
Marshall, Richard, 46
Marti, Cristina, 119, 182
Martinez, Rodrigo, 238
Mason, Charles, 176
Mason, Linda, 101
Massaro, Jeff, 24, 30, 67
Mattix, Tom, 38
McCargar, Victoria, 63
McCartney, Don, 108
McClard, Jerry, 108
McCloud, Nancy, 38
McConnell, Ben, 48
McCormick, Pat, 80, 95, 159
McCrea, Jerry, 159

McCulley, Dennis, 71
McDonald, Ken, 22, 58
McDonald, Michelle, 97
McDonough, Doug, 110
McFarlane, James, 231
McIntire, Larry, 159
McIntosh, Jean, 37
McKee, Rick, 225
McKeon, Dennis, 230
McNaughton, Sean, 32
McNeal, Stan, 32
McNulty, Ruth M., 190
McQuaid, Carol, 93, 166
Meade, Annette Ney, 135, 226
Meier, Raymond, 172
Meislin, Rich, 74, 247, 249
Mencher, Eric, 176
Menchin, Scott, 123, 190-191
Merzer, Martin, 140
Meson, Luis, 70
Metzner, Sheila, 124, 172
Meyer, Lawrence, 161
Miguel, Manuel de, 38, 43-44, 112-113, 140
Mikami/AP, Sadayuki, 77
Miller, David, 42, 206, 231
Miller, Doug, 38
Miller, Lloyd, 242
Miller, Randy, 22, 173, 244, 247, 252
Mina, Val, 108
Minister, Scott, 38, 102-103, 195, 204
Mitchell, Patricia, 63
Mode, Michael, 73, 220
Monahan, Iona, 101
Mondon, Karl, 168
Mones, Jim, 38
Monroe, Bryan, 249
Monsees, Peter, 71
Moody, Matt, 63
Moore, Steve, 135
Moores, Ian, 212
Morris, Burton, 166
Morris, Chris, 216, 230, 239
Morris, Don, 197
Moses, Monica, 135
Motichka, Dolores, 82, 91, 194
Moxam, Jean, 140
Mundet, Rosa, 74, 81, 131, 238
Murdoch, Sarah, 84
Murphy, Mary, 34
Murphy, Richard J., 25, 135, 176
Murray, Noah K., 32
Mutchler, Kurt, 24, 42, 74
Myers, Reggie, 140, 199

Nakamura, Joel, 89
Natoli, Sharon, 105
Nead, Julia, 98
Needham, Steven Mark, 159
Needleman, Deborah, 122, 164
Nelson, Constance, 237
Nelson, Eric, 84, 157
Nelson, Hulda, 31
Nelson, Patti, 108
Neumann, Jeff, 135, 208
Newman, Robert, 160
Nigash, Chuck, 33
Niklewicz, Adam, 206
Norgaard, Fred, 34, 247
Nunes, Teresa, 42

O · P

O'Connell, Frank, 221
O'Connor, Margaret, 29, 34, 74, 213, 247, 249
O'Gorman, Kathy, 220
O'Neill, Michael, 120
Odom, Dennis, 39, 135, 219, 226
Oistad, Linda Hawks, 48
Oliver, Merrill, 41
Oliver, Terence, 252
Oliver, Tim, 32, 150
Omori, Dale, 183
Oren, B.C., 215
Ortega, Jo´se, 97
Ortiz Lopez, Dennis, 142, 242
Osmundson, Glenn, 34
Ostendorf, Bill, 34
Outing, Steve, 75, 223, 230
Owens, Ed, 226
Owens, James, 61, 63

Palmer, Randy, 23, 35, 197, 248
Papasian, John, 213
Paris, Jordi, 74, 238
Parker, Sue, 22, 26, 58
Parsons, Donald, 247
Pattison, Neal, 26, 140, 168, 184
Pauer, Frank, 69
Pauli, Luiz Gustavo, 42
Pelavin, Daniel, 139
Pench, Randy, 180
Perez, Carlos, 38, 74, 81, 131, 238
Perez de Rozas, Carlos, 74, 81, 131, 238
Peskin, Dale, 22, 41, 43-44, 50, 54-55, 133, 141, 145-147, 251
Peters, Anne, 174
Pett-Ridge, Christopher, 72, 91, 250-251
Peyton, Tom, 161
Philbrick, Andrea, 17, 161
Philippidis, Evangelia, 195, 204
Piccirillo, Gary, 153
Pickel, David, 183
Pictures, Culver, 37
Pierce, David, 43, 54, 56, 214-215, 221, 227-228
Pinchin, Neil C., 97, 108-109, 123, 139, 154, 225, 235
Pinkhassov, Gueorgui, 173
Pitt, Dave, 48
Pitts, Ted, 195, 248
Pitzer, Bill, 74, 138, 215, 224, 229, 232, 240, 248
Pollard, Susan, 168
Pompa, Frank, 222
Poon, Albert, 40
Porter, Carol, 96, 98, 148
Porter, Tom, 48
Potelle, Jocelyne, 200
Power, Ed, 138
Prast, Rhonda, 80, 95, 99, 199, 207
Press, Rick, 152
Prochnow, Bill, 46-47
Prouse, Marcia, 173
Puckett, David, 60-61, 63, 235
Putrimas, Peter, 48

Q · R

Quinlan, Jim, 48
Quinn, Michael, 30
Quinn, Molly, 26, 168
Quinn, Sara, 48

Rachles, Ed, 230
Rafferty, Mike, 32
Ramberg, Anders, 62-63, 233
Ramirez, Pedro J., 44
Ramos, Josep, 74, 238
Rasa, Greg, 42, 70
Rauch, Laura, 46
Ravenscraft, Stephen, 39, 135, 219, 226
Redman, Trich, 197
Redondo, Amparo, 119, 182
Reeder, Mona, 133
Reep, Sam, 29, 247, 249
Reese, Nancy I.Z., 219, 226, 236
Reichl, Ruth, 96
Remillard, Lisa, 70
Renfroe, Don, 23, 30, 57, 149
Reynolds, Bob, 75
Rhodes, Elizabeth, 70
Ricceri, David, 159
Richards, Robert, 43, 54, 214-215
Richer, Barbara, 104, 141
Rickard, Tim, 249
Rickerd, Carolyn, 102
Ritchie, Rachel, 119, 169, 175
Rini, Pat, 197
Rivenbark, Maurice, 133
Rivoli, Kevin, 163, 168
Roberts, Charmaine, 80
Roberts, Randall K., 135
Rochon, Dick, 201, 227
Rodriguez, Claudio, 90
Rodriguez, Enrique, 226
Romare, Jan, 111
Romero, Javier, 148
Rorick, George, 58-59
Roschuni, Gil, 16
Rose, Thorina, 107
Rosen, Joan, 54
Ross, Andrew, 40, 211
Ross, Wendy C., 251
Rota, Kathi, 127, 192
Roth, Eric, 97
Rotner, Shelley, 106
Rudnak, Theo, 121, 163
Russ, Jim, 33
Russo, Anthony, 89, 201
Ryall, Zach, 43
Ryan, Greg, 37, 223
Ryan, Kathy, 6, 78, 120, 127, 169, 173

S · T

Salas, Rafael, 74, 238
Salazar, Fernando, 46
Salgado, Sebastiao, 6, 78
Salvador, Ricardo, 123, 182
Sampedro, Gorka, 44, 213, 222, 238
Sanchez, Rodrigo, 119, 123, 182
Sargent, Chris, 212
Saul, Kathleen Triesch, 70
Scheffler, Tony, 90

Schidlovsky, Dimitry G., 223
Schiegel, Erich, 136
Schlegel, Erich, 186
Schmitt, Tom, 232
Schneider, Iris, 135
Schneider, Sandra, 19, 114
Schofield, Mark, 114
Schubarth, Cromwell, 166
Schwartz, Sara, 92
Scopin, Joseph, 16, 22, 42, 57, 80, 82, 150
Scott, John E., 229
Sedlar, Patrick, 23, 33, 36, 43, 84, 87, 157, 190, 214, 227-228, 248
Seib, Al, 135
Seibold, Jotto, 159
Seifert, Channon, 152
Seiffer, Alison, 93, 114, 143, 242
Seline, Rex, 252
Sena, Don, 226
Sevick, Joe, 46
Shames, Stephen, 177
Shannon, David, 192
Shaughnessy, Janet, 99, 240
Shechter, Therese, 144
Sheer, Julie, 39, 135, 226, 236
Shelby, Bob, 46
Shema, Bob, 81, 100-101, 156, 244
Sherman, Whitney, 161
Shew, John, 90, 195
Shoulak, Joe, 40, 108, 211, 239
Shoun, Brenda, 23, 39, 67, 148
Shriver, Sandy, 17
Siciliano, Karin, 20
Silverstone, Stuart, 134
Sim, David, 111
Simonson, Ellen, 98
Sims, Geoffrey, 73
Sines, Scott, 26, 140, 168, 184-185
Sinkler, Becky, 82
Sinnamon, Glenda, 96
Sky, Alice, 25, 46, 48
Sloan, William, 123
Smith, Jack, 200
Smith, Lane, 192
Smith, Mike, 173
Smith-Rodden, Pam, 26
Snyder, William, 48, 177, 186
Soble, Anne, 250
Soler, Angels, 74, 238
Sonsky, Steve, 95
Soutar, Paul, 46, 48
Spain, Tom, 69
Spino, Pete, 88-89, 95, 163, 194, 203
Spitza, Anne M., 102
Staley, Lynn, 97
Stallcop, Brian, 71
Stallons, Malcolm, 71, 184
Stamm, Alan, 221
Stano, Randy, 36, 80, 86, 95, 140, 147, 158, 199, 207, 228, 252
Stanton, Laura, 136, 144, 226
Stemgold, Nancy, 223
Stephan, Eliane, 42
Stephen, Diane, 231
Stern, Sherry, 119
Sterngold, Nancy, 109, 158, 206
Stevens, Heidi, 97
Stevens, Susie, 34

Stigg, James, 119
Strawser, Kristine, 75, 223, 230
Stuart, Guy, 134
Sullivan, Joe, 32
Sullivan, Paul, 116, 118, 165, 246
Sundstrom, Tommy, 171
Sutter, Mike, 43
Sutton, Tony, 246, 252
Sveningson, Ulf, 83, 99
Swanson-Scott, Linda, 43
Sweat, Stacy, 37, 46
Sweeny, Glynnis, 23, 197, 207
Swisher, Molly, 71, 199
Syrek, David, 102
Syrek, David, 102
Syska, Bozena, 37
Szerlag, Hank, 46, 220

Takushi, Scott, 37
Talcott, Julia, 97
Tarlofsky, Malcolm, 163
Tascon, Mario, 44, 75, 213, 222, 238
Tellez, Carol, 81
Thayer, Bob, 170, 174-175, 179
The Douglas Brothers, 94
Thewes/Der Larm, Thomas, 191
Thierry, Martha, 46, 220
Thomas, Pat, 26, 71
Thomassie, Juan, 63
Thompson, Phillip, 197
Thomson, John, 23, 35, 69, 248
Thurber, Jon, 41, 147
Timmons, Bonnie, 159
Tobias, Randy, 25, 46
Toner, Mike, 219
Topor, Roland, 84
Torbjern, Kjeld, 199
Townsend, Bob, 71
Trapnell, Tom, 93, 96, 147
Treston, Lauri Hopple, 37
Tuckwood, Jan, 72
Tuma, Rick, 219, 226
Turk, Stephen, 96
Turney, George, 218
Turnley, David C., 59, 173
Tusa, Susan, 173
Tuttle, Jeff, 25, 46
Twohey, John, 88, 144

U • V

Ulmer, Mary, 33
Ulrichsen, Rolf Chr., 30
Uria, Juan Carlos, 90
Usabiaga, Pedro, 182

Valdez, Patti, 102
Valenti, Michael, 84
Valera, Juan, 46
Valone, Beth, 22, 41, 50, 54-55, 147
Van Orden, Clark, 178
Van Pelt, John, 14, 130, 134, 160, 236
Van Zoetendaal, W., 93
Vancura, Cliff, 43
Varela, Juan, 27-28, 42, 70-71, 119, 123, 171
Varon Brown, Laura, 46, 58-59, 220
Vazquez, Claudio, 106
Vega, Herman, 80, 95, 140, 158, 199, 228
Vegella, Patricia, 56,

214, 221, 227-228
Velasco, Juan, 213
Velasco, Samuel, 44, 112, 189, 213, 222, 238
Victoria, Alison, 186
Villa, Roxana, 104, 159
Villar, Sandra, 74, 238
Vincent, Kathleen, 48
Visci, Chip, 46, 58
Vitt, Shawn, 108
Volpp, Terry, 226
Vondracek, Woody, 36, 140, 199
Vondracke, Raul, 199
Vorlet, Christopher, 161

W • Y • Z

Wada, Karen, 135
Waigand, Lee, 191, 194, 244
Wakely, Rick, 17, 161
Walstrom, Susanne, 171, 181
Ward, Joe, 213, 223, 247
Warren, Karen, 43
Waters, Phil, 93, 119
Watson, Warren, 17, 161
Watters, Jim, 36, 147, 252
Watters, Pete, 224
Watts, Paul, 80, 82
Weinberger, Peter, 46
Weinstock, Nancy, 29
Weiss, Diane, 141
Well, David H., 169
Wesch, Hank, 40, 230
Westman, Marty, 59
Widebrant, Mats, 81, 83, 99, 158
Widmer, Mark, 19
Wigginton, Mark, 132, 220, 229, 234, 248
Wigstrand, Kerstin, 111
Williams, Dave, 46
Williams, David, 104
Williams, Genevieve, 92, 140
Williams, Mike, 220
Williamson, Ted, 46, 220
Wilson, Diane, 47
Wilson, Jonathan, 184
Wilson, Scott, 75, 230
Wilson, Wade E., 47
Wilton, Nicholas, 159
Winfield, Paul, 223
Winters, Dan, 123, 164, 169
Wirtz, Michael S., 177, 180
Wise, Michelle, 73, 82, 248
Wisnewski, Andrea, 196
Withey, Deborah, 35, 81, 91, 96, 103, 121, 139-140, 157, 164, 173, 191, 196, 201, 227, 248, 252
Wolff, Tom, 122
Wolin, Glenda, 80, 158
Wolley, Janet, 122
Woodward, Paul, 22, 42, 57
Woolley, Janet, 125, 192-193, 202
Workman, John, 139
Wray, Wendy, 142, 243
Wyatt, Don, 39, 48
Wynne, Patricia J., 109, 206

Yang, James, 123, 161, 202
Yarosh, Lee, 22, 58
Yates, Dave, 101
Yemma, Mark, 22, 41, 48, 66-67
Youngblut, Shelley, 118
Yu, Kam Wai, 80, 95, 159
Yuill, Peter, 110

Zedek, Dan, 245
Zeff, Joe, 250-251
Zelz, Eric, 195
Zisk, James, 74, 216
Zollinger, Lisa, 159, 232

By Paper

A • B

Aberdeen American News, The, 71
Aftenposten, 24, 30
Akron Beacon Journal, 35, 38, 208, 224, 244, 247, 252
Albuquerque Tribune, The, 71, 135, 208
American Medical News, 192
Anchorage Daily News, 25, 84, 88-89, 94-96, 135, 162-163, 176, 194, 203
Anchorage Times, The, 178, 191, 194, 244
Arizona Daily Star, The, 224
Arizona Republic, The, 102, 224
Army Times, 72
Asbury Park Press, 32, 35, 150
Atlanta Journal & Constitution, The, 43, 219, 225, 236
Atlantic City Press, The, 34
Augusta Chronicle, The, 225
Austin American-Statesman, 43

Bangor Daily News, 195
Berlingske Tidende, 22, 84
Boston Globe, The, 77, 79, 86, 91, 97, 104, 106-109, 121, 123, 126, 128, 139, 154, 156, 163, 170, 225, 235
Boston Globe Magazine, The, 77, 121, 123, 126, 128, 156, 163, 235

C • D

Charlotte Observer, The, 225
Chicago Tribune, 39, 88, 102, 135, 144, 219, 226, 236
Christian Science Monitor, The, 14, 47, 69, 81, 130, 134, 160, 236
Citizen, The, 153, 163, 168
City Paper, 110
Columbus Dispatch, The, 38, 102-103, 195, 204

Computer Reseller News, 206
Concord Monitor, 170, 178
Contra Costa Times, 168

Dagens Nyheter, 111, 171, 181
Daily Journal, The, 152
Daily Press, 245
Daily Republic, 133
Dallas Morning News, The / Dallas Life Magazine, 177, 186
Dallas Morning News, The, 43, 48, 76, 81, 96, 100-101, 103, 136, 144, 156, 171, 177, 186, 226, 234, 244
Dallas Observer, 190, 245
Dayton Daily News, 23, 35, 69, 195, 197, 248
Denver Post, The, 134
Des Moines Register, The, 245, 247
Detroit Free Press, 13, 22, 26, 35, 46, 58-59, 81, 84, 91, 96, 103, 121, 139-140, 157, 164, 173, 191, 196, 201, 220, 227, 248, 252
Detroit Free Press Magazine, 121, 164, 173, 191, 196, 201, 227
Detroit News, The, 13, 21-23, 33, 36, 41, 43-44, 49-50, 52, 54-56, 84, 87, 96, 133, 141, 145-147, 157, 190, 197, 207, 214-215, 217, 221, 227-228, 237, 248, 251
Diario 16, 38

E • F

Eagle-Tribune, The, 248
Eastsideweek, 19, 114
Edinburgh Evening News, 111
El Mundo / Metropoli, 119, 197
El Mundo, 38, 43-44, 75, 85, 112-113, 119, 140, 188-190, 197, 205, 213, 222, 238
El Norte, 99
El Nuevo Dia, 87, 191, 194
El Nuevo Herald, 95, 111, 191, 198, 207
El Sol, 15, 27-28, 42, 46, 70-71, 119, 123, 171, 182
El Sol Magazine, 182

Financial Times, 36, 197, 246
Financial Times of Canada, 36, 246
Folha de São Paulo, 42
Fort Worth Star-Telegram, 99, 105

G • H

Gannett News Service, 222
Gannett Suburban Newspapers, 135
Gazette, The, 101

Gazette Telegraph, 17, 23, 33, 43, 150
Globe and Mail, The / Business Traveller Magazine, 128
Globe and Mail, The / Magazine Network-West, Toronto, Montreal, 145, 165
Globe and Mail, The / Montreal Magazine, 246
Globe and Mail, The / West Magazine, 116, 118
Globe and Mail, The, 84, 116-118, 126, 128, 157, 165, 246, 252
Goteborgs-Posten, 81, 83, 99, 158
Greensboro News & Record, The, 249
Hartford Courant, The / Northeast Magazine, 121
Hartford Courant, The, 108, 121
Honolulu Star-Bulletin, 222
Houston Chronicle, The, 215

I • K • L

InfoWorld, 173

Kansas City Star, The, 140, 198

La Presse, 200
La Vanguardia, 74, 81, 131, 238
Lansing State Journal, 151
Lexington Herald-Leader, 71, 184, 199
Los Angeles Times / Orange County Edition, 33, 60-62, 221, 235
Los Angeles Times / TV Times, 119
Los Angeles Times, 33, 41, 60-63, 93, 96, 119, 135, 147, 210, 221, 233, 235

M • N

Maine Sunday Telegram & Press Herald, 17
Malibu Surfside News, 250
Miami Herald, The, 36, 80, 86, 95, 99, 140, 147, 158, 182, 199, 207, 228, 252
Monterey Herald, The, 178
Morning News Tribune, The, 229

Naples Daily News, 152
National Sports Daily, The, 221, 229
New York Times, The, 6, 12, 29, 34, 37, 48, 74, 78, 82, 84, 89, 92-93, 104, 109, 120, 124-125, 127, 140-141, 158, 169, 172-173, 192-193, 206, 213, 217, 223, 247, 249
New York Times Magazine, The, 6, 78, 120, 124-125, 127, 169, 172-173, 192-193

THIRTEENTH EDITION 255

News, The, 22, 25-26, 28, 30, 32, 34, 36, 38, 40, 42, 44, 46, 48, 149, 152
News-Leader, The, 33
Newsday, 24, 30, 37, 67
Novedades, 90
NRC Handelsblad, 93

O · P

Orange County Register, The, 22-23, 38-39, 41, 48, 66-67, 139, 148, 218, 237
Oregonian, The, 73, 82, 132, 220, 229, 234, 248
Orlando Sentinel, The / Florida Magazine, 119

Palm Beach Post, The, 72
Patuxent Publishing Company / Holiday Entertaining, 139
Philadelphia Gay News, 252
Philadelphia Inquirer Magazine, The, 78, 123, 169, 172, 176-177, 180, 184, 186, 190, 200, 206, 244
Pittsburgh Post-Gazette, 72, 91, 250-251
Pittsburgh Press, The, 200
Plain Dealer, The, 183, 224
Plain Dealer Sunday Magazine, The, 183
Portland Press Herald, 17, 161
Post and Courier, The, 249
Post-Standard, The, 69, 213, 230, 249
Press Democrat, The, 200
Providence Journal, The, 26, 34, 46, 119, 148, 169-170, 174-175, 179
Providence Sunday Journal, The, 119

R · S

Record, The, 71
Reno Gazette-Journal, 215, 246-247
Reporter, 33, 46, 70, 75, 111, 113, 215, 220, 226, 231, 237
Richmond News Leader, The, 190

Sacramento Bee, The, 41, 180
Saint Paul Pioneer Press, 37, 46, 98, 135
San Diego Union, The, 32, 40, 108, 230
San Francisco Bay Guardian, The, 166
San Francisco Chronicle, 31, 75, 223, 230
San Francisco Examiner, 26, 40, 46-47, 75, 108, 211, 216, 230, 239
San Jose Mercury News / West Magazine, 170
San Jose Mercury News, 26, 40, 47, 75, 170, 191, 200, 208, 249
Seattle Post-Intelligencer, 231
Seattle Times, The, 42, 70, 206, 231, 239
South Bend Tribune, 231
Spokesman-Review, The & Spokane Chronicle, 26, 140, 167-168, 181, 184-185
St. Louis Post-Dispatch, 90, 195
St. Petersburg Times, 104, 113, 133, 197
Star Tribune, 47, 237
Star-Ledger, The, 105, 113, 159, 232
Sun, The, 93, 166
Sun-Sentinel, 101
Sunday Times, The, 73, 212, 218
Syracuse Herald American, 232
Syracuse Herald-Journal, 27, 41-42, 64-65, 151

T · V · W

Times, The, 73, 151
Times Advocate, 30, 69
Times-Leader, The, 178
Times-Picayune, The, 24, 37, 42, 74, 98, 207, 216
Toronto Star, The, 80, 95, 159
Tribune, The, 47

Vagabond, 171
Vendsyssel Tidende, 199
Village Voice, The, 160, 191
Virginian-Pilot / Ledger-Star, The, 71, 74, 138, 199, 215, 232, 240
Virginian-Pilot, The, 18, 26, 71, 74, 99, 138, 215, 232, 240

Wall Street Journal Classroom Edition, The, 20
Wall Street Journal Reports, The, 114, 137-139, 142-143, 155, 242-243
Washington Post, The, 86, 96, 98, 106, 122, 126, 148, 159, 161, 164, 169, 201-202, 251
Washington Post Magazine, The, 122, 126, 164, 169, 201-202
Washington Times, The, 4, 16, 22-23, 25, 27, 30, 42, 57, 80, 82, 90-91, 105, 114, 149-150, 161, 197
Wichita Eagle, The, 25, 46, 48, 68-69

1992 SND Officers

President: Randy Stano, The Miami Herald

1st Vice President: Nancy Tobin, University of Buffalo, NY

2nd Vice President: George Benge, The News-Leader, Springfield, MO

Treasurer: Deborah Withey, Detroit Free Press

Secretary: Jim Jennings, Lexington Herald-Leader, Lexington, KY

Immediate Past President: Jacqueline Combs, Chicago Tribune

The Society of Newspaper Design

Executive Director: Ray Chattman

The Newspaper Center, Box 17290
Dulles International Airport
Washington, DC 20041

(703) 620-1083

Special Thanks

Liz Doherty, National Geographic, Washington, DC

Oscar Diaz and Tony Espetia, El Nuevo Herald, Miami, FL

J. Ford Huffman, Gannett News Service, Arlington, VA

Tom Wood III, Lexington Herald-Leader, Lexington, KY

Editor & Designer: David Griffin, National Geographic

© 1992 THE SOCIETY OF NEWSPAPER DESIGN

All rights reserved. No part of this book may be reproduced in any form without written permission of the copyright owners. All images in this book have been reproduced with the knowledge and prior consent of the artists concerned and no responsibility is accepted by producer, publisher or printer for any infringement of copyright or otherwise, arising from the contents of this publication. Every effort has been made to ensure credits accurately comply with information supplied.

FIRST PUBLISHED IN THE U.S. BY:
ROCKPORT PUBLISHERS, INC.
P.O. BOX 396
FIVE SMITH STREET
ROCKPORT, MA 01966

(508) 546-9590
FAX: (508) 546-7141
TELEX: 5106019284 ROCKORT PUB

DISTRIBUTED TO THE BOOK AND ART TRADE IN THE U.S. AND CANADA BY:

NORTH LIGHT, AN IMPRINT OF
F & W PUBLICATIONS

1507 DANA AVENUE
CINCINNATI, OH 45207
(513) 531-2222

OTHER DISTRIBUTION BY:
ROCKPORT PUBLISHERS, INC.